P9-CML-797

THE VANISHING IRISH

THE VANISHING IRISH

THE ENIGMA OF
THE MODERN WORLD

Edited by
JOHN A. O'BRIEN

"The rural population is vanishing and with it is vanishing the Irish race itself. Rural Ireland is stricken and dying and the will to marry on the land is almost gone."

MOST REV. CORNELIUS LUCEY, D.D., BISHOP OF CORK

McGRAW-HILL BOOK COMPANY, INC.
NEW YORK   TORONTO   LONDON

THE VANISHING IRISH

Library of Congress Catalog Card Number: 53–11487

PUBLISHED BY THE MC GRAW-HILL BOOK COMPANY, INC.

PRINTED IN THE UNITED STATES OF AMERICA

To

*Ireland and her brave sons
and daughters in all lands
this volume is dedicated
in token of esteem and love*

ACKNOWLEDGMENTS

We acknowledge our indebtedness to the contributors, on both sides of the Atlantic, who favored us with articles from their gifted pens. These contributions reflect not only their prolonged thought and study but also their deep personal interest and concern. Each, we think, is a little masterpiece. To W. T. Cosgrave, former Prime Minister of Ireland, we are indebted for the data on the mass emigrations and evictions in the years following the Famine and for other valuable information which we have used as the historical background in Chapter 2.

R. C. Geary, Director of the Central Statistics Office, not only sent us all the publications of his office on the recent census but also carefully checked the statistics in the original draft of that same chapter and brought them up to date with his revised census figures. For this kindness and for additional advice and suggestions we extend our sincere gratitude.

We acknowledge likewise the valuable suggestions and help given us by Dr. Oliver St. John Gogarty, T. O'Connor Sloane III, Joseph D. Brennan, Counsellor at the Irish Embassy, and our own confreres, Eugene P. Burke, Patrick J. Carroll, Michael A. Mulcaire, Raymond W. Murray, and Felix D. Duffey of the Congregation of Holy Cross. We are indebted to *The Ave Maria* for permission to reprint Father Noonan's article, to *Dublin Opinion* for "The Inheritance," and to *St. Joseph's Magazine* for permission to reprint our article, "The Vanishing Irish."

To the prelates, priests, scholars, and friends in Ireland and in America who favored us with their views on the subjects treated in this volume we are indeed grateful. The entire project absorbing our thought, study, and research over many years has been for us a labor of love, from which we shall accept not a penny of remuneration. We shall feel more than repaid for our years of labor on this project if it helps in a small way to stem the population decline in Ireland, to stimulate the growth of the Irish at home and abroad, and to multiply their descendants in all lands. Then shall Ireland take her rightful place among the nations of the world, and her numerous children in all lands shall be still more fruitful in all good works.

JOHN A. O'BRIEN

CONTENTS

THE VANISHING IRISH

THE IRISH ENIGMA

John A. O'Brien

NOTHING IN RECENT CENTURIES IS SO PUZZLING OR SO CHALLENGING AS THE strange phenomenon being enacted before our eyes: the fading away of the once great and populous nation of Ireland. If the past century's rate of decline continues for another century, the Irish will virtually disappear as a nation and will be found only as an enervated remnant in a land occupied by foreigners.

What makes this phenomenon all the more surprising is that it has taken place during the very century when the other nations of Europe achieved their most spectacular growth, most of them tripling their populations. The enigma deepens when it is recalled that Ireland has been traditionally a nation of large families. Today Ireland is teetering perilously on the brink of near extinction as the habits of the past century persist.

What are the causes of her decline? Can the present trend be reversed? What measures must be launched to save Ireland from extinction? These are the chief questions which this volume seeks to answer. As the ones best qualified to treat these questions are native Irish men and women, wrestling with these problems day by day for many years, we have asked some of the most brilliant and scholarly writers of Ireland to supply the answers. In this roster of distinguished names are scholars, playwrights, novelists, biographers, historians, sociologists, educators, and journalists. Other gifted writers there are in Eire today, but these will rank with the best.

Common to all these contributors are a burning love of Ireland, a profound solicitude for her welfare, and an anxious concern that a solution be found for the grave dangers threatening her very existence. They yield

3

to no one in loyalty and devotion to the land of their birth, endeared to them by the sufferings and sacrifices of their forebears throughout long centuries of struggle for freedom.

We have requested all to speak with utmost frankness and fearless honesty: otherwise the study would be worthless. At the same time we have made it clear that "our aim is to secure not mere destructive criticism but helpful constructive suggestions offered in a spirit of friendliness and love." Unless this good will is transparent in every constructive criticism and in every proferred suggestion, there is danger that antagonism will be engendered and hostile emotions will close the gateway to the mind.

When one's feelings are hurt, his thinking usually gives place to mere "emoting": no matter how valuable and helpful the counsel offered, it generally falls upon deaf ears. We have been most anxious to avoid the wounding of feelings and the hurting of racial sensitivity and national pride. This is not always an easy task, but we have done our best.

In conformity with our twofold request the contributors have spoken with complete candor and evident kindliness, good will, and love. We hope that our own contribution is not devoid of these same qualities.

Since this is a cooperative study, in which each contributor presents independently the results of his own thought and observation, it is inevitable that there will be differences of opinion. It is good to have these differences aired and placed side by side and thus stimulate frank and full discussion among the readers and in the press. Such discussion is badly needed. Until recently, few in Ireland showed any awareness of the anomalous situation in which they have been and still are in the matter of few and late marriages as compared with other nations. The same is substantially true among the Irish abroad.

The more it is discussed, the better it will be and the more quickly will the Irish seek to lose the unenviable distinction of having more of its members kept from marriage than those of any other nation or race in the civilized world. To help achieve both these purposes, we have given the contributors freedom to express their convictions even when we anticipated that others might have a different opinion and even when we differed.

Indeed, when the viewpoint concerns details in the picture in Eire, we of the Diaspora must respectfully stand aside and allow the Irish there to pound out the truth on the anvil of open, frank, and free discussion among themselves. Hence the expression of any opinion in this book does not necessarily imply agreement on the part of the editor or of the other contributors; it is simply the considered thought of the individual writer, submitted for what it may be worth.

If at times a reader encounters a viewpoint which is contrary to his previous conception, may we suggest that, instead of yielding merely to a hostile emotional reaction and dismissing it as "all rot," he do two things: First, ask, "Is this true or not?" Second, investigate and find out. Truth sometimes falls like a cinder in the eye: it stings and smarts. This is especially so when the previous conception was clustered about with emotions of a racial or national character. It is a truism that clear thinking is at a minimum when national feelings are aroused.

This study aims to engender light, not heat. It seeks to heal, not wound. It aims not to tear down but to build up. It seeks not to stir dissension but by disclosing the causes of Ireland's decline to pave the way for united action to arrest that decline and promote her growth and her progress in all the arts and sciences, for which she was so long famous.

For many centuries Ireland was known as the "island of saints and scholars." She held aloft the torch of learning when many of the countries of Europe were in darkness. She sent scholars to spread learning and missionaries to carry the gospel of Christ to the far corners of the earth. She has woven into the tapestry of the world's culture the design with the brightest colors of all—those which symbolize the noblest spiritual ideals of the human race. Beneath that design might well be carved the tribute inscribed on the Colossus of Rhodes to the Greeks who lit the torch of learning for the ancient world, "Not over sea alone but over land as well they set the exquisite lamp of unsubdued freedom."

The flourishing condition of the Church in many lands and even her preservation in some are due in large measure to the generosity with which Ireland has provided priests, brothers, and sisters to carry on the many-faceted apostolate of religion, education, mercy, and charity. Without stint she has poured out her lifeblood to supply the needs of people in every land. With bowed heads and grateful hearts we pay our tribute of gratitude and love to a nation whom only God can adequately reward.

It is precisely because we love Ireland as our spiritual homeland and wish to see her survive and prosper that we undertake this clinical in-

vestigation into the malaise which threatens her with death. While every
foreign land has been enriched with her sons and daughters—and none
more than America—there comes a point where continued hemophilia
can mean only death. Charity begins at home, and every nation has a
right to preserve her own life. It is time for Ireland to look to her own
health and welfare and forget others for a while. "We've been polishing
the silver," says Sean O'Casey, "to shine in everybody else's place and
leaving our own to sink into the dullness of lead." Yes, to sink perilously
close to the dullness of death.

Hence it is of the utmost importance for the reader to understand the
reasons which have led, and even compelled, us to undertake this cooperative study. If he sees in it only the disclosure of gaping wounds and
not the effort to heal those wounds, he will miss the whole purpose of
this work as well as the spirit in which it is performed.

The Irish are an old race and, some have said, a proud race. Indeed,
they have reason to be. And we think no one is prouder of the folks on
the "auld sod" than her children of the Diaspora—her far-flung army of
exiles in distant lands. We want them to understand that we would not
knowingly hurt their pride or wound their sensitivities. If we err here
and there, as well we may, in seeking to bandage Erin's wounds, it is
due to a defect in our technique or to our clumsy fingers but not to a defect of our hearts or a lack of love.

Indeed, we exiles in far-off lands have often found the words of
Alfred P. Graves forming on our lips and their sentiments stirring in
our hearts:

> Oh, if for every tender tear
>   That from our aching exiled eyes
> Has fallen for you, Erin dear,
>   Our own loved shamrocks could arise,
> They'd weave and weave a garland green,
>   To stretch the cruel ocean through,
> All, all the weary way between
>   Our yearning Irish hearts and you.

Ireland is one of the few nations whose children can say with truth
the words spoken of them by John Boyle O'Reilly:

"We have wronged no race,
We have robbed no land,
We have never oppressed the weak!"
And this in the face of Heaven is the nobler thing to speak.

Ireland is a Catholic nation. As its great leader Eamon de Valera said recently, "Ireland is the foremost Christian nation in the world today." The activities of the Church and her priests are intertwined with the daily life of the Irish people. They touch at a thousand points. The Irish love the Church and revere her priests. Many are the families which have given a hostage to God in the form of a priest or brother or sister.

The Church is divine in her foundation and in her teachings but human in her ministers and in her membership. Because the Church stands calm and unruffled in the sure possession of the full deposit of divine truth, she can listen with a serenity greater than that of any merely human institution to constructive and respectful criticism of the policy and activities of herself and of her ministers in all the fields outside the strict domain of divinely revealed truth. It is inevitable that in the closely intertwined life of priests and people in a Catholic country divergent reactions to complicated questions of political, social, educational, and economic natures will ensue.

Those differences can be stated irenically and without offense. Indeed, they must be expressed, or resentment, bitterness, and ultimately rebellion rankle in one's bosom. Cooperation is a venture in sharing, and it implies sharing thoughts and feelings as well as following a common program. It is a two-party line, in which no one does all the talking or all the listening but in which each one both talks and listens. It is of supreme importance that our laity talk, but always with respect, and express their honest convictions. Only in this way can there be a real meeting of minds and of hearts. Only out of such mutual sharing is genuine cooperation instead of mere lip service possible.

In the fields of marriage and family life, as well as in those of social mingling and courtship, which in most modern countries are their necessary preliminaries, the laity have a wide and intimate experience from which, by virtue of their celibate state, the religious of both sexes are excluded. It is the bride and groom who administer the sacrament of matrimony to each other, with the clergyman merely serving as the official witness. Without the free mutual consent of each of the contracting parties there is no valid marriage.

The lay person has the exclusive right to select his marriage partner. To make a suitable and wise choice, it is generally necessary for individuals to meet a reasonably wide circle of young people. In this way they can find partners with the maximum of congenial qualities, interests, and tastes. "Company keeping" and courtship serve a useful purpose in enabling young people to verify through such association the wisdom of the choice they will make for life.

In all these matters lay people have rights which pastors are glad to have them exercise with prudence and discretion. A healthy social life in a parish, enabling young people to meet often and under pleasant conditions, will foster not only suitable marriages but also the spiritual life of the members.

Love of God has as its corollary the love of neighbor. But we cannot love him unless we first know him. Hence the importance of promoting social acquaintance and friendship among our people, old as well as young. It is earnestly to be hoped that the frequently expressed appeals of the bishops of Ireland for more and earlier marriages will be implemented through a vigorous and well-balanced social program in each parish, with priests and people working hand in hand for the achievement of a common goal.

We would like to think that friendly meetings and discussions between educated lay leaders and their spiritual shepherds on all moot questions, such as suitable opportunities for wholesome socials for young people, courtship, the censorship and banning of books, the importance of elbow room for creative work in writing and in all the arts and sciences, and kindred matters, would enable them to solve these problems to the satisfaction of all. With intelligence, good will, and a willingness to see both sides, any problem, no matter how serious and complicated, can be solved. Without those qualities, no problem, no matter how simple, can be solved.

With the exception of Arland Ussher, all the contributors are Catholics, earnest, faithful, and genuinely devoted to the Church. Ussher is a well-known Irish writer, scholar, and patriot, and we are honored to have his distinguished company. The contributors were selected without regard to political viewpoint or party affiliation or previous inquiry as to their views. Our one simple objective was to ascertain the truth and to have it presented clearly, fearlessly, and with transparent kindliness and friendliness. Each contributor assumes responsibility for the views and opinions which he expresses and for them alone. The inclusion of any chapter in this joint study does not necessarily imply agreement with the views expressed therein either on the part of the other contributors or on our part.

One word about ourselves. Since publishing our first study on *The Vanishing Irish* we were surprised to discover that some Irish people construed this effort to awaken the citizens of our ancestral homeland as an act of hostility on our part. We hasten to assure them that the exact opposite is the case. Our four grandparents came from Ireland, and the love for Erin has never ceased to burn within us. For years we have spoken and written for the freedom of Ireland. We were chairman of the drive for the sale of bonds for Irish freedom when De Valera was leading the struggle at home. We yield to no one, native of Ireland or descendant of Irish forebears, in love for the Republic of Ireland and its people.

We know Ireland, not merely through the haze of books and tradition, but at first hand. We have made repeated visits of a prolonged character to Ireland, and we have lived with friends both in the cities and on the farms. We have journeyed on foot and on bicycle through the Irish countryside. For forty years we have been deeply concerned with the problem of Ireland's declining population and the strange reluctance of so many Irishmen to marry—a phenomenon we had previously noted among the Irish in America. We have talked about these matters with men and women in Ireland in all walks of life—farmers, merchants, young men and women, teachers, writers, priests, professors at Maynooth, where we sojourned at length, bishops, members of the Dail, and the beloved Prime Minister De Valera and members of his cabinet.

Furthermore we write from the campus of a university which is known not only throughout America but the whole world for its proud Irish traditions. Hither have come sons of Irish families from every state in the Union and from every province of Canada to secure a higher education. Perhaps no institution of higher learning in the New World has so large a proportion of Irish in its student body as well as on its faculty. Its football team has carried the fame of the "Fighting Irish" to the far corners of the world. We mention this background simply that readers can be assured of the sympathetic interest and affectionate concern with which we approach this problem.

Despite our intimate knowledge of the customs and attributes of the people of Eire, we thought it more seemly to call upon outstanding native scholars and writers to diagnose the ailments of contemporary Ireland and to prescribe the remedies. With them it is a daily, and even a lifelong, preoccupation. Hence we can be sure of getting as accurate and penetrating an analysis of the strange enigma of modern Ireland and an insight into the methods of solving it as is humanly possible to obtain. We believe that the answers of these distinguished scholars and writers will have a profound and far-reaching effect in hastening the solution of a problem that has long been causing uneasiness and concern not only to Irish people at home and abroad but also to their friends throughout the world.

The solution of the problem in Eire will undoubtedly help to solve the secondary problem this volume attacks: Why do the Irish in the United States, Canada, Great Britain and Australia tend to persist in a non-marrying tradition where not a shred of economic justification exists for such a race-suicidal practice? Several discerning writers discuss the Irish scene in America and show the perpetuation of the nonmarrying mores which characterize such a large proportion of the Gaels in their homeland. Hence the volume undertakes to get at the very root of the strange malady which for more than a century has been blighting the growth of the Irish in every land.

While there are flashes of wit and humor in these pages, as might well be expected from the pens of Irishmen, the contributors have written not with their tongues in their cheeks but in a spirit of deep sincerity and anxious concern for the continued existence of the Irish race. It is because they love Ireland and are proud of her historic contributions to the culture of the world and wish to see them continued and enlarged that they have taken up their pens. The stakes for which they are fighting are the greatest which ever challenged the courage and resourcefulness of any warriors: the saving of a great nation from extinction and the rescue of her sons in other lands from the nonmarrying mores which they have unconsciously carried with them to the detriment of themselves, their race, their religion, and the countries of their adoption.

THE VANISHING IRISH

2

John A. O'Brien

Canon Matt Lavelle is dozing before the fire in the rectory in the seaside village of Lorcan, County Louth, in Ireland. His legs, paralyzed by a recent stroke, are resting on a cushioned footrest. Awakening with a start, he calls, in a bit of a panic, for his housekeeper Rosieanne. It's just like her, he feels, to let him doze off that way while she's off "blatherin'" with tradesmen at the door.

"Sure I can't be running in and out all day for you," says Rosieanne. "Then, too, I'll be leaving in a week."

It's not because she has any idea of marrying, as the Canon suspects, but because she has come to believe that no one but a saint could stand the new Father Shaughnessy who has come to administer the parish while the Canon is convalescing.

Canon Matt is sure he can adjust that matter, for he is still the Canon, and he'll be speaking to Father Shaughnessy.

"Listen to me, Rosieanne: where is he now?"

"He's down in the church hall havin' a meetin'. Sure he's always havin' meetin's inside and outside and everywhere."

"The divil if such a man for meetin's I ever met."

"If you had to hear him last night below at the pier, standin' on the promenade wall. Down with the drink, down with the dancin', down with the lovemakin' . . ."

Complications increase when Phelim Fintry, the vegetable man, comes to protest the action of Father Shaughnessy in putting his daughter Nora off the hockey team. Rosieanne relays the protest to the Canon.

"And what's he got agin *her?*" asks the Canon. "Sure Nora's a fine little bit of a girl."

"It was for going with—with a boy," replies Rosieanne.

"A boy! And what the divil does he want her to go with, an elephant?"

"He has the girls in the team pledged agin boys an' courtin' an' kissin'. "

"And the marriage rate the lowest in Europe!"

Thus does Paul Vincent Carroll set the picture for his play *The White Steed*.

When wise old Canon Matt Lavelle uttered the words "And the marriage rate the lowest in Europe!" he placed his finger upon the most disturbing fact in Ireland today. No nation can long survive if it loses faith in the institution of marriage and its sons and daughters have little truck with it. While Ireland has not formally disowned wedlock, her children enter into it so seldom and so late that the Irish nation is slowly but surely vanishing from the face of the earth.

This comes as a surprise and a shock to most people. Sure, they ask in amazement, isn't Ireland famous for its lovely colleens whose smiling beauty is sung in song and story? For its gallant sons with their rollicking good humor and sidesplitting wit? Aren't the Irish known throughout the world for their warmheartedness, their wealth of affection, and the readiness with which their love goes out to others? What about all those songs which echo with a refrain like "When Irish eyes are smiling, All the world seems bright and gay"? Are they all a mockery?

WEDDING RATE LOW IN ERIN

By Associated Press

DUBLIN, Aug. 8.—Although Ireland once had a reputation as a land of romantic lovers, statistics show that the marriage rate is far below most European countries.

The 1946 census showed that only two out of five Irishmen between 30 and 34 years old were married, the lowest proportion in the world.

No, the Irish have the endowment of tenderness, warmheartedness, and affection to a degree unsurpassed by any race, as their literature and history eloquently attest. But the strange and paradoxical fact remains that fewer of the men and women in Ireland marry than do those of any other country in the civilized world. Because of their widespread failure to marry—we don't say their aversion to marriage—and the custom of many young people of emigrating, Ireland has had a steadily declining population for more than a century. Economists and sociologists are agreed that, if this ominous trend continues, in another century the Irish race will have vanished much like the Mayans, leaving only their monuments behind them.

Indeed, many sober students think that the Irish are already far along on the path to extinction—much farther than they realize. After an exhaustive study of their declining population, Dr. Clement S. Mihanovich, director of the Department of Sociology at St. Louis University and a specialist on population, reaches the conclusion that Ireland is rapidly becoming a nation of a meager handful of old men and women—a vanishing race whose glory will be contained not in the souls of living men and women but in old tomes covered with dust and tucked away in some remote corner of the bombproof libraries of the world.

Such, too, is the grim and melancholy conclusion which Father P. B. Noonan, C.S.Sp., a native of Ireland, reluctantly reached as a result of his painstaking investigation. "It is an indisputable fact," he says, "that the Irish are a vanishing race. If the present rate continues, they will be counted among the extinct people in less than a hundred years. The saddest feature of the tragedy is the universal unconcern of the Irish themselves. Only a few, even among the thinking elite, have uttered a cry of warning. The ordinary folk still cling tenaciously to a system which is more deadly than either the plantations or the rack, while successive governments have done little or nothing to avert the evil."

It is a piece of tragic irony that such a doom is impending upon a people who respect so highly the sanctity and the indissolubility of Christian marriage and among whom artificial birth control is at a minimum. Yet cruel and ironic though such a fate be for a nation which scorns divorce, abhors abortion, and holds in the highest reverence the divinely instituted sacrament of matrimony, there can be no escape from the sinister threat of impending extinction which the grim figures of a century of unbroken national decline cast before them.

Let us look at those figures. From a total population of 8,177,945 in 1841, Ireland had dwindled to a nation of but 4,330,172 on the night of April 8, 1951. During that period the population of the six counties in Ulster, now constituting Northern Ireland, fell from 1,648,945 to 1,369,-579—a loss of 279,366.

Far more striking and even more appalling, however, was the decline of the population of the 26 counties, now constituting the Republic of Ireland, from 6,529,000 to 2,960,593—a loss of 3,568,407. This means that Ireland has shrunk to less than half its former size! At every census taken since the disastrous Famine of the 1840's until 1946, the record showed an unbroken decline. Not till the 1946–1951 census was taken did the record show an increase, and then it was the exceedingly slight gain of but 0.2 per cent.

These statistics, sent us by Dr. R. C. Geary, director of the General Statistics Office in Dublin and the foremost authority on this subject,

The Population of Ireland

reveal more clearly than a volume of words that Ireland as a nation has been vanishing for more than a century from the face of the earth. Instead of tripling in the course of a century, as the other nations of Europe did, it dwindled to less than a half, numbering but 2,992,034 in 1941. By 1946 it had ebbed to an all-time low of 2,955,107.

The unbroken decline, decade by decade, is shown in percentages in Table 1 and is depicted even more vividly in Chart I. Let any Irishman or a descendant of Irish forebears look at that chart with its telltale line

TABLE I. *A Century of Decline: Percentage Changes in Ireland's Population*

(+ = INCREASE   — = DECREASE)

YEARS	PERCENTAGE CHANGE
1841–1851	— 21.7
1851–1861	— 13.9
1861–1871	— 7.9
1871–1881	— 4.5
1881–1891	— 10.4
1891–1901	— 7.1
1901–1911	— 2.6
1911–1926*	— 5.3
1926–1936	— 0.1
1936–1946	— 0.4

* Fifteen-year period.

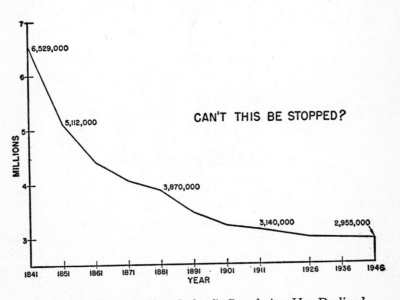

CHART I. *Showing How Ireland's Population Has Declined for More Than a Century*

tracing the tragic path to near extinction, and he will see that his home-land has been bleeding to death for a hundred years. Contrast that de-cline to less than half its population with the growth of little Denmark, which more than tripled its population during the same period. How long can this racial hemophilia continue without Erin's becoming a desic-cated, withered body from which the throbbing lifeblood has been drained? Year after year has witnessed a continuous stream of young men and women leaving their farm homes, wending their way by lorry and train to the ships to sail for foreign lands—most of them never to return.

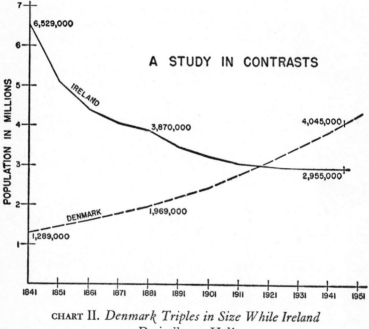

CHART II. *Denmark Triples in Size While Ireland Dwindles to Half*

"Twenty-six left Tuam Station last week for England!" begins a feature story in the December 15, 1951, issue of the Tuam *Herald,* Tralee, Ireland. "This," it continues, "is just a trivial verbal news item; rarely, indeed, does it find its way into print. So frequently down the years have we heard the likes that we have now come to accept such melancholic tidings with a nonchalance savoring of fatalism."

Linger long over that simple chart, stripped of all nonessential details, and its silent message will come home to you. It will tell you why some of the statesmen, bishops, priests, and other discerning observers are now sounding the alarm that Ireland is stricken and dying.

When we sounded a similar note of warning in a magazine article in January, 1952, we were deluged with thousands of letters from Irish people in this country declaring that Ireland was noted for its large families and ridiculing the idea that the Irish were vanishing. Not a few even asserted that we were an enemy and a traitor to Ireland for stating that the population had dwindled to an alarming extent and the prospect of extinction was ahead if countermeasures were not adopted. Refusing to look at the blinding evidence, refusing to make any effort at calm reasoning, all too many engaged merely in vituperation and abuse, for which we Irish seem to have such an unusual capacity.

If the problem with which this book comes to grips is to have reality and not to appear as the mere creation of an excited imagination, it will be necessary then to present at some length the evidence of Ireland's danger of extinction as a nation and the interpretation of those facts by her own scholars and leaders. We present the evidence not gleefully but sadly.

There are three outstanding causes of Ireland's declining population: (1) emigration; (2) too few marriages; (3) too late marriages. For more than a century Ireland has had the highest emigration rate in the world, the lowest marriage rate in the world, and the latest marriage rate in the world. Any one of these factors would seem to be enough to thwart the growth of a nation. But with all three sapping her vitality the wonder is that Ireland is still extant at all. Apparently Providence has stepped in, as Paul Vincent Carroll predicted, and saved her in spite of herself.

Let us look first at emigration. The decline in Ireland's population began in the 1840's when the Famine, the potato blight, the plague, and sickness took the lives of an estimated million people. In 1841 and for many years before, Ireland was under the control of the government of Great Britain. Much of the land of Ireland was owned by absentee British landlords and by the "planted" English, who were interested chiefly in enriching themselves through the sweat and toil of the tenant farmers.

The historian Michael Davitt estimates that in one year, when hundreds of thousands of Irish were starving, the British exported from Ireland 45 million dollars' worth of food, taken under the guise of rent. So great were the misery, suffering, and starvation of the people, who sought to stave off death by eating grass, that even the Sultan of Turkey was moved to send food.

In an address delivered in New York on March 20, 1847, Archbishop Hughes declared, "It is manifest that the causes of Ireland's suffering have been multitudinous. Nearly the whole of the soil is under the ownership of persons having no sympathy with the population except the cold tie of self-interest. Since her union with England, her commerce has followed capital to the sister isle. Nothing has remained but the produce of the soil; and that is sent to England to find a 'better market,' for the rent must be paid, but neither the produce nor the rent is ever returned.

"It has been established that the average exportation of capital from this source alone (indeed, it is the only resource that has been left) is equal to some twenty-five or thirty million dollars annually for the last seven-and-forty years; and it is at the close of this last period, by the failure of the potato crop, that Ireland without trade, without manufactures, without a return from her agricultural exports, sinks beneath the least feather; not that the feather was so weighty, but that the burden previously imposed was far above her strength to bear."

From his seat in the House of Commons, Benjamin Disraeli, later Prime Minister, thus defined the "Irish question": "A dense population in extreme distress inhabit an island where there is an established Church which is not their Church; and a territorial aristocracy, the richest of whom live in a distant capital. Thus they have a starving population, an absentee aristocracy, an alien Church and in addition the weakest executive in the world. . . . Well, what then would honorable gentlemen say if they were reading of a country in that position? They would say at once, 'the remedy is revolution.'

"But the Irish could not have a revolution, and why? Because Ireland is connected with another and more powerful country. Then what is the consequence? The connection with England became the cause of the present state of Ireland. If the connection with England prevented a revolution, and a revolution was the only remedy, England logically is in the odious position of being the cause of all the misery of Ireland. What, then, is the duty of an English minister? To effect by his policy all those changes which a revolution would do by force. That is the Irish question in its integrity."

The picture of the magnitude and the root causes of the Famine is presented not to stir smoldering embers of racial hatred, for the Irish are willing to forget and to forgive those ancient wrongs, but simply to convey to the reader an understanding of the origin of that wild and frantic exodus which has continued to the present day. The Famine had the catastrophic proportions of a continuing earthquake that shook the inhabitants from their ancient moorings in the green island and sent them scurrying in headlong haste to America, Canada, Australia, Great Britain, New Zealand, and all the countries of the world. Its terror and horror have gnawed their way into the inner marrow of the race's memory and would seem to have left upon the Gaelic soul a wound so deep that even the passage of a century has failed to heal it.

The Famine started the exodus more than a century ago. Is the racial memory of it still continuing it? Has it set up some unfathomed psychosis deep down in the Celtic psyche which fills the heart of the Gael with an insatiable restlessness, a cosmic wanderlust, a sort of wild demiurge that goads him to the waiting ship and the far-distant shore? However the prober into the unconscious motivation of the racial psyche may some day answer these questions, the fact remains that the Gael has presented to the modern world the most amazing spectacle of a wild, frantic, unbroken flight from his native land—a flight which continues strangely undiminished even after he had achieved its long-sought freedom.

A glance at Table 2 shows that, beginning in 1845, the annual migrations assumed the proportions of tidal waves. They tapered off to a mere 100,000 in 1865, then underwent a further decline, and owing to bad harvests and evictions mounted again in 1880. During the eight-year period 1845–1853, when the Famine, starvation, and sickness were taking the lives of hundreds of thousands, a total of 1,495,000 fled from the island in fear and terror.

Second only to the Famine in starting the Irish on their long exodus was the continued eviction of the people from their homes by their greedy landlords. This factor is of particular interest to me for it was as a consequence of being evicted from their farm home in Kilkenny that my father's parents migrated to America. These ejections were carried out by the constabulary with gun and bayonet and were often accompanied with acts of brutality and cruelty difficult to imagine in these enlightened days. Families with eight and ten children, some so young as to be still in their mother's arms, were thrown out, frequently half naked and starving, to flee or perish. Among the vivid memories of my

TABLE 2. *The Emigration from Ireland Following the Famine*

YEAR	EMIGRANTS
1845	75,000
1846	106,000
1847	220,000
1848	181,000
1849	219,000
1850	214,000
1851	255,000
1852	225,000
Total in 8 years	1,495,000

early childhood are the harrowing stories grandfather told of such oustings.

After a family had been suddenly pounced upon and brutally thrown out, even in midwinter, the constabulary would often tear down their humble shelter before their very eyes. This would prevent them from creeping back into it at nightfall in the pitiful effort to stave off perishing from cold and hunger. Often the family would cower for days and weeks in the ditches by the roadside, depending upon the bits of food which other families could bring from their meager cupboards.

Describing this savage warfare against peasants' homes, Isaac Butt wrote, "Let any man tell me the difference between an expulsion of the whole population of the highland regions of Glenveigh by a squadron of Cromwell's troopers in 1650 and an expulsion of its population in 1850 by the man who has inherited or purchased Cromwell's patent.

The very 'pomp and circumstance' are the same. Military force ejects the people now as it would have done then. The bayonets of the soldiery drive now, as they did then, the old population from their homes. Cruel men come now as they would have done then, and, amid the wailing of women and the cries of children, level the humble habitations that have given shelter to the simple dwellers in that glen.'"

TABLE 3. *Number of Families and Persons Evicted from Their Homes from 1849 to 1882*

YEAR	EVICTED		YEAR	EVICTED	
	FAMILIES	PERSONS		FAMILIES	PERSONS
1849	16,686	90,440	1867	549	2,489
1850	19,949	104,163	1868	637	3,002
1851	13,197	68,023	1869	374	1,741
1852	8,591	43,494	1870	548	2,616
1853	4,833	24,589	1871	482	2,357
1854	2,156	10,794	1872	526	2,476
1855	1,489	9,338	1873	671	3,078
1856	1,108	5,114	1874	726	3,571
1857	1,161	5,475	1875	667	3,323
1858	957	4,643	1876	553	2,550
1859	837	3,872	1877	463	2,177
1860	636	2,985	1878	980	4,679
1861	1,092	5,288	1879	1,238	6,239
1862	1,136	5,617	1880	2,110	10,457
1863	1,734	8,695	1881	3,415	17,341
1864	1,924	9,201	1882	5,201	26,836
1865	942	4,513			
1866	795	3,571	Total	98,723	504,747

William T. Cosgrave, the former Prime Minister of Ireland, has graciously secured for us from the official reports made by the Royal Irish Constabulary to Dublin Castle the number of such evictions from 1849 to 1882. These findings, assembled in Table 3, show that during those 33 years not less than 98,723 families and 504,747 persons were evicted from their homes. This is an astonishing total, and yet it is modest compared with the estimates made by other historians of those bleak and tragic years. It enables everyone to see how this factor accelerated still further the exodus started by the Famine.

TABLE 4. *Natural Increase and Emigration,*
1871–1881 to 1946–1951

PERIOD	AVERAGE YEARLY DECLINE (+ = INCREASE)		AVERAGE YEARLY NATURAL INCREASE (BIRTHS LESS DEATHS)		AVERAGE YEARLY NET EMIGRATION		NO. OF FEMALES EMIGRATING PER 1,000 MALES
	MALES	FEMALES	MALES	FEMALES	MALES	FEMALES	
1871–1881	8,003	10,314	16,955	14,900	24,958	25,214	1,010
1881–1891	18,384	21,749	10,873	8,727	29,257	30,476	1,042
1891–1901	11,852	12,836	8,463	6,491	20,315	19,327	951
1901–1911	2,058	6,156	9,706	8,234	11,764	14,390	1,223
1911–1926	5,508	5,672	8,426	7,396	13,934	13,068	938
1926–1936	+1,357	1,714	8,612	7,706	7,255	9,420	1,298
1936–1946	2,558	+1,226	8,700	8,680	11,258	7,453	662
1946–1951	+2,390	1,271	12,699	12,804	10,309	14,075	1,365

Long after the Famine ended, however, the emigration continued. Chart III shows that over the eighty-year period 1871–1951 emigration took a total of 2,637,520 people from Ireland! Table 4 presents the average annual increase for each intercensal period in those eighty years and shows how that increase was more than nullified—except in the last five-year period 1946–1951—by a still larger number of young men and women emigrating. During the decade 1936–1946, births exceeded deaths by 173,798, while the decrease in the population was 13,313, so that the sum of 187,111 must represent net emigration (passengers outward less passengers inward).

This is an average of 18,711 per year, compared with 16,675 per year during the decade 1926–1936. Although this continuous drain of youthful blood and energy is threatening Ireland with extinction, emigration instead of slowing down is continuing to climb to alarming proportions. Thus in the last intercensal period the annual emigration jumped from the previous average of 18,711 to 24,383—the highest in the last twenty-five years! Disturbing too is the fact that most of the emigrants in the last five years are women and girls: potential mothers of families lost forever to Ireland. Hence we can see that for more than a century emigration has been like a huge open sore on the bosom of Ireland, robbing her of her lifeblood.

By far the major portion of this vast stream of emigrants poured into the United States of America. Speaking English, they quickly took their places in the developing American scene and rose to positions of power and influence in the cultural, political and social life of the Republic. The overwhelming majority migrated to the cities, especially the larger ones, and they have given much of the tone and color to these great

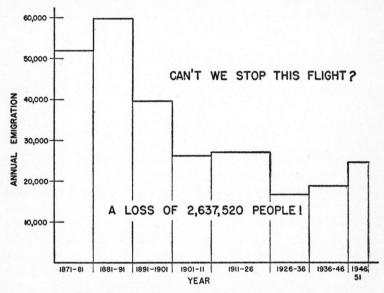

CHART III. *Showing Enormous Emigration from Ireland over Eighty-year Period, 1871–1951*

urban centers. While the century-long migration has enriched America, Great Britain, and Australia with youthful life and vigor, it has weakened Ireland to the degree that her own existence as a nation is now in grave jeopardy.

"We're everywhere," observes Sean O'Casey in a bit of whimsical "St. Patrick's Day in the Morning" reminiscing, "fleeing through every gateway from our own corner, while we're young, content to wear a sprig of shamrock once a year, and think ourselves at home again. There's not a state of America that hasn't an Irish sod on its soil; or some Irish fellow, pale as ever, wandering about its desert places. Well, we've survived through the tare of things down the ages, but listen, whisper.

"I'm afraid we're withering. Even the shadow of what we once were is fading. What's our exports now to them of the time when we roofed the cathedral of Salisbury with our Irish oak? Someone or something is ruining us, Sean. What do we send out to the world now but woeful things—young lads and lassies, porther, greyhounds, sweep tickets, and the shamrock green. We've scatthered ourselves about too much. We've spread ourselves over the wide world, and left our own sweet land thin. We're just standing on our knees now." How true! Ireland has fallen to half size, a dwarf alongside her former stature.

So great has been the stream of emigration in the years immediately after the Famine that in the 1850 United States census Irish immigrants totaled almost a million, forming 43 per cent of all the foreign-born. The immigration continued over the next forty years, and in 1890 the total of Irish immigrants residing in this country reached an all-time high of 1,871,509, constituting 20.2 per cent of all the foreign-born.

"The very large numbers of Irish that came to this country throughout the nineteenth century," observes Prof. T. Lynn Smith in his scholarly work *Population Analysis,* "have done much to give the Irish stock a primary place in the ethnic composition of the United States. Throughout the entire span of our republic, the immigration of Germans comes nearest ranking alongside that of the Irish in importance. Actually more Germans than Irish have come to our shores, but the Irish came first in greater numbers and consequently, have made large contributions to the present composition of the national blood stream."

Most influential among the forces drawing so many young men and women from Ireland is the enormous number of relatives and friends which they have abroad. There is scarcely a family in Eire which doesn't have an uncle or aunt or brother or sister or cousin overseas. Many of these frequently send funds back home to enable other members of the family to join them.

In addition, they make the transition from life in the Old World to life in the New World easy by sheltering the immigrants and getting jobs for them. As Ireland has now more of her children and their descendants in the countries overseas than at home, there is a constant centrifugal force pulling more and more of her children from their homeland.

Somewhat akin to emigration from her shores is the flight of her people from the land into the cities, especially Dublin. It is well known that it is the country districts which constitute the chief wellsprings of population. Cities are notorious for consuming their populations; unless constantly supplied with fresh recruits from the rural areas, they would decline and ultimately disappear.

Ireland is essentially an agricultural country. The ancient Irish established no cities: with fierce independence they clung to the land. At odds with this ancient tradition is the pronounced drift in recent decades into the towns and cities. Despite the repeated pleas of statesmen and prelates the young continue to flee incontinently from the farms, seeking an escape from its alleged monotony and boredom to the bright lights of the city.

The last census, 1946-1951, shows that this flight continues unabated. Of the four provinces of Eire, Leinster is the only one which shows an increase in population. This is due chiefly to an increase of 56,829 in the aggregate overswollen population of Dublin, County Borough and County. The heaviest declines again occurred in the great farming districts in the west and northwest of the country, in Counties Leitrim, Roscommon, Cavan, Kerry, Longford, Clare, Mayo, Donegal, Monaghan, Galway, and Sligo.

Leitrim lost nearly one-thirteenth of its population in the five years. With the exception of Galway, these were also the ten counties which showed the largest percentage declines in the previous intercensal period, 1936-1946. In that ten-year period there was a decrease of 37,629, or 6.2 per cent, in the number of persons engaged in agriculture. Map I vividly depicts the flight from the land, the counties with few cities showing the greatest relative losses.

The second cause of Ireland's declining population is her low marriage rate. It is a strange phenomenon, indeed, that for many decades Ireland has had the lowest marriage rate in the civilized world. In 1864-1871 it was 5.10 per 1,000 population; in 1871-1881 it declined to 4.5, and in 1881-1891 it ebbed to the all-time low of 4. There was a slight rise in 1891-1901 to 4.4, and in the next two decades it rose to 4.8 and 5.0, only to fall back to 4.6 in 1926-1936.

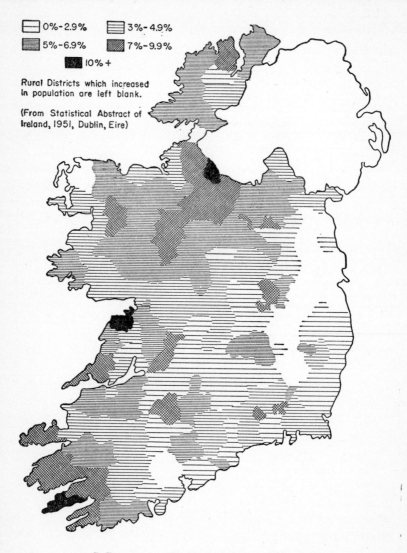

0%-2.9%   3%-4.9%
5%-6.9%   7%-9.9%
10%+

Rural Districts which increased
in population are left blank.

(From Statistical Abstract of
Ireland, 1951, Dublin, Eire)

MAP I. *Percentage Decline in Country Population
in Each Rural District, 1946–1951*

During the last two intercensal periods it remained stationary at the 5.4 mark. Chart IV presents a comparison of the marriage rate in Ireland with rates in the six Ulster counties, in England and Wales, and in the United States and shows how far it lags behind the other three. It is less than half that of the United States, and even the war years, which caused sharp upshoots of the rate in the other three countries, had but a feeble effect upon the rate in Eire.

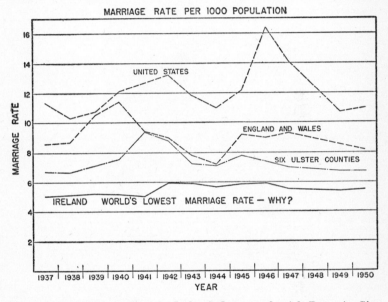

CHART IV. *Marriage Rate in Ireland Compared with Rates in Six Ulster Counties, England and Wales, and the United States*

Taking cognizance of this tragic situation, the *Irish Monthly* declares, "In 1936 Ireland had 73 married women under 45 per 1,000 of population; the U.S.A. had 145. *We are 25% lower in this figure than any other country in the world:* the Northern Ireland figure, one of the lowest, being 97 per 1,000; Scotland 105; England and Wales 123. . . . The proportion of unmarried males in this country of each age is much higher than in any other country."

Further light upon the almost incredibly high number of bachelors in Ireland is afforded us by the following breakdown of the 1946 census figures, made for us by Dr. R. C. Geary. Of the males in the 15- to 29-year group, 92 per cent are unmarried; of those in the 20- to 29-year group, 88 per cent are unmarried; and of those in the 25- to 29-year group not less than 80 per cent are bachelors.

The strange reluctance of the Irish male to marry persists even when he grows older. Thus of those in the 15- to 39-year group 78 per cent are bachelors, and even of those in the 20- to 39-year bracket bachelors constitute 72 per cent. Moreover, 73 per cent of the males and 59 per cent of the females, 15 to 44 years old, are single as contrasted with but 30 per cent of American men and women at those ages.

Furthermore, the average age at which the comparatively few Irish men and women who finally marry is the oldest of any nation in the world. The average age at marriage as derived from the results of the 1926 census, Dr. Geary's office informs us, was 34.9 years for men and 29.1 years for women. The corresponding figures for the 1946 census were 33.1 years for men and 28.0 for women. The questions from which this information was derived were not asked at the 1936 and 1951 censuses.

Contrast this, too, with the fact that in the United States half of the men are married at 24.3 years of age and half of the women at 21.6 years. Indeed the median age at which they have their first child is but 25.3 for the men and 22.6 for the women. At the age when more than half the men and women in the United States are not only married but raising families, the overwhelming majority of Irishmen and women are still bachelors and spinsters to whom marriage looms up as something in the distant future—if it looms up at all.

The proportion of bachelors is even higher in the rural areas of Ireland. In their monumental work, *Family and Community in Ireland,* Conrad M. Arensberg and Solon T. Kimball report almost unbelievably high percentages of bachelors in the 25- to 30-year group in the following dominantly rural counties: Clare, 88 per cent; Sligo, Galway, Mayo, and Leitrim, 90 per cent; Roscommon, 91 per cent. In County Clare 90 per cent of the women in the 20- to 25-year group were unmarried.

In their chapter on "Marriage Rates and Birth Rates in Ireland," the authors present the table shown as our Table 5.

TABLE 5. *Number of Married Women of Childbearing Age per 1,000 Women*

Ireland	74	Germany	125
U.S.A.	142	Denmark	112
England	121	Italy	119

It is seen that the percentage of Irish colleens who marry is just about half of that which obtains among the women in our country. One can scarcely blame them for seeking to escape from a land where the opportunity for marriage is the poorest in the world.

In short, 64 per cent of Ireland's population is single, 6 per cent widowed, and only 30 per cent married—the lowest in the civilized world! While family life is dying out in Ireland, the land is teeming with bachelors who seem strangely unaware that their refusal to marry is dooming the nation to extinction and is driving the girls and women in ever-increasing numbers to flee in desperation to other lands. Instead of engaging in the social life common to men and women in other countries, the Irish bachelors spend their evenings in "pubs," engrossed in cards, drinking, and endless chatter about horse racing.

They seem never to have heard of the words spoken by the Most High at the dawn of creation: "It is not good for man to be alone. . . . Wherefore a man shall leave father and mother and shall cleave to his wife, and they shall be two in one flesh. . . . Increase and multiply and fill the earth." No echo of these words reverberates in their hearts or minds. Without doubt, the strangest species of male on the face of the earth today is the Irish bachelor. He is the enigma and mystery of the world.

It is doubly ironic that the lowest national percentage of marriages should be recorded in what is probably the most Catholic nation in the world and among a people whose religion constantly emphasizes the dignity of marriage and encourages large families. In probably no other country is the percentage of merely civil marriages so small. Thus out of a total of 17,525 marriages in 1946, only 31 were celebrated by civil contract in the registrar's offices, while all the others were religious ceremonies.

Commenting upon this ironical condition, *Time* remarks, "Thoroughly Roman Catholic Eire has one of the lowest birth rates in the world. . . . Eire is behaving more or less as the Neo-Malthusians want all countries to behave. It is not industrializing, it is not greatly increasing food production. Vast numbers of her men and women do not marry at all. 'Ecologists' might call this balance; few ecologists would call it healthy."

All investigators, whether they be native Irishmen or not, are in agreement upon this finding: The percentage of men and women who marry in Ireland is by far the lowest in the civilized world. For more than a century, Irish men and women, contrary to their traditions and the ideals of their religious faith, have been committing racial suicide. Though the extermination of the race was not deliberately planned, their century-long abstinence from marriage on such a large scale has been ruthlessly effective in reducing the nation to a handful of old men and women, well on its way to extinction. Death comes as inexorably to the person who sleepwalks out the window of a tall building as it does to the person who, with open eyes, deliberately jumps.

Upon returning from a recent visit to Ireland, a confrere reported that more than half of his old schoolmates, now in their fifties, were still unmarried.

"Don't they have," I asked, "the normal hunger for a wife, children and a home? Are they somehow deficient in the biological and psychological endowment which prompts men of other races to leave their fathers and mothers to seek marriage partners?"

"No,"—he grinned—"they're not totally devoid of the mating impulse but they have nearly strangled it. They have the unfortunate custom of waiting in the homestead till the parents die before the eldest son inherits the farm.[1] By that time the younger ones have emigrated and the eldest is probably forty and his bachelor habits are deeply grooved. He's a confirmed old bachelor and if he thinks of marriage at all, he thinks of it . . . for others."

"But don't those bachelors," I asked, "ever think of the slow suicide they are inflicting upon the race?"

"Apparently not. They're a self-centered lot . . . a disgrace to the nation. A good stiff tax on them and on spinsters to help young couples get started would spur many to action. Such a tax is badly needed to change the celibate character of the nation and to rescue it from extinction."

---

[1] The homestead may be inherited also by a younger son or daughter, thus increasing the uncertainty of the plans of all for their future.

"Has the high esteem for the religious—priests and nuns—who are all celibates, been carried over to esteem for celibacy as a state of life in the world?" I asked him.

"Unfortunately it has. This is particularly true in families where one of the children has become a priest or nun. The number of the remaining children who remain celibates is as a rule unusually high. It is sad to reflect that while Ireland is sending priests and nuns like my sister and myself to minister in foreign lands, the folks back home, through their persistent refusal to marry, are dooming the nation to extinction.

"The Irish need to be reminded," he continued, "that marriage is also a vocation . . . in fact, the one intended for 95 per cent of the people upon whom rests the indispensable duty not merely to continue the race but to increase it. God said: 'Increase and multiply.' If I were a priest in Ireland, I would preach that in season and out of season. In fact, I'd shout it from the housetops. It's the message most needed by the Irish today . . . or else Ireland will soon be peopled by foreigners."

"Yes," I said, "and that's the message that needs to be shouted to the Irish in America as well."

The *Ave Maria* recently proposed the following drastic method of reducing the enormous number of bachelors in Ireland: "We suggest that all the culpable Irish bachelors in country districts be taken into custody and held in prison until such time as they make a promise to find a mate within six months. This may seem drastic, but Ireland's falling population, due to infrequent marriages, calls for definite action to diminish widespread bachelorhood."

Apparently some such means will be needed likewise to stir the grossly disproportionate number of Irish bachelors in America to nuptial activity.

The decrease in the number of school children in Eire during the last 100 years is without a parallel in any nation in the civilized world. From 1851 to 1861 the magnitude of the decline was catastrophic. Then occurred a slight increase, followed by a sharp decline from 1881 to 1901. The rate of decline then became less steep and the period from 1946 to 1951 shows a slight increase. No nation can long survive if its children wither away, and a glance at Chart V shows how real is the threat of Ireland's extinction.

Not all the colors in the Irish picture, however, are a somber black. There is one white color, full of hope and promise. It is the generosity with which the couples who do marry pass on the precious heritage of life to offspring. Despite the fact that they marry later than the people of any other nation, Irishwomen have an unusually high fecundity rate. The 1946 census inquiry into fertility of marriage shows that the average size of the completed family in 1946 was slightly over 4 children. During the decade from 1936 to 1946, births exceeded deaths by 173,798. Hence if all emigration had been stopped during that period, Eire would have experienced a sizable gain. Unfortunately it was more than nullified by an emigration of 187,111, causing a decrease of 13,313 in the population.

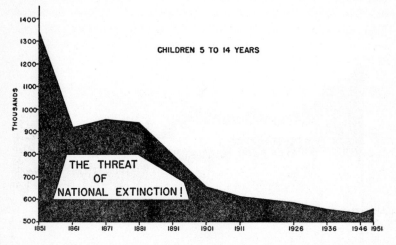

CHART V. *The Tragic Decline in Number of Irish Children—
A Catastrophe Unparalleled in Any Nation*

The 1946–1951 census is even more favorable. The annual average birth rate per thousand of the population rose from 20.3 for the previous decade to 21.9. During these last five years the average annual natural increase (births less deaths) was 12,699 males and 12,804 females. This again was almost nullified by an average annual emigration of 10,309 males and 14,075 females.

It is then more accurate to say that the people of Ireland are not exactly dying out but are moving out and that the *nation* in consequence is dying. The emigrants are absorbed into other nations and are for all practical purposes lost to their native land. They are like snowflakes melting as they fall and disappearing forever from sight. Since each of these young emigrants has cost Ireland about $5,000, it is evident that the continued mass migration is impoverishing Ireland economically, socially, culturally, and spiritually.

"If all emigration were to cease," Dr. R. C. Geary points out in a letter to us, "the population of this country would reproduce itself with a substantial margin of safety." That is a point well worth keeping in mind in all the discussion of the vanishing Irish. But it is also true that if Eire had a higher and therefore a more normal marriage rate, say something like that of the United States or even congested England, the natural increase would then be sizable, even if the emigration rate persisted.

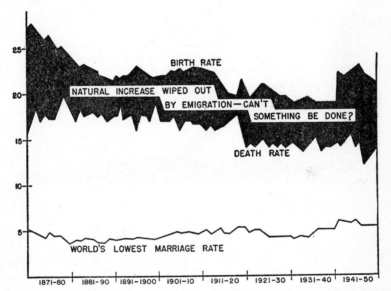

CHART VI. *World's Lowest Marriage Rate and Highest Emigration Rate Bring Ireland to Near Extinction (marriages, births, and deaths per 1,000 population)*

Likewise, if the Irish married at ages comparable to those in other countries instead of at their present unusually late ages, it is likely that the number of births would mount considerably higher and thus in-

crease still further the nation's margin of safety. Since the net emigration rate, despite all efforts to lower it, has risen during each intercensal
period since 1926, it would seem advisable to foster both more marriages
and earlier ones. The wisdom of this policy would seem to be clearly
indicated by Chart VI, which shows how emigration has more than
wiped out the natural increase over the eighty-year period 1871–1951.

It is this nonmarrying tradition that Irish immigrants bring with
them to America—so that today the percentage of bachelors and spinsters
among them and among Americans of Irish descent is probably more
than double that among other extractions. Thus recently the Bishop of a
Middle Western diocese told us of a country parish composed almost
entirely of Irish from the "auld sod." They were so numerous that the
parish originally was a thriving and prosperous one. But over the years
their numbers thinned out, and because of the scarcity of marriages
among them the Bishop was compelled to reduce the parish to a mission.

"If those settlers," said the Bishop, "had been Germans, Poles, Italians,
Lithuanians, or any other nationals save Irish, they would have more
than doubled their numbers. The countryside would be studded with
the prosperous, children-filled homes of their married sons and daughters. But the strange propensity of so many of the Irish to keep their
offspring, even when grown men and women, about the home has
yielded a crop chiefly of bachelors and spinsters, and has spelled their
gradual disappearance.

"It is a great pity," he added sadly, "and a great loss to the Church
and to America. It's the reenactment in America of the tragedy that has
been going on in Ireland for a century. We need to preach to the Irish
in America as well as to those in Eire that marriage, too, is a vocation
and a great and noble one and they should not look upon it with Jansenistic aversion."

The instance cited by the Bishop could be duplicated in thousands of
communities across the nation. The parish in which we were raised was
almost 100 per cent Irish—a large settlement from County Kilkenny.
The pastor and most of the assistants were from Ireland, and St. Patrick's
Day was celebrated with as great enthusiasm as in Dublin. But if one
visits there now, he finds Germans, Syrians, and Italians in abundance
and a dwindling number of Irish. But the gravestones are covered with
their names. It is the old story of the strange failure to marry, which has

made Eire a nation of bachelors and spinsters, writing its tragic tale anew in America.

This is all the more inexcusable in our country because the economic conditions are so much more favorable here. After boasting about the greatness of the Irish race, they proceed to doom it to extinction—a strange manner in which to manifest their belief. One may well wonder if the Irish and their descendants in America haven't an underlying taint of Jansenism, which Bruce Marshall so aptly characterizes as "the impression that God made an artistic mistake when He planned the mechanics of procreation."

The story is much the same in Canada. Recently a pastor from Canada remarked to us: "What you say about the Irish in the United States not marrying and reproducing themselves like members of other nationalities certainly holds true for Canada too. For years I have witnessed the slow death of a number of once flourishing Irish parishes."

"Why?" I asked.

"Because so few of them marry. If it were not for the influx of a great number of Dutch immigrants, some of those parishes would either have to be reduced to outmissions or closed altogether. I don't understand that peculiar strain in the Irish nature which freezes so many of them in a lifelong bachelorhood. They're a mystery, especially to the French Canadians, who think of marriage as the normal goal in life for those not called to the religious life."

To return to Ireland. We have presented the figures furnished us by the Irish government, showing the century-long decline of Ireland and the threat of extinction facing it. We have presented these in graphs so simple that even a child can read the story at a glance. But there are some people who are allergic to statistics and say they prove nothing. Hence we shall supplement the hard, factual, statistical evidence with the testimony of a few witnesses whose words will surely carry conviction even if statistics fail.

Our first witness is the Rev. Jerome Dennehy, C.C., of Tuosist, who tells what has happened in his typical parish. *The Kerryman,* Tralee, January 31, 1953, gives a vivid account of the testimony which Father Dennehy presented to the county committee of agriculture in Tralee. He said in substance: Every mother of a grown child in the parish is a lonely mother, lonely for her children scattered over the earth. The priests and teachers decided in December, 1951, to conduct a survey to find out how many of the people between the ages of twenty and forty who were born in the parish are still there.

Omitting the people who were dead, they learned that of the 746 people who had passed through the schools of the parish from January, 1917, to December, 1946, 192 are still left in the parish, 151 had left for other parts of Ireland, mainly Dublin and Cork, and 403 had left, mainly for England and America.

In other words, 26 per cent were left in the parish, 20 per cent were in other parts of Ireland, and 54 per cent had gone abroad!

These figures, he continued, are out of date now because quite a number of those who were in the parish in 1951 and quite a number of those who were in other parts of the country in 1951 have now gone abroad. Even more disturbing is the fact that of the 379 girls who left the schools during that period only 51 were left in the parish in December, 1951, and that figure was already out of date, for only about 40 of the 379 are now left in the parish. In 1840 the population of the parish was 7,400, and in the spring of 1952 it was down to a mere 1,171. In 1845 the birth rate was 347, and in 1950 it was down to 18!

Now silent, decaying monuments to something or other, continued Father Dennehy, were the forty-one houses in the parish which had been completely closed down in the past eight years. Some of these were erected in the 1930's.

Here is a close-up of the withering away of life in a typical parish in Ireland. It is a mirror of what is taking place in many such parishes, especially in the rural areas.

Our second witness is the Most Rev. Cornelius Lucey, Bishop of Cork. In a recent confirmation address at Ballingeary, Bishop Lucey declared, "For a hundred years now, during which the population of every other civilized country has increased by leaps and bounds we have been the vanishing Irish. Two-thirds of our people have vanished in that time, and the end is not yet. The decline goes steadily on. Not Partition, then, not the balance of payments, not every other Party crisis of today or yesterday is Ireland's major national problem. That problem is rural depression and decay—the disappearance of so many uneconomic holdings, so-called, the drying up of the very wellsprings of national population."

Referring to the large stream of young men and women leaving Ireland each year for foreign lands, never to return, the Bishop said: "If only the seed for a new crop of families were left, there would be no cause for alarm. But the tragedy is that it is not being left. Too few marriages, too few big families, too many holdings with the houses closed for good, too many schools with the attendance not half of what it was a generation ago—that is what is so lamentable in so grand a people up and down the countryside. The rural population is vanishing, and with it is *vanishing the Irish race itself.* For the rural families are the wellsprings from which the towns and cities replenish themselves, and if they are drying up, then inevitably we are doomed to wither away as a nation. Rural Ireland is stricken and dying and the will to marry on the land is almost gone."

Our third witness is the Most Rev. Joseph Walsh, Archbishop of Tuam. Addressing the Tuam Young Farmers' Club the Archbishop declared, "Anyone who has the least love or pride in his country cannot but feel sad when he sees the countryside denuded, while the finest of boys and girls drift to the towns, or worse still, leave the country altogether to place their talents at the disposal of foreigners. During the past ten years, one thing especially has brought me great sadness—the flight from the land.

"There is no use in one's boasting," continued the Archbishop, "that this country has attained freedom, if the land of Ireland is not worked to provide sustenance for all our citizens, if our men are not given the chance of earning a decent livelihood, so that they can marry and rear a family. Our population in the country districts is falling; already economists view with alarm the low marriage rate in these districts and the fall in the number of pupils attending the national schools."

Our fourth witness is the Most Rev. James McNamee, Bishop of Ardagh and Clonmacnois. In a recent Lenten Pastoral the Bishop called attention to a recent census report showing a continued decline in the population, especially marked in the rural districts of his diocese. "Thus we are faced with the sad and discouraging paradox that on the one hand this motherland of ours was never so prosperous in her long history as she is today, and yet her children flee incontinently from her shores in an exodus only comparable to that consequent upon the great Famine of a hundred years ago. . . . This perennial stream of emigration from our shores is surely Ireland's supreme problem: it is the life-blood of the nation that is being drained away. The solution of a problem so truly and literally *vital* demands the cooperation of all in a unity of purpose that should transcend all party differences and sectional interests. Whatever can be done should be done without delay to stem the tide both of emigration to the cities and of emigration beyond the sea."

The Bishop then turns to the other great cause of Irish decline: "Emigration is unfortunately not the only social bane affecting our country to a degree unknown elsewhere: there is also the alarmingly low marriage rate that prevails amongst our people. Along with the highest emigration rate in the world, we have the lowest marriage rate! Either would be a serious threat to the national life; but their combined effect, if not checked, can only lead to near extinction of the Irish race in Ireland. It is especially ominous that this low marriage rate should be lowest of all in the rural districts and amongst the agricultural community; which, in normal circumstances, should be the abounding life-spring of the nation.

"In so far as this low marriage rate is due to economical causes, the remedies would be the same as those discussed above for migration from the rural districts. But, as in the case of emigration we cannot attribute our low marriage rate solely to economic causes. Many remain unmarried who might easily support a family, because for one reason or other they had not the opportunity earlier in life and have now sunk into a lethargic and fatalistic acceptance of permanent bachelorhood. In some cases parents are, or have been, at fault, either through unreasonable opposition to the marriage of their children, or through an obstinate refusal to make such domestic arrangements and settlements as would enable them to marry and found a family. Such an attitude to the marriage of their children is deplorable on many counts."

Enumerating the evil consequences of such an attitude, the Bishop continues: "It is injurious to the happiness of the parents themselves and unjust to their children who are frustrated of their natural right to marriage by such opposition or want of cooperation on the part of parents. Rather should parents on the contrary encourage their children to marriage, and to early marriage where possible; instead of practically compelling them to an enforced celibacy until well on in middle age. By so doing they would consult for their own happiness; for the spiritual welfare of their children; for the revitalising of the country side; and for the future strength and prosperity of the nation."

The testimony of Father Dennehy and of the three members of the Hierarchy reflects the warnings now being sounded by all the priests and bishops of Ireland. Since the fifth century, when St. Patrick planted the Faith in Ireland, they have labored ceaselessly for the welfare, spiritual and temporal, of the Irish people, and no voice commands greater attention or respect than theirs. No one can read their wise pronouncements without detecting therein the notes of anxious solicitude and deep concern over the plight of Ireland today.

Our fifth witness is *The Standard,* the Catholic newspaper of Dublin. In its February 27, 1953, issue it featured a three-column editorial with a caption in huge type shouting, "IRELAND! YOU'RE IN DANGER!" The subtitle runs "Your Population Is Falling. Your People Are Leaving You. Face Up to the Dangers!" Then it proceeds to tell the Irish people how imminent is the danger of extinction as a nation.[1] That threat is depicted graphically in Chart V.

Our last and chief witness is none other than Eamon De Valera, the Prime Minister of Ireland and one of its most respected and beloved leaders in our generation. De Valera recently made a public appeal to the thousands of Irish immigrants to England to return to their homeland because it stands in such dire need of them. The appeal was unusual and attracted wide attention in both Great Britain and Ireland. It mirrors the growing concern of the government over the desperate plight of the nation, bleeding slowly to death while its children continue to flee to other lands.

The *Chicago Tribune* recently sent a trained journalist, Arthur Veysey, to depict the high lights of his observations in the various countries of Europe. His dispatch, cabled from Galway, describes the scenes of desolation he saw all around him. "It is a sad thing," he said, "to drive through the green hills of western Ireland. All is so still among the piles of stone which were once the cottages of the Irish who have gone away. For more than 100 years, the chief export of Ireland has been its

---

[1] Further evidence of the anxiety of the nation's leaders to alert the people to the danger of extinction is the article featured in a recent issue of *The Landmark,* the monthly journal of Muintir na Tire, entitled "Can Ireland Survive?"—the title printed in huge type on the front cover.

sons and daughters. For more than 1,000 years the Irish have been going out into the world, but the mass exodus really began with the great Famine.

"Between 1845 and 1851, a sixth of Ireland's population fled, seeking something to eat, and a sixth of those who remained at home died. For 100 years the flight has continued until today Ireland is the only nation in the world with half the population it had a century ago. Although the flight from Ireland has slowed, the flight from the farms continues. Rural counties today have only a third the population of a century ago and some have even less."

The desolation stretches, however, even into the cities and towns. "Walk the back streets of Limerick," continues Veysey, "of Galway or other important centers and you see whole buildings abandoned. Some villages of the west are also half derelict. Nor is it just cottages that stand empty. Everywhere are the castles and manors—all ruins since the landlords lost their grip on the land. And everywhere are remnants of churches and abbeys."

Yes, a ride through the Irish countryside is a melancholy experience today. Everywhere the discerning traveler sees signs of abandonment, decay, and incipient death creeping like paralysis over what was once a great and populous nation. On repeated trips over the last thirty years through the Irish countryside, sometimes bicycling and sometimes walking, I found myself saddened by the unmistakable marks of abandonment everywhere I looked.

"What!" I found myself saying, "are these places being closed and abandoned? Is this the land and are these the green hills for which my forefathers fought for more than seven centuries? Only in recent years have their sons come into ownership of the land and achieved freedom and independence. How strange and how sad that they should now turn their backs upon the land for which their forebears fought and died. Crimsoned by their blood and moistened by their tears, this green island deserves a better fate than abandonment."

With heavy heart and moistened eyes I prayed that some day a clarion blast would be sounded throughout the length and breadth of Ireland and reach clear over to her children across the seas and awake the Irish race throughout the world to the threat of doom closing in upon their homeland. Erin is the physical and spiritual homestead of many millions of sons and daughters across the seas, the sanctuary of their spiritual ideals, and the island enshrined in the loveliest memories of their race. It is sad to think of her falling into decay, denuded of her youth, likely to fall in increasing measure into the hands of foreigners, gobbling up farm after farm.

The government is keenly aware that the population has sunk so low that now the very existence of Ireland as a nation is in jeopardy. That government is composed of wise and able leaders, and we have complete confidence in their ability and statesmanship. Already it has launched various measures, and its efforts are deserving of the support of its sons and daughters at home and abroad. These and other measures will be discussed by the Irish contributors to this study. The aim is not only to save Ireland from extinction but to see her grow in strength and power as a great and flourishing nation of ten or more millions ... and ultimately a united Ireland as well.

The Irish have a great and glorious past; they have enriched all lands with their talents. Everywhere they have spearheaded the struggle for human liberty and have drenched a thousand battlefields with their blood. That is why the spectacle of their uninterrupted population decline for a century—until now they totter perilously close to the abyss of extinction—is distressing to every friend of the Irish race. Particularly distressing is it to Ireland's sons and daughters in other lands, who are brokenhearted at the prospect of the Irish becoming an enervated minority in a land occupied by foreigners—and, even worse, to be found like the vanished Mayans only in mausoleums, tombs, and graves of the buried past.

WHY FEW IRISH MARRY

3 _____

Patrick B. Noonan, C.S.Sp.

Patrick B. Noonan was born in Askeaton, County Limerick, on April 11, 1914. Raised on a farm, Patrick got a close-up of Irish rural life, with its distinctive economic and social problems, which has enabled him to write with insight and understanding of the conditions confronting all who live on the land. As a young boy he attended Cappagh National School, then under the direction of William Murphy, an able and distinguished teacher.

Patrick received his secondary education at Rockwell College, County Tipperary, a large boarding school conducted by the Irish Holy Ghost Fathers. In 1933 he entered the novitiate of that community, and upon its completion he enrolled at the National University of Ireland, where he took degrees in science and art. He taught for two years at his alma mater and then completed his studies in philosophy and theology at the Senior Scholasticate, Kimmage Manor, Dublin, being ordained on July 16, 1944.

His first appointment was as bursar at the novitiate, Kilshane, Tipperary, where he remained for three years. Father Noonan, C.S.Sp., was then sent to St. Mary's School, Nairobi, Kenya, East Africa, where he teaches science. The school has an enrollment of some 400 students drawn chiefly from the European families living in Kenya, Uganda, and Tanganyika.

Despite the pressure of his educational duties, Father Noonan has contributed articles to various magazines. Far from lessening his interest in the welfare of his native land, his temporary absence has increased it. Indeed, the absence has given him a perspective which enables

*him to write with both revealing insight and judicious concern about
the Emerald Isle so dear to the heart of every Irish exile.*

IT IS A STARTLING REFLECTION THAT THE IRISH ARE A VANISHING RACE, AND
if the present[1] rate of decline continues, they will be counted amongst
the extinct peoples in less than a hundred years. Moreover, the saddest
feature of the tragedy is the universal unconcern of the Irish themselves.
Very few, even among the thinking elite, have uttered a cry of warning.
The ordinary folk still cling tenaciously to a system which is more
deadly than either the plantations or the rack, while successive governments have done little or nothing to avert the evil.

Many, no doubt, will question the truth of the statement that the
Irish race is in danger of extinction. Does it not sound unreasonably
pessimistic to foretell the total disappearance of the very people among
whom Christian marriage is respected and birth control is at a minimum? Would it not seem that the nation which permits unlimited
emigration can have no fear for its future welfare? It will be argued with
a certain degree of plausibility that emigration, instead of being a
menace to the preservation of the race, is the natural sign of overpopu-
lation and of healthy expansion.

However, when we examine the question in the light of the available
data and national perversive tendencies, it will be seen that the outlook
is anything but optimistic. Even the Black Famine of 1848 is a minor
catastrophe in comparison with the deadly but hidden blight which now
saps the vitality of the Celts as a nation.

The modern trends which affect the stability of the Irish population
—emigration, rural depopulation, and town crowding—are the heralds
of racial decay. They are grave national evils. In other countries emigration is perhaps the normal expansion of a surplus population; in Ireland it is depriving an underpopulated country of the fairest of its sons
and daughters. It is a sign, not of progress, but of inevitable doom.

In contrast with all the other European countries, Ireland has the
smallest average rural population and the figures are lowest where the
land is best. This is why it is so hard to explain the excessive emigration
figures. Rural Ireland could and should support three times the present

[1] Editor's note: This refers to the census of 1936 to 1946—the last decennial census
taken when this was written.

number in comfort and prosperity. It would seem that country life is being subordinated to the city. This process of urbanization is relentlessly weaning the youth of Ireland from the bosom of mother earth.

An underpopulated nonindustrial country which panders to the gay life of a swollen metropolis of over 550,000 inhabitants, one-sixth of the total population, has lost due respect for the struggling farmer and cottier. Ireland has become top-heavy, and the foundations, which should rest deep in the soil, are beginning to crumble.

Appalling as this drainage by emigration must appear, there is still a greater source of alarm. I refer to the prevailing system of late marriages. Emigration is a great evil, but it might be condoned to some extent if those at home married at an age when they are capable of producing large families.

Up and down the country there is the same lamentable, if amusing, spectacle of bachelors and old maids who still cherish the hope of capturing a suitable spouse. A recent writer who visited a country district stated that he found the young people waiting for a ship and the old people waiting for the grave. Apparently he did not notice the middle-aged group waiting for a partner. Some men defer matrimony to an age when a nurse would be more appropriate than a bride.

In no other country in the world is marriage undertaken so late in life, and perhaps in no other country in the world is there such a high proportion of the unmarried. Worse than the number of bachelors and old maids is the custom of deferring marriage until the man is almost sterile and the woman incapable of producing more than one or two children. If we take the system as it is at present, the average family will be less than three, excluding the parents.

These are the somber facts. They require little elaboration to reveal the seriousness of the Irish racial question. Unless immediate and drastic measures are taken, the Irish race will either disappear altogether or continue to survive only as an enervated minority in a planted country. Already Ireland has become the land of promise for many adventurous or tax-fleeing foreigners who eagerly purchase the lands and property vacated by the emigrant. I have heard that great numbers of aliens have settled in the country in recent years. Some of the best farms are passing into the hands of unscrupulous men whose love of Ireland is on a par with their love of God. As native life and culture dwindle with the decreasing population, its foreign counterpart will become more dominant, and native Paddy will soon find himself a stranger in his own land.

A large number of thinking men outside the country look with dismay at the spectacle of the racial suicide of an old Catholic nation. They find it difficult to fathom the bland indifference with which the Irish authorities, religious as well as secular, regard the major problem of their people. It is indeed a problem which should concern Church as well as state. There are serious moral consequences in a system which prevents young men and women, not called to a life of celibacy, from getting married at an age when marital union is most necessary and fruitful. Priests unfortunately are perhaps more vehement in condemning incontinency than in promoting early marriages. What really calls for condemnation is not the immorality—which in the circumstances is remarkably rare—but rather the system, which is the root cause of the immorality.

It is not easy to assign any one particular reason for the low as well as the late marriage rate in Ireland. No two bachelors will attribute to the same motives or conditions their failure to marry. Nevertheless a close acquaintance with the people and the country reveals certain major factors and universal trends which account for the system of belated marriages.

In the first place, the very mentality of the people is opposed to youthful unions. The present faulty system, which originated in the stress and poverty of a bygone age, is now regarded as the ideal system. What was once imposed as a necessity has become the accepted standard. People, especially in the country districts, consider thirty-five the lowest suitable age for a man to marry, while the woman is scarcely considered mature at thirty.

Personally I believe that no less than 40 per cent of the bachelors and spinsters in Ireland are the product of this erroneous outlook, plus a modicum of selfishness and inertia. The average man does not regard the prospects of matrimony seriously until he has reached his thirties. Then too often he finds himself in a groove, a fixed mode of existence, which he is loath to abandon even in order to secure a worthy partner or to promote family life.

Frequently it is the man in possession of all the normal comforts of life who emerges into confirmed bachelorhood. He does not require a wife to cook his meals or to keep his home in order. He can pay a maid, or he may have a loyal unmarried sister. In his eyes marriage is more of a disability than a blessing. While terminating his gay independence, it makes demands on his generosity and self-sacrifice. Even if he does marry, he is too old to be capable of adjustment and in consequence his married life will be unhappy.

While thus conceding that a large percentage of the marriage evasions is due to the wrong attitude and inertia of the people, we must, however, admit that the prevailing economic conditions are by far the greatest factor. It is a fact of experience that a falling marriage rate in a Catholic society is always a sign of economic distress. Christianity promotes fruitful family life rather than barren stagnation. In spite of what the unobservant visitor or the prosperous native may think, conditions in Ireland are far from satisfactory.

It is true, of course, that the past twenty-five years have seen many improvements in the general way of life. Better housing and domestic comforts are available for those who can afford them. But we must not conclude that the well-being of some is an index of the prosperity of all. It is estimated that in the west of Ireland, where native blood is purest and native culture strongest, over 75 per cent of the young people are unable to settle down because of economic conditions. They are eager to work and to reproduce, but they are the hapless victims of a regime which imposes idleness and poverty.

It is beyond the scope of this chapter to outline the errors of the present economic arrangement. The problem is extremely complex, involving the analysis of a faulty financial system, vested interests, the uneven distribution of land, the progressive subordination of rural life, lack of housing, the coexistence of bureaucracy with inefficiency, and finally the inheritance of all the national evils, including a party system of government, which follows centuries of alien domination.

Were the youth of Ireland in a position to earn an honest living and establish a home in their own land, it is certain that emigration would almost cease and the marriage rate would be higher. Surely then a country which is deemed to have more reclaimable territory than all Central Europe together, which has over 300,000,000 pounds sterling of its money invested abroad, and which provides a sanctuary for all kinds of undesirable aliens could do more for its own sons and daughters. It is no exaggeration to state that Ireland could feed and support two or even three times its present population in comfort and prosperity.

The fact that it has not already achieved that happy condition, or at least that it has not made this the major issue of its social policy, is a serious slur on the ruling authority, past and present. The position seems altogether hopeless when one of the leading political figures declares publicly that rural prosperity will be in direct ratio to the accelerated thinning of the population by emigration.

In addition to the economic status, there are certain customs inherent in the Irish way of family life which impede early marriage. Chief among these is the custom by which the parents retain the ownership and administration of their property even into the seventies and eighties. Only the grave will terminate their rule. Meanwhile the eldest son, who is frequently the only boy of the family not to emigrate, is prevented from introducing a new mistress into the home. In the eyes of his parents he is still a "child," and he dare not go counter to their wishes.

Normally he abandons all prospects of marriage until they are laid to rest. If he is courageous enough to broach the subject of matrimony, he is likely to incur their wrath. Even if they grant him a sympathetic hearing, they still retain the exclusive right of admitting or rejecting the proposed daughter-in-law. In a word, she must be their choice, not his. Before she is deemed worthy of admission to the family circle, she must be endowed with certain qualifications: a social status equivalent or superior to their own, various personal attributes, and last, but not least, a handsome dowry. Thus it is the man's parents who are the judges of the girl's worthiness.

Perhaps in no other country and among no other section of the people is family pride so deep as among the rural classes in Ireland. Social status is usually a greater consideration than personal goodness. When it comes to marriage, social discrimination goes beyond the bounds of reason and charity. Hence it often happens that a happy union is prevented or postponed, simply because an excellent young girl cannot satisfy all the exaggerated demands of two old grave-dodgers whose days would be better spent at prayer than at domestic administration.

It does not seem that the road to matrimony will in time become easier for the young men of Ireland. Since the proportion of female emigrants is rapidly increasing, the number of female candidates for matrimony will be correspondingly reduced. Even those who return and marry in their native land will reject the attentions of the hard-working farmer in favor of the businessman, the civil servant, or the lout. Their urbanized manners will no longer be compatible with the healthy but arduous duties of a farmer's wife.

The past decade has indeed witnessed a striking change in Irish girlhood. The combined influences of emigration, the tourist influx, the craze for pleasure, and all the modern trends in thought and conduct have well-nigh transformed the traditional colleen into a sophisticated miss. A rural existence no longer appeals to her. The obvious consequence is fewer marriages and a further subordination of rural life.

What then of Ireland's future? When a crisis threatens the very existence of a nation, only an inspired nationwide movement can possibly provide a remedy. Mere pronouncements and spasmodic efforts on the part of a few are of little avail. The lead must come from authority, and the means adopted must be enlightened and far-reaching.

The changing of the attitude of the people in regard to the proper age for marriage is the task of education. They should be taught, not merely in the schools, but from the pulpit and through all the modern channels of information, that the normal age for marriage is before, not after, thirty. The constant and universal insistence on the desirability of youthful marriages would soon destroy the old attitude and encourage lovers to end an aimless courtship and effect an early union.

Likewise judicious legislation should safeguard the freedom of the son who wishes to marry. It is not in the interests of national prosperity that selfish parents should retain to the grave a quasi-dictatorial authority. Their work will be all the more efficiently executed if transferred to younger hands. The law should entitle the dependent heir who enters the married state to the ownership, partial at least, of his father's property and wealth. There is no injustice if the parents are guaranteed a home and adequate provision for old age.

The economic factors provide a far more difficult problem. Only an enlightened and courageous government can provide the solution. The altering of a bad financial system, the interference with vested interests, the stabilization of rural life, and the provision of work and housing for all present a major task. But, on the other hand, where in all the world is there a more compact state or a more uniform culture?

If rural Ireland were to provide greater opportunities for enthusiastic youth and present a brighter aspect, the flight from the land would be quickly retarded. Emigration will be effectively stopped, not by any legal enactments, but by removing the causes of emigration. Until rural life is rendered more attractive, until the government gives the farm-house and cottage all the attention it now gives to the luxury hotel, until every village and parish offers work and security for its sons and daughters, there can be no solution to the Irish question.

Thus the state should provide those economic and social conditions which render youthful marriages not only possible but desirable. Young couples should be the recipients of special benefits. Marriage and family allowances, while perhaps not being an ideal procedure, may be neces-sary owing to the high cost of living. A system of graded taxation affect-ing old maids (over twenty-five) and bachelors (over thirty) would have the dual advantage of providing funds for marriage endowments and of stimulating the tardy and fainthearted toward the goal of matri-mony.

Of late there are some indications that the Irish authorities have taken up the matter seriously. Recent pastorals have decried the evils of emigration and late marriages. The same problems have been discussed in Parliament, and a commission has been formed to inquire into their causes and to suggest remedies. There is a growing sense of uneasiness and apprehension which may well be the herald of an all-out effort to save the country and the people. In the meantime let us cherish the hope that God will not allow to vanish the nation which, at the price of poverty and persecution, chose the "better part."

WOMAN-SHY IRISHMEN

4

Maura Laverty

Starting as a journalist, Maura Laverty became a novelist and later a playwright and now ranks among the leading dramatists of Ireland. In early life she spent some years in Spain, where she worked as a secretary for Princess Bibesco, did some foreign correspondence for a bank, and had various newspaper jobs on "El Debate."

She drew upon this experience in writing her book "No More Than Human." It embodies episodes about Delia Scully, whose earlier life is depicted in "Never No More," which is partly autobiographical. Her novel "Touched by the Thorn" met with instant success and was published in England under the title "Alone We Embark."

In recent years Maura Laverty has turned her hand to the drama, and in this difficult field she has achieved probably her greatest success. Her first play "Liffey Lane" proved popular with Dublin audiences, and her producers commissioned her to prepare another script. "Tolka Row" was the result, and it further enhanced her reputation as a dramatist of skill and with something to say.

Her latest play "A Tree in the Crescent" drew packed audiences in Dublin and won acclaim even from dramatic critics, who had been somewhat reserved in their praise for her previous efforts. This play deals with love, marriage, housekeeping, flat finding, childbearing, and child rearing among the common things of each indifferent day. The story is unfolded with a quiet insistence, an intense poignancy, and an enveloping sense of humor.

In addition to editing a woman's magazine and contributing plays, stories, interviews, and cookery talks to Irish radio programs, Maura

*Laverty is running a weekly radio feature for women. She is married to
a journalist, has two daughters, and resides in Dublin.*

A FEW YEARS AGO, "ESQUIRE" PUBLISHED AN ARTICLE DEBUNKING THE REPU-
tation which Latins have been building up for themselves ever since
Ovid wrote *Ars amoris*.

"For one Irish-American," wrote, in effect, the author, "I would trade
you five Cubans, three Italians and two slightly-used Spaniards."

I know Latins. I know Irishmen. I know nothing about Irish-Americans beyond what James Farrell and Betty Smith have taught me; so I
will content myself with saying that if such a swap represents a fair
exchange, the air and diet in the United States must have a highly
beneficial effect on men of Irish breed. No woman in her senses would
trade even one very moth-eaten Spaniard for a whole team of All-Ireland
Hurling Finalists, referee included.

For there is this to be said for Latins at their lousiest: they have a
happy knack of making a woman feel that in merely being a woman
she enriches the world. There is nothing but degradation for her in the
shamed, apologetic approach of the average Irishman. The "insults" to
which she may be subjected abroad are not nearly so shattering to her
self-respect as the cold indifference she encounters at home.

I realize that in saying all this I am laying myself open to being called
a frustrated, middle-aged, anti-Irish hag.

Middle-aged? Certainly. I am forty-five.

Hag? Possibly—although my husband does not seem to think so.

Frustrated? Hardly. I am, thank God, a happy and contented woman,
married to that rarest of rare creatures, a full-blooded and warmhearted
Irishman. We are blessed with a delightful family, of whom the eldest
is twenty-one and the youngest is four years.

Anti-Irish? As to that, I like to believe what the late Stephen Gwynn
wrote of me when reviewing one of my books in *Time and Tide:* "She
is one who loves Ireland and yet sees Ireland clear."

It is precisely because I love Ireland that I would quote from Frank
O'Connor's translation of "The Midnight Court" and be one of those

> ... women in scores who come to attest
> That the youth of the country's gone to hell,

And the population in decline . . .
And what have you done to restore the nation?
Shame on you there without chick nor child
With women in thousands running wild.
What matter to you if their beauty founder,
If belly and breast will never be rounder,
If ready and glad to be mother and wife,
They drop unplucked from the boughs of life?

The two hundred years which have passed since Bryan Merryman wrote his scathing denunciation of woman-slighting Irishmen have done nothing to mend matters—chiefly, I believe, because the men of Ireland have never acknowledged that there is anything to mend. In this smug attitude they have been aided and abetted by the subservient adulation of Irishwomen and by a religious education which concentrates on St. Paul's insistence on the inferiority of females while ignoring that some acquaintanceship with women is a necessary preliminary to following his advice about marriage.

The sorriest aspect of this whole sorry business is that our milk-and-water celibates actually believe themselves to be the gay, romantic fellows who have kissed and made love and eloped through the pages of thousands of lying Irish works of fiction.

You know how it goes: All the world loves a lover, and all the English-speaking world is crazy about an Irish lover. He is so dashing and impetuous, this Irishman of the novel and film. His most endearing quality is his romantic approach to life. Young heart aflame, he sweeps the girl of his choice to the altar rails, throwing to the winds such dull considerations as dowries and parental approval.

That is the Irishman of fiction.

May I recommend to you a non-fiction best seller which gives another picture of the Irishman? In this book his character is delineated not with fancy but with facts—cold, hard incontrovertible facts as disclosed by our latest census. The title of the book is *The Statistical Abstract*. The author is that unimaginative entity, our Department of Industry and Commerce. The Irishman who emerges from its pages is representative of 400,000 males of marriageable age which in this country usually means anything from middle-age to senility. Counting from teen-age girls to would-be brides of forty-five, there are 300,000 women from among whom our representative Irishman may select a wife, which makes him one of four possible husbands for every three women. In view of this surplus of males, unparalleled in any other European country, he might be pardoned if he made sure of a wife by rushing into an early marriage.

If he is the marrying kind (which happens only 56 times in every 100), he looks the women over and makes a choice. Then he settles down to a lukewarm courtship which lasts from five to fifteen years, or until he reaches the age of thirty-five. This is the average marrying age of the supposedly warm-blooded Southern Irishman. Compare it with the unromantic Englishman's thirty or the cold Belfastman's twenty-five.

If our Irishman belongs to the farming class—and 49 per cent of Ireland's population is engaged in agriculture—he will not give a thought to marrying until he is forty-five or fifty or more. At that age, he will arrange a satisfying transaction which will bring him money and cattle and land. The charms of the wife will be incidental. Even if his holding is no bigger than a head scarf, he will demand a dowry with his wife.

In a recent breach-of-promise case, the defendant, a small Meath farmer, swore stoutly, "I would not marry any woman for less than 500 pounds." In parentheses, let me state that the Irishman's reputation for openhandedness is just another fiction. There is not a French peasant living who could hold a candle to the average Irishman in matters of penny-pinching. The improvident Irishman will, of course, be with us always, but it is not in such nonsense as presents for women that his money will be spent, but on liquor and gambling.

Should the prospective bridegroom be a shopkeeper, he will be equally careful to ensure that the woman whom he endows with his name and his declining years shall pay for these favors with a handsome dowry. Should he be a townsman of the civil-servant or bank-clerk class, he will continue to spend his money on himself until the shortcomings of landladies drive him to undertake the support of a wife.

He is not an attractive fellow, this Irishman who emerges from the pages of *The Statistical Abstract*. He is cautious and cold and unromantic. He forces his fiancée to waste her best years waiting for him to make her his wife, often delaying beyond the years when she might normally hope to have children. A feature of the figures disclosed in the present agitation for a legal-adoption bill is the number of childless couples in Ireland—childless, for the most part, because of late marriage.

Here is another intriguing fact which merges from *The Statistical Abstract:* Youth in a wife does not appeal to the average Irishman. The figures show that, while 50 per cent of women in England, Scotland, and Wales marry in the early and middle twenties, the Irishwoman is not given a chance to start a home and family until she is thirty and more. Nowhere else in the whole world does such a high proportion of women marry at the age of forty.

Let me offer you a few stories from real life which may help to bear out those statistics. The little tragedies of Betty and Mary occurred not long since. The girl in each case is known to me personally, and I am ready to vouch for the truth of her story on the Bible.

Betty is a young girl who would be remarkable for her good looks even if she were living in Hollywood. Some time ago, she met and fell in love with a man of thirty—a man who, if he belonged to any other race, would have been married five or more years ago. He has health, wealth, and no dependents. But, to balance these assets, he has his share of native caginess in courtship.

However, when he started to keep company with Betty, he seemed to be prepared to become a real daredevil. There were frequent phone calls and drives in the country and film dates. He even ran the risk of getting her name linked with his (a risk which every Irish bachelor shuns) by taking her on two occasions to dinner in a big Dublin hotel.

This hectic courtship went on for six months. Then, one evening, the girl came home in tears.

"He doesn't want to see me any more," she told her mother through her sobs. "He says that he daren't—that every time he kisses me I give him bad thoughts."

Yes, I know. One's first reaction is laughter, peal after peal of laughter. And the laughter could go on for an hour were it not checked by the sad realization that this half queer is not just one isolated case of a monk gone wrong, but a typical example of a race of men whose abhorrence of their Christian, social, and racial duty has led them to persuade themselves that a natural impulse is an evil thing and that women are the devil's handiwork.

I have known Mary since the early years of my marriage. She was an attractive and gentle girl, a secretary. While efficient at her job, she was no career girl. Her greatest ambition in life was to have a husband to love, a family to rear, and a home to run. It was a happy day for all of us when, at twenty-four, she announced her engagement to a young man who had just opened his own business.

"But we won't be marrying just yet," she told us. "My fiancé is a very practical man. He feels it would be lunacy to rush into marriage before he has his business well established. He says that no one but a fool would take on the responsibilities of married life without making sure of financial security. But we're both going to save hard, so it shouldn't be too long before the banns are called."

My friend saved her money. During an engagement that lasted for seventeen years, she denied herself all the little extravagances dear to the hearts of women. All her spare cash—which was little enough because her salary was small—went into the bank as an insurance against the insecurity which her fiancé felt was not compatible with a happy marriage.

Early this year he told her he had taken counsel with his confessor and had decided to break off the engagement because as a married man he would not be able to save his soul. Four months later he married a girl who stood to inherit a considerable fortune.

Why, oh, why must Irishmen commit the blasphemy of using God as a cloak for their only sincere passion—the passion for money and temporal advancement?

Let us examine the reasons which contribute to making the Irishman in his attitude toward women the laughingstock and contempt of the world. Why have they, as a Spaniard once said of them, *la sangre de nabos*—"the blood of a parsnip"?

It has been said that our clergy, in denouncing the company keepers, have frightened the sex out of our men. If by clergy you mean the hard-working parish priests and curates who look after the young men and women of this country, I cannot agree that they are in any way to blame. Go into any parish in Ireland and you will find priests working like slaves to raise funds for the building of parish halls where young people may be brought together. They are wise men. They realize that only by providing facilities for dancing and card games and social intercourse may our countryside be saved from the complete depopulation with which it is threatened as much because of boredom as because of unemployment.

Admittedly, in days gone by, we had many a priest who resembled the curate in Paul Vincent Carroll's *The White Steed*. When I was a child in Kildare, Father Loughlin (God be good to him) made a practice of walking through leafy Boran's Lane in the dim summer evenings where, with the aid of his horsewhip, he tore boys and girls from their lovers' embrace. Today, the horsewhip castigation of courting couples is as obsolete as the bay mare on which Father Loughlin used to ride to his sick calls.

If we must blame the clergy, let us blame the educationists. Most of us remember with a shiver those three-day retreats at school ending in a general confession in the course of which the confessor—no doubt with the best of intentions—put questions to us concerning sexual habits of which in our genuine innocence we had never dreamed in the worst nightmare and which so shocked and sickened us that we remained sex-frightened for years.

I have compared notes, and I have found that in this matter nuns are not nearly so much to blame as priests and teaching brothers. Is it because nuns, being women, have a larger, wider wisdom touching these things? Because they realize that the quivering antennae of young and innocent souls must be respected? And that the natural delicacy of children must not be outraged? Whatever the reason, no one will deny that the nun-educated women of Ireland do not suffer from the morbidity which is the curse of our cleric-mauled men.

The July 28, 1952, issue of *Time* published the following interesting item concerning the Kogis, an isolated tribe of aborigines who flourish in the Santa Marta Mountains of Colombia. An anthropologist, Gerardo Reichel-Dalmatoff, has recently disclosed the results of his work among these peculiar people.

"Kogi men," says Reichel-Dalmatoff, "loathe sex and shrink from it, an attitude they learn as boys from priests who spend nine years in darkness studying the tribal rituals. The priests, called *mámas*, teach that women are evil—but a necessary evil because they provide men with food. . . . Since a woman's place in this man's world is to grow and prepare his food, a Kogi man's idea of a good catch is a lass with a workhorse physique. . . . Once a wife is with child, a Kogi man may throw himself without reserve into the male community's fervid philosophical life. He gathers nightly with other men in a big conical ceremonial house to chew cocoa leaves. . . . The drug dispels the physical and sexual hunger which he despises; at his nightly talk-fest he is content."

Why, in the name of all that's cold-blooded, should *Time* or Gerardo Reichel-Dalmatoff believe that there is anything new or unique about the Kogis? Substitute teaching Brothers for *mámas,* the local pub for "big conical ceremonial house," Guinness or whisky for "cocoa leaves," and arguments about greyhounds, horses, and politicians for "fervid philosophical life," and you have a faithful portrait of any town or village in Ireland.

Next to the clerical teachers, I blame the mothers of Ireland for its marriage-shy and sex-denying sons. Here again the Irishman bears a strong resemblance to his Kogi twin as described in *Time*:

"Reichel-Dalmatoff, turning to psychiatry for an explanation of such behavior, says the Kogi man's aversion to sex stems from a cult of love for a world-mother spirit. Kogis think life is only a larger womb than the one from which they sprang, and death only a return to the womb of the great All-Mother."

With all due respects to Reichel-Dalmatoff, I say that the Irishman is the world's prime example of the Oedipus complex. He is anchored to his mother for as long as she lives. If this should seem an exaggeration, consider the following facts: An Irishwoman's life expectation is sixty-eight years. Her marrying age is thirty. Her son's marrying age is thirty-five. It follows that an Irishman does not marry until after his mother has died or is about ready to die.

In this matriarchy, men cannot help being mother-bound. Mothers prize their sons far above their daughters—and they have no compunction in showing this favoritism while their sons are young. (Query: Do Irishwomen lavish this inordinate love on their sons in an effort to compensate themselves for inadequate husbands?) Sisters are taught at an early age that their duty is to dance attendance on their brothers. I myself remember that my nightly duty was to clean my brother's boots. The inevitable result is that the Irish boy grows up with an exaggerated affection for and dependence on his mother and with a contempt for all other females.

The Kogis chew cocoa leaves to deaden their natural impulses. The Irishman has resort to alcohol—and here we have one of the prime causes of our low marriage rate. No one will deny that an occasional drinking spree will stimulate the passions. (In the Rotunda Hospital, Dublin, the spate of babies born around Christmas time is known as "St. Patrick's Day rush.") But steady toping, the kind of day-in day-out drinking to which so many Irishmen are addicted, has, equally undeniably, a blood-chilling effect.

"Put an Irishman in a room," they say, "with a woman and two bottles of stout, and he'll choose the stout every time." And by the time he has had his two bottles of stout, all he will ask from life is two bottles more. With wages so low and the cost of drinking and the incidence of alcoholism so high, it is not surprising that so many Irishmen plead economic reasons for our low marriage rate.

All these factors apart, I am forced to the conclusion that the principal cause of our dwindling population is sexual apathy on the part of Irishmen. Thomas Moore was mistaken when he wrote, in "Rich and Rare,"

> For though they love woman and golden store,
> Sir Knight, they love honor and virtue more.

The lady of his song could certainly journey through Ireland knowing that she need not "fear the least alarm." But her safety lay not in the honor of the sons of Erin but in their indifference to women. The truth is that where the charms of a woman are considered, the average son of Erin couldn't care less.

Most people will agree that, unless a man is vowed to chastity for the love of God and receives thereby special graces, a womanless existence is unnatural and wrong. Years ago, when I was young and intolerant, I looked around me and saw the preponderance of Irishmen who prefer the company of their own sex to that of women. In Rabelaisian mood, I wrote verses to an air made popular by the late Count John McCormack. The title of my song was "The Fairy Males of Ireland."

Although the years have brought me a certain amount of tolerance, I have not become deaf or blind or idiot, and I know that in this Catholic country we have a shocking number of "queers," too many of them practicing homosexuals, the others unconscious perverts. I know, too, that cowardice in one form or another has caused others of our woman-hating males to become addicted to the little-boy habits of the hero of Patrick Kavanagh's "The Great Hunger." I know (and I sometimes wonder if this is not even more pitiable) that the great majority of Irishmen are completely indifferent to sex in any shape or form.

To sum up, I would say that our male population today consists of 10 per cent full-blooded warmhearted men, 10 per cent libertines (most of them owing a duty to wife and children), 20 per cent soaks, and 60 per cent a mixed collection of what in various countries are known by various names. Here in Ireland, we call them "ould Mary Annes."

THE MYSTICAL IRISH

5 ———————————————————

Paul Vincent Carroll

Among contemporary Irish playwrights Paul Vincent Carroll stands in the top rank. His plays have scored successes in the theaters on both sides of the Atlantic and have stamped him as a dramatist with a nimble and provocative wit and a faculty for satire.

Born on July 10, 1900, at Blackrock near Dundalk, Ireland, he was educated at his father's school until he was thirteen and later at St. Mary's College, Dundalk, and at St. Patrick's Training College for Teachers in Dublin. There he was pitched right into the Irish armed rebellion against England and got caught up breathlessly in the seething literary and dramatic activity that was finally to roll Ireland in battle smoke from 1916 to 1921.

At the Abbey Theatre he learned the rudiments of playmaking and acquired that unquenchable love of the drama that became the chief impetus in his life. At the age of twenty-one he sailed out of Dublin on a cattle boat and landed in Glasgow, where he began his teaching career and where he spent the happiest days of his life. There he met Helena Reilly, a gown designer, whom he married in 1923; they now have three daughters.

"I do not believe," declares Carroll, "in a Gaelic-speaking smug Irish Republic. I believe that the future greatness of Ireland lies in her full cooperation with a spring-cleaned British Commonwealth of Nations. I am not a republican doctrinaire. I believe the monarchy is the best form of government for Britain."

Strongly influenced by Swift, W. B. Yeats, and Ibsen, Carroll feels indebted also to Synge, from whom he caught color and rhythm. In 1932 he won the Abbey Theatre prize for the best play of the year with

"Things That Are Caesar's." It was not until 1937, however, that he won recognition as a professional dramatist. In this year "Shadow and Substance" scored a dramatic hit at the Abbey Theatre in Dublin and the following year in New York. The play received the Casement award of the Irish Academy of Letters and the American foreign award of 1937–1938. Refused production in all the theaters of Ireland, "The White Steed" was pronounced by George Jean Nathan "the best play of the Broadway [New York] season 1938–1939." "It deals," says Carroll, "with the clash between clerical fascism and the old liberal Catholicism of wayward love, divine mercy and pity and the redeeming grace of God."

His other plays are "The Old Foolishness," "Kindred," "The Strings, My Lord, Are False," "Coggerers," and "The Wise Have Not Spoken." George Jean Nathan said his work was "stippled alternately with tenderness and dynamite." "I write," says Carroll, "as Ibsen did. I take the life of a small village and enlarge it to encompass all human life." He and his family now make their home in Kent, England.

THE DESTINY OF THE IRISH RACE IS SHROUDED IN A MYSTICAL HAZE, AND HE would be a brave prophet indeed who would purport to foretell whither the race is bound. Providence will surely be a not unkind contributing factor in determining its final fate. As one garrulous old woman on the quays of Dublin put it to me, "What the hell do we want with systems and the like? Isn't *God* lookin' after us!" Or shall I put it more poetically in the words of the late poor Tom Kettle:

> It's Paddy this, and Paddy that,
> But when roses droop and fade,
> It's Ireland in the firing line,
> When the price of God is paid.

And that just about sums up the Irish attitude to themselves and their mystical future: "Leave it to God!"

If the Irish had not always been an extraordinary race, the terrifying period from the disastrous battle of Kinsale to the black year of 1847 would have wiped them off the face of the earth. Yet, miraculously it would seem, they survived the ignominy of the Wild Geese, the unparalleled barbarism of Cromwell, the Penal Laws that rank alone in history for severity, the smoldering fury of the eighteenth century that burst into battle flame in 1798, the crucifixion of young Robert Emmet, and the heartbreaking land hunger and evictions of the respectable Victoria.

Not only did they survive this incredible series of ordeals, they actually emerged out of the bogs, dumb with grief and hunger but with Faith immaculate and love unsullied, and in their last ordeal from 1916 to 1922 swept the ancient persecutor finally from their shores.

For such a race, there is surely something better in store than the synthetic doom prophesied for them by that chief of humbugs, the statistician!

I have stated my belief in the profound inner wisdom of the race. Let us examine some facets of their peculiar lives and their even more peculiar and contrary characters.

First of all—and let us face it squarely—the Irishman is a mystic. He may be a drunkard, a playboy, a rebel, a fanatic, a cynic, an Anglophobe, even a gombeen [grasping] man, but fundamentally he is a mystic. His roots are as old as time, and no matter what his class or station, peasant or professional, the stirrings deep in his nature are profoundly spiritual. As Æ [George W. Russell] put it in one of his poems, "You cannot all disguise the majesty of fallen gods!"

Because he is a mystic, his inner knowledge, learned from no mere study book, makes him tend inevitably toward the cynical. He knows, even when he is making a fool or an exhibition of himself, that all life is a gloriously disguised fake. He is only too pathetically aware that all these foolish things will pass. As Pearse put it:

> Things young and green, things white and beautiful,
> And then my heart hath told me these will pass,
> Will pass and fade, will die and be no more ...

To be precise, materialism has never seriously captured the inner being of the Irishman, as it has completely captured the entire being of, say, the American. Give a materialist a plenitude of this world's good things, and he will wallow childishly in them until he dies pathetically of dyspepsia and his own idiocies. But give an Irishman the king's robes and jewels, and at the mystical fall of evening the illogical fellow will go hungering after some undefined something that is positively unattainable. He knows he is the lost child of some celestial hall of high splendors and that there is no real satisfaction for him in the tinselries of earth. So, deep underneath his humbugging and his jollifications, there is a restless yearning that has no name.

Because the Irishman is as I have alleged above, woman is no mystery to him. Deep in him, he knows her every move and wile and caprice. She is to him the greatest and most final illusion in a strangely unsatisfying existence. But for goodness' sake, let no reader deduce from this unqualified assertion that the Irishman is a celibate. That is an international fiction that greatly amuses him, for in the full tide of sex love he is as intense as an Italian and as ruthless as a Spaniard.

But mark one thing carefully—he is known in Anglo-Saxon countries and their offshoots, where women expect and even command meticulous attention, as a terrific and indeed even a promiscuous lover, but by other standards a very poor husband. There is a deep and very subtle reason for this. As a mystic he simply refuses to accept the popular sentimental fiction that woman is a romanticist and that her avid earth lover is continually tying her down to the drab realities of the common day. He knows only too well the emptiness of that widely accepted and expensively advertised notion!

He is only too tragically aware that it is the woman who is the materialist under the alluring veils and the sweet petticoats and the doelike eyes and that she is the mentor who captures him from his dreaming and his lofty preoccupations and binds him to the marriage bed, which he dislikes, and the grinding stone, which is the nightmare of his private raptures. As a consequence, if he can possibly avoid it, he will not marry or, if he does, he will do so only at an age when the blood runs cooler and he requires the comfort of a nurse and housekeeper. But that is only one reason for his aversion to matrimony; there are others which I shall deal with presently.

From this yearning and preoccupation of his with mystical abstractions, the world has gathered a rich literary harvest. Some of his plays are among the masterpieces of dramatic art, his poetry at its best has astonished what is left of the classic world, his novels when good are outstanding in their profundity. No one in the English-speaking world can equal him when it comes to setting standards of fine writing. He is equally at home with angels or demons, for he knows both sides of the mystical coin on which the puzzle of the purpose of the whole human race is written in code.

When in company, he shines, for his wit is proverbial, his brogue pleasing, and his dissertations piquant and arresting. Yet after such an exhibition of his powers in public, he turns down the covers of his lonely bed and is well aware that he has been a fake and even a charlatan! I once knew an old priest, a distinguished thinker in his way, who took a dram and had a mighty gift for fecund discussion. Every night in his incongruous nightshirt he used to look at himself in his cracked bedside mirror and exclaim: "You old fool! You talked utter rubbish all evening, and you know it!" That, indeed, is like the Irishman.

His woman in Ireland has one great and outstanding virtue, born of tolerance, experience, and understanding of him—she expects not a great deal from her husband. That belief is part of the Irishwoman's nature, and because of it Ireland remains essentially a *man's* country, while England follows America down the incongruous drain of matriarchy.

No opposites could be more completely different than the average American woman and the average Irishwoman. The American woman runs her husband like a business, tells him what to do and how to do it, controls the number of his family for him, regulates and regiments him, and for these gifts of hers he is, I fear, paradoxically none too grateful to her!

The Irishwoman accepts her husband's orders in a mannerly way, cleans his shoes and shirts, bears him as many children as he desires, expects him home only when he actually arrives, makes his children pray for him, and in spite of all these thankless woes and worries miraculously she loves him! The American woman kisses her dog and allows him in her living room and even her bedroom. The Irishwoman kicks his backside and puts him outside to guard the house; yet she commendably likes a dog on the strict condition that you don't, as Chesterton said, "spell him backwards."

The American woman dresses magnificently but has little time for love. The Irishwoman dresses anyhow, but if she loves you, she is only too prepared to give you a "little court" under any given tree, for she knows that life without love is a barren monstrosity from which her maternal mind recoils. I point out these differences so that we can get a picture of the woman in Ireland who has to contend with that diffi-cult and contrary puzzle, the Irishman.

The Irishman courts well—he is charming to his sweetheart, gentle, solicitous, passionate, and generous to a fault. But let her just get one step ahead of him in his wooing and transgress his male prerogatives, and he is off like a shot to seek a more *mannerly* woman who knows her place in the scheme of things!

He is never in a hurry to burden himself with matrimonial responsi-bilities, for he hates the traces and the matrimonial bit in his mouth and has a strange and shrinking fear of "bed and board." They are the twin realities that will murder his illusions and preoccupations. As a conse-quence, Irish girls, only too tragically often, have to wait for matrimony and natural fulfillment until the late thirties, and so the nation is robbed of masses of healthy children born of young parents in love with each other.

Of course, it only too often happens that Irish girls emigrate in droves to England, where the Englishmen, who make good and understanding husbands but are phlegmatic and indifferent lovers, fall head over heels in love with their accents instead of their ankles and marry them in great numbers. Too often these marriages are mixed, and the children grow up as young English boys and girls in an alien faith, and with no particular interest in the "quaint and comic" sister isle that gave birth to their mother.

In the last five years, I have had here in southern England four young nursemaids from Ireland. Of these, three have married charming Eng-lish boys whom they literally swept off their feet, and this poor deprived scribe is now the godfather of three bouncing Englishmen! The fourth, my present one, has the Cockney postman "astray in the head"; so I am grimly prepared for the worst! And so the tragedy of Ireland continues.

But as I have said previously, there are other reasons which militate strongly against the vital Irish birth rate, which is unhappily the lowest in Europe. Let us expatiate.

It is a well-known fact that the elderly Irish mother is about the most jealous and unreasoning female on the face of the earth. Between her and "the self-seeking hussy" who aims to "trap" her son—the son being between thirty and forty—there is just no compromise this side of the grave. The *bean-a-thoigh* (woman of the house) sits squat and solid in the chimney corner, and no younger woman, not even her unmarried daughters, will question her authority or experience in matrimonial manners, until the undertaker finally puts his tapes on her to measure her for her coffin and says: "Ah, sure the parish won't be the same without her at all."

If we could get round that maternal dog in the manger, we could get round a lot, but we can't, and so the rot goes on. She dies, always too late and always, as the local paper puts it, "fully fortified by the rites of Holy Church." But in the other world when she rejoices and is glad, I often wonder does she ever realize the utter ruin she has caused to the lives of her sons and to the future of the comely girls who wait interminably to marry them? Oh, love! Oh, patience! Oh, crass prejudice that only death resolves!

It is a well-proven fact that no two women have ever been known to like each other in the same kitchen, and nowhere on the earth is this so belligerently true as in Ireland. The elderly Irish mother, far from being a sentimental old lady who prays by her bed in red petticoats, or indeed a metaphorical candle in a window to light her wayward sons home, is often in strict reality a garrulous termagant who tolerantly allows her aging son to grow a moustache but forbids him to give expression to the urgent and morally endorsed life with which she has endowed him.

Of course, the ideal way out of this whirlpool of the aged matriarch is to build one or more small cottages on the land near to the parental home so that the sons could marry their sweethearts early and have priceless clutches of healthy young children. But grim economic exigencies meanwhile rob the country of the benefits of such a solution. These cottages, tragically conspicuous by their absence in rural Ireland, could in harmony with other factors banish the horrid emigration skeleton from the creaking Irish cupboard.

Let us turn to the villages which should be the charming ivory keys of a perfect Irish harmonium. Anyone like me who lives, or has lived, in southern England knows how that lovely land is dotted with villages of superb beauty. Indeed the English have a natural genius for the making and preserving of really lovely villages. But unfortunately England, during her long domination of Ireland, never thought it worth her while to apply a little of that same genius to the lovely island she so cruelly coerced and despoiled, with the result that the average Irish village has emerged out of the welter of history looking like an odd collection of crude houses thrown at random out of a giant's box.

. There were high hopes when the Revolution was successfully achieved that such ugly pictures would be obliterated by Irish brawn and vision and that Irish villages would spring up that would be fit for intelligent young men and women to live in. But no such thing has happened. Ireland's barren villages, imprisoning thousands of frustrated lives, have not been made fruitful. Nor indeed has the Revolution taught the Irish to love, live, and pray with greater dignity, although one outstanding priest, a man of real foresight and genius, has been, and still is, making commendable efforts through a movement called Muintir na Tire (The People of the Land) to develop village life and to give blossom and flower to sterile lives. I shall return to this exceptional priest later.

Partisan passions do not die easily in Ireland, and such passions, bred by the disastrous civil war that followed the defeat of the Black and Tans, are still bitterly alive, confusing vital national issues and impeding essential economic progress. Indeed the day that W. B. Yeats foresaw threatens with "public life moving from violence to apathy, Parliament disgracing and debauching those who entered it, and men of letters living like outlaws in their own country."

The necessity for the guidance of a nation by its men of letters, working within its constitution, and vitalized by its moral, aesthetic, and traditional forces, simply cannot be overstressed. As Plato put it: "Where there is no art, the people perish." And today, the Irish psyche, in spite of regular and multitudinous churchgoing, stands in the shadow of that very danger. The Irish men of letters, who must perforce as a first principle swim against the popular current of mass opinion, stand suspect by the Irish Hierarchy and clergy.

The *official* government censorship is pernicious and even foolish, for it has admitted to the nation that historical stranger, the Puritan, and in fact presented him with the freedom of Dublin city. But the *unofficial* censorship, prevalent throughout the rural areas where the local priest— sometimes an old and crusty stick-in-the-mud, often a young and inexperienced cleric—bans an activity in circumstances from which there is no appeal, and is a national disgrace and a cowardly expedient to safeguard an ignorance that is only too often confused with natural innocence.

The combination of the two censorships has reduced Irish literature and drama to the mediocre and the merely pious and directly brought about an eclipse of Irish letters. The Church, and more especially the Catholic Church, with her infinitely wide fields of opinion on which internal major battles can be fought without damage to her eternal fabric, should never have any fear of the creative artist. They should be complementary to each other and each should be fully cognizant of its profound responsibilities.

But such is unhappily not the case in Ireland, with the result that Anglo-Irish literature, the vital link between Ireland and the English-speaking world, has been deliberately sabotaged. Ireland has sulkily and under clerical guidance turned inward from Britain and the Continent and has developed, as Æ (George W. Russell) feared, into "a smug, peasant republic."

This state of affairs makes for internal decay, and that decay is reflected in emigration, reckless spending on luxuries, slipshod agriculture, neglect of the great staple industry of fishing, undredged harbors, and general ennui. In fact, a state of affairs that the young are glad to escape from, as soon as possible. Yeats, with his unerring vision, put his finger on Ireland's greatest need when he asserted that the Irish have always had *political* leaders but have never had social leaders. The crying need of Ireland today is for *social* leaders who would educate the people in essential social principles within the Christian framework and encourage them to throw their corrupt and bombastic political leaders in the dustbin or, better still, in the Liffey.

The natural *social* leaders in Ireland are of course the priests, who should be passed out of the seminaries excellently equipped socially, mentally, morally, and intellectually. Their efforts to rehabilitate the rural areas should be tireless and their labor a labor of love. They should ask for little in return except the Christian guarantee that "the laborer is worthy of his hire."

The remarkable priest I mentioned above, Father Michael Hayes, foresaw the necessity of all this when he started his excellent movement Muintir na Tire. Let us be just to this tireless working bee among so many drones and record that the small number of thriving villages in Ireland, with their village councils, their cooperative schemes, their parochial factories, workshops, and libraries, their draining schemes, and their excellent social activities in the local hall are all the highly beneficial work of this priest's brain and vision.

This is, and must remain, the key to the solution of Ireland's fundamental problems—problems that must be solved if the nation is to endure and survive. Ireland needs hundreds of such priests as Father Hayes, but unfortunately they are not there. Indeed, some of the younger clergy are not sufficiently learned or experienced to know that the present dangerous drift in Ireland must some day come to a violent stop and that the priceless things they are supposed to safeguard may be regretfully damaged by a people who, though they are generous and kindly, are violent and dangerous when tempers are lost. Anyone who has read Dorothy MacArdle's truly shocking book on the atrocities during the Civil War in Ireland will know only too well what I imply.

The danger is there, and the rumblings are audible enough to those who have ears to hear. It is not a communist danger or an anti-Catholic one but is best interpreted as a determined undercrying of the Irish nature against the bombastic and corrupt politicans, both lay and clerical, who have made the gombeen man respectable, the iniquitous secret forces that covertly oppose social reform in medicine and child welfare, and the clerical Rip van Winkles who subtly use the Eternal Church as the sounding board of all their petty taboos and rural tyrannies.

The explosion, when it comes, will not be a gentle one, but out of its violence Ireland may emerge again and prosper, for it will obliterate the present politician, with all his mean crudities, in favor of the genuine social reformer, and it will be a signal to the priests to man their action stations and pull their genuine weight in the battle for the future.

Yet, taking a broad view of our tear-drenched history, and taking into account the peculiar composition of the Celtic mind and soul, it may well be that Ireland will never become either populous or prosperous like Denmark or Belgium. She may well be destined to be the savior of idealism in a world jungle of rank material weeds, and perhaps distracted foreigners, driven to despair by the ever-multiplying complexities of a machine- and gadget-ridden age, will visit her to try to relearn, from that tattered woman trudging her way to the slum hospital to have her baby or from that peasant lost in wonder at the yellowing barley, the unutterable simplicities of living.

Perhaps, after all, an inscrutable providence has decreed that Ireland will always export her mystical children and that these will forever roam through other lands, dropping their pearls and their vermin, but carrying with them a light, tossed in the tumult of their wayward souls, that will rekindle the lamps of human liberty when these burn low and splutter out in their sockets and so ensure that the Name of the Author of all life shall not wholly be forgotten on the earth.

If *that,* instead of prosperity, population, and efficiency, is the destiny of Ireland, then surely she is the divine instrument of a pitying God, and I, as one Irishman, will be well content. Let me conclude with that mystical and typically Celtic outburst of Joseph Plunkett who gave his life for her before the English firing squad in the Easter Rebellion:

> We sail into the Dark
> With laughter on our lips . . .

THE KEY TO THE PROBLEM

6

Edmund J. Murray

Born on April 14, 1907, in Bridgeport, Connecticut, Edmund J. Murray is the son of John A. and Margaret McMahon Murray. Upon graduating from the local high school, he went to work for the Jenkins Valve Company, where he remained for a couple of years. Deciding to study for the priesthood, he entered the novitiate of the Congregation of the Holy Cross in November, 1929, and graduated from the University of Notre Dame in 1934.

He received his theological training at Holy Cross Seminary in Washington, D.C., and was ordained to the priesthood on June 24, 1938. He was an assistant professor of theology at Notre Dame for several years and served as a chaplain for four years with the United States infantry in World War II, leaving the service with the rank of captain.

Returning to Notre Dame, he resumed his teaching duties and served also as assistant prefect of religion to the whole student body, in which position his experience as a military chaplain served him in good stead. He was also assistant editor of the "Religious Bulletin," issued daily to each student at the university.

In the autumn of 1950 he left for Ireland to do research work for his Ph.D. degree at the National University, and he is at present at University College, Cork. His research work occasions him to travel rather extensively through Ireland, where he has paid particular attention to the causes of Ireland's declining population. His observations are made at first hand, and he reports them with the candor and honesty characteristic of all the contributors to this study.

TODAY WHEN THE THREAT OF NEAR EXTINCTION IS STARING HER IN THE FACE, the fate of Eire is a matter of deep concern, not only to her own inhabitants, but also to her sons and daughters in many lands. It is of the utmost importance, therefore, to plumb the causes of this strange phenomenon of a people on the verge of vanishing and to see what, if anything, can be done to save them from the doom that has fallen upon many other races in the past.

Attention will be directed, of course, to the economic factors back of the continued mass emigration and especially to the strange marriage moratorium which for so many decades has been thinning Irish blood until it is now a mere trickle. A careful study of the reports released periodically by the Central Statistics Office in Dublin discloses the pathetic story of Ireland's decline and lays bare the economic factors working to that end. I shall supplement the story told by the statistician by presenting the observations which I have been able to make on this problem during several years of study in Ireland, where I am writing this chapter.

One of the strangest paradoxes in Ireland today is the perennial and justifiable demand for the ending of Partition, *i.e.,* the return of the six Ulster counties to the Republic, while at the same time there is an ever-increasing flow of English gentlemen of means into the Republic—men who are leaving the burning ship of the English state and crossing over to John Bull's former island, buying up estate after estate and settling down to the traditionally Irish leisurely way of life. It is a new plantation movement in Anglo-Irish history. Whereas in the days of the Henrys and Elizabeth the loyal followers of the Tudors were transplanted to Ireland as a reward for conquering the Irish, nowadays this new ascendancy crowd is staging a peaceful but no less a real invasion on a money-for-acre basis, rather than by royal grant, as was the case in the fifteenth, sixteenth, and seventeenth centuries.

The saddest feature of Ireland's current population decline is the flight from the land. The Republic is essentially an agricultural country even though there may be potentialities in Eire for small industries here and there. Without an interest in things rural and without encouragement to farming the nation just cannot survive. Its climate and condition of soil call for a rural way of life rather than an urban one. Nevertheless there has been a disastrous decline in tillage acreage in the land.

Whereas during the years of World War II Irish farmers had more than 2½ million acres of land in tillage, since the end of the war this has fallen off to approximately 1¼ million acres. In 1952 Prime Minister De Valera, in a message to the Irish people, made an urgent plea to the farmers to meet the coming world emergency by increasing their efforts at tillage for more food for both human and animal consumption as well as for export purposes. De Valera made it clear that the chances for Irish survival were hopeless unless immediate steps were taken to get back to the land and to get more out of the land.

The sad feature of this flight from the land is the undeniable fact that other small countries such as Belgium, Denmark, Holland, Norway, and Austria are getting twice and sometimes three times as much out of their less arable lands! Recently in another message to the people, this time from his hospital bed in Utrecht, the Prime Minister repeated his previous appeals for more efforts at agriculture. "I regret," said De Valera, "that my appeal, and the many appeals by the Minister of Agriculture and other members of the Government, were left unheeded. We need a much larger increase in our tillage generally."

In 1952 Irish farmers (with only 50 per cent of their land in tillage) produced about 250,000 acres of grain, although the land could have yielded twice that much within the year had the time been spent to work the additional acreage. According to the present Minister of Agriculture, Tom Walsh, potential buyers are putting in bids from all over the world—if only the Irish farmers would plant the seed and harvest the crop. Whereas last year the Republic brought in 9 million pounds' worth of wheat, the Irish farmers could have sold that much wheat during that time. "Irish farmers could get the highest price in the world for wheat," said the Minister. "Increased tillage is the necessary basis for increased agricultural production in general. . . . It is a matter of vital importance which affects every man, woman and child in the State."

Recently Joseph Lyons, M.Sc., professor of agriculture at the University College in Cork, prepared a study on Ireland's current agricultural problems and showed that there has been no significant increase in the agricultural output of Ireland since the days of landlordism—*i.e.,* for more than one hundred years! "This is all the more disturbing despite the fact," points out Professor Lyons, "that many favorable factors have been introduced, such as security of tenure and reduction of rents to farmers, considerable improvement in animal and plant strains, increase in the use of labor-saving machinery, introduction and extended use of chemical fertilizers, improvement in the means of combatting and controlling animal and plant diseases, and the establishment of a Department of Agriculture in 1901 for advising and assisting farmers."

Commenting on the above study, Prof. John Busteed, head of the Department of Economics at University College in Cork said: "For all that has been written about the Irish economy no satisfactory analysis has yet been made of the reasons for our backwardness. It is indeed considered something in the nature of treason to point out that we are backward. Yet it would be unreasonable to say that the Irish farmer is not as intelligent, as hard working and indeed as enterprising as his like elsewhere. Where then is the key to the mystery? It must be found. For we are facing perilous days."

In a recent talk in the town of Bantry, the Most Rev. Cornelius Lucey, Bishop of Cork, emphasized the tragedy of the young people leaving the rural areas of Ireland. "Too many of the young people are going away," said His Lordship. "If only the seed for a new crop of families were left, there would be no cause for alarm. But the tragedy is that it is not being left. Too few marriages, too few big families, too many holdings with the houses closed for good, too many schools with the attendance not half of what it was a generation ago—that is what is so lamentable in so grand a people up and down the whole countryside. The rural population is vanishing, and with it is vanishing the Irish race itself. For the rural families are the wellsprings from which the towns and cities replenish themselves, and if they are drying up, then inevitably we are doomed to wither away as a nation. Rural Ireland is stricken and dying and the will to marry on the land is almost gone."

We have in the facts just presented a clear indication of the very causes of Ireland's present-day gradual suicide as a race. It is a problem primarily and essentially of emigration, especially the departure from the land, late marriages, and—what is more disastrous to Ireland—the departure of Ireland's fair ladies to other lands, where they eventually accept offers of marriage and foreign citizenship.

There have been other causes attributed from time to time to the problem: some biological, others economic. It has been suggested, for instance, that the life expectancy of the Irish female has been traditionally lower than among the males in comparison with other countries throughout the world, thereby resulting in the higher proportion of males to females in the over-all population. But this reason is hardly acceptable because prior to the beginning of the present century the males did not outnumber the females in Ireland as they do now.

It has been said, too, and not without justification, that the lure of the less wholesome, materialistic aspects of American standards of life (due to the influence of the cinema to which the Irish are inordinately attached) has distracted many of the young people to such a degree that they are in grave danger of losing their traditionally high spiritual values, including a love for the home and family life. In the minds of many Irishmen also there is the thought that the artificial prosperity which the country enjoyed during and immediately after World War II has been a great contributing cause to the nation's present plight inasmuch as the people of Ireland are reluctant to accept the fact that this temporary period of prosperity is a thing of the past.

The author recently came across the following letters in Irish newspapers which shed much light on the thesis that emigration and the failure to marry are the prime causes of the "vanishing Irish." The first, appearing in the *Illustrated Magazine* of May 10, 1952, is from a girl, Irish-born, but by her own choice currently working and living outside of London: "As one of the girls who has left Eire, I would say that we go to other countries for two major reasons: 1. Economic necessity. Eire's great need is for industrial development to provide for her own fold. 2. The nature of Ireland's bachelors. Too many of them are merely seeking help for their farm at a cheap rate; too few of them think of their wife's comfort."

Another letter appeared in the *Illustrated Magazine* of May 17, 1952. It was signed by a young man living not too far from Dublin in the village of Maynooth: "Eire is indeed a land of paradoxes. Irishmen are leaving our farms in thousands, yet hundreds of foreigners are buying farms here. Irish girls are leaving, yet we are bringing in domestic servants from Germany and Italy. An agricultural country, we are importing butter from Denmark and New Zealand. We have the lowest birth rate of any comparable country, yet we have the largest families."

When De Valera recently made a public appeal for the Irish exiles to return home from across the Channel, one disillusioned exile, Mickaleen Og, made this reply through the medium of the Dublin *Evening Mail* of January 5, 1952: "When Mr. De Valera made his flowing eloquent

speech and spoke about the conditions that his poor countrymen were
living and working under across the Irish Sea and urged them to return,
perhaps he wasn't fully conversant with the living conditions that pre-
vail in the capital city of our Emerald Isle. Does he know of the people
who exist in the dirty, ill-lit, unkempt, windowless hovels in the back
streets and alleys of Dublin? If he doesn't, I can assure him that they do
exist in the twentieth century just the same as they did in Charles Dick-
ens' time. If the floating Irish population did return, what in God's
name is he going to do with them all? Where is the work coming from?
Where is he going to house them? Perhaps he is going to move them all
to the Kildare Plains and let them live on the abundance of green herbs
that I am told abound there. Or were they going to live on his promises
and his fine sounding words?

"I have no wish to be sarcastic at his or anybody else's expense, but I
think I have the right to criticize his rash words, when they are nothing
but words, and no further steps are taken. So come home, Paddy Reilly,
to Ballyjamesduff and Rathfarnham and Ballyfermot; come home,
Brigid, *alannah acushla;* come all ye Micks and Johns and Kevins and
Seamuses, the whole caboodle of ye. Father Dev has a candle in the
window and a welcome at the door—but very little in the cupboard.

"We're all right and the ship's name is Murphy, and if we can't live
in our Ireland, be the holy fly we'll die in it—but we'll be cursed if we
stay in England, where all we can do is work and get paid for it; and
although we can't fill our tummies with all we would *like* to fill them
with, we can at least fill them with the fruits of the work of our own two
hands and not with the paltry few shillings from the Labor. Good luck
to you."

Since it is the author's conviction that the abnormal emigration from
Ireland is not due primarily or entirely to economic reasons, then
wherein does the real cause lie? At the risk of hurting the sensibilities
of the thousands of Eire's unbagged bachelors—and their mothers—we
do not hesitate to place most of the blame for the Republic's high emigration, especially of women, and the subsequent depopulation of the land
on the male species. Call it selfishness, lethargy, indifference, love for
independence, laziness, the fact of the matter seems to be that Ireland's
young and not so young men are at fault more than the women or economics or any other cause one might suggest.

There is too much reluctance on the part of the *men* of Eire to assume the Christian responsibilities of marriage and family life. A cruel and unfounded accusation? Let the girls bear me out! In answer to the complaint made sometimes by Ireland's males that the girls are more interested in becoming waitresses, factory workers, and domestics in London, New York, Toronto, and Melbourne than in marching down the aisle, listen to this lament made by one Kerry maid whom I met on the Cork to Dublin Enterprise Express a few months ago.

She was off to Liverpool, she said, not because she was seeking a career but because "I'm just sick and tired of waiting for one of my own kind to pop the question." This young lass had been engaged to a local laddo for ten years. Twice the engagement was broken because his mother didn't think the time was right for him to go off on his own and take unto himself a wife. The man was twenty-nine. The girl had just passed thirty.

"Every time I came home from England on holiday," she said, "he would say, 'We'll get married as soon as Mom gives her O.K. You know I can't leave her even though I do love you. But we can't go off if she disagrees, and she doesn't think I ought to get married just yet.' That sort of thing went on since 1942. Last night before I left the town we were both born in, I gave him the ring—for the third and last time. I told him I had met an Englishman and had been dating him for the past year. He is a Catholic like myself, and he wants to marry me. We both want a large family. We've settled the date and made the first payment on a house outside of London. I would have married one of my own, but what can you do when a man is tied to his mother's apron strings all his life?"

Within the past week we have conversed with another happily married Irish girl who was home from England—with her British-born husband and three children. Said she, "I didn't see any prospects of marriage during the days when I was back home here in Ireland. So I took off for England seven years ago, got a teaching position in a large industrial town, was courted by another teacher over there who was more interested in settling down and raising a family than chasing dogs at the races or playing football. We were married during the Christmas season of 1945. It has been tough going from time to time, but we wouldn't have it any other way, and our marriage is a success. I don't

deny that there is more to eat and things are much cheaper by far in
Ireland, but what girl wants to spend her whole life slaving away as a
frustrated schoolma'am?

"You ask me if I am happy. Don't these three lovely children demonstrate my happiness? I have been reading about the low marriage rate
in Ireland, and we in England often discuss it. I have come to the conclusion that it is not emigration so much that is the cause of Ireland's
decline as a nation; it is rather the reason why the women of Ireland
emigrate—and that's the marriage shyness of Irishmen and their selfishness as well as the selfishness of their families who won't release them.
I don't think I am being unfair in saying this because I now have two
brothers at home who are approaching forty-five, and neither they nor
my mother are interested in their getting married."

Similar complaints have been voiced by countless other girls who
have left Ireland for other lands either because the boy friends back
home were too lazy to settle down and found a family or because the
traditional matriarchal system and undue attachment of the mothers of
Ireland to their sons long after marriage age have prevented the break
from home ties. No marriageable young lady anywhere wishes to remain unwooed and unwed all the days of her life.

It has been shown that Ireland's women want marriage and long for
family life more than anything else in this world. The selfish females
who prefer the independence and freedom of a celibate life outside of
religion are far in the minority. Ninety-five per cent of Ireland's eligible
women would marry tomorrow were the eligible men of the nation to
transfer their affections from horses and dogs and football matches and
"pubs" to the nobler activities of courtship and marriage.

As for the Irish maidens, they are today to the same high degree in
possession of those six gifts demanded by Cuchulain of old when he
was courting Emer—that beautiful soul and star of ancient Irish womanhood. There are indeed few Irish maidens today who lack those
same gifts: beauty, singing, needlework, sweet speech, wisdom, and
chastity. But though the maids remain unchanged, the male descendants of Cuchulain have indeed changed with the times.

One County Leitrim lass remarked to me recently, "The modern
Irishman is not interested in his future wife's beauty of countenance or
natural gifts of song and wit. All that really matters is her ability to

milk a cow, fetch water from the pump, and pitch hay. The bigger the muscles, the greater the catch for the young bucko—and that goes for the city slicker as well—because his first concern is always the size of your bank roll and other financial inducements."

The lassie could be more right than wrong were one to believe the classified matrimonial ads in the local newspapers. Within the past month we have carefully observed these connubial bids in the three largest dailies in Ireland. Out of 78 pleas "with a view to matrimony" it must be admitted that 51—about two-thirds—of these matrimonial requests were initiated by lovelorn males. And here's the catch, girls! There is the inevitable demand by the Gaelic Don Juans that the female party be "well heeled" before there is any decision to say, "I do."

Thus in the *Cork Examiner* appeared the ad, "Young man, 30, wishes to meet nice girl, 25 to 30, *with good home and earning good money,* with view to matrimony." In the *Dublin Mail* on October 20, 1952, there appeared this date bait, "Gent in good circumstances wishes to meet Catholic girl *with means,* genuine view to marriage." In the *Daily Times,* "Country man, single, young, with 2,000 pounds, wishes to hear from girl *with small farm and home."* Same paper, same date, "Man, 39, with 1,000 pounds, wishes to meet young lady *with own country home.* View to matrimony." And "Protestant gentleman, very respectable, 37, with means, would be interested in corresponding with young lady *with position and means.* View to matrimony."

An ad in the *Dublin Mail* on October 9, 1952, from a Lothario with an eye to riches, read, "Barman, large capital, good family connections, desirous of acquaintance with young lady *with own business, cash or capital*; view to marriage." Finally in the *Cork Examiner,* "Tradesman, 34 years, with nice home of own, wishes to meet a *working girl with some money,* view to marriage"; and in the *Dublin Mail* on October 13, 1952, "Respectable country widower, T. T., anxious to meet respectable girl or widow, *with business or a home.* View to matrimony." Though not at all marriage-shy as the generality of Eire's bachelors, these hopefuls are hardly the type described by the Irish poet Edward Walsh in his *"Cashel of Munster"*:

I would wed you, dear, without gold or gear, or counted kine;
My wealth you'll be, would fair friends agree, and you be mine.

Indeed it would appear that the young ladies of Ireland who claim that their swains are more given to financial considerations in their loves than to real romance cannot but be right. All of which reminds one of the young couple who were putting the finishing touches on their wedding plans, when the future husband, looking most unromantic but truly businesslike, said to his bride-to-be, "Remember, Mary, we don't want to forget a single thing—not even the slightest detail." To which Mary replied, "We won't. I'll be there."

Any crisis in any nation is at least half solved when there is a common recognition of the problems involved and when there is an awakening of public opinion to the grave danger of doing nothing in a concrete way about the situation. Both Church and government authorities in Ireland are working together to improve the standards of living in those areas that are not so well off as Dublin and other urban centers. Higher wages have been promised and, in many instances, have been given to meet the higher cost of living. The fear of poverty and insecurity is being removed by higher maternity allowances, dependent allowances, more houses, and lower rent scales.

To keep more people on the farm, the drab living conditions are being alleviated by more amenities, such as, light, heating, sanitation, and more adequate housing facilities. The findings of modern agricultural scientists and other technical advisers are being utilized by the farmers, who are also being given more modern and timesaving machinery as an encouragement to greater initiative and production. But most important of all, the people on the farms are being made to realize the dignity of their labor and the need the nation has of them if Ireland is to survive.

In recent times tremendous contributions in the agricultural and rural life of Ireland have been made by the Muintir na Tire society (The People of the Farm), the Macra na Feirme (Young Farmer's Society), and the Countrywomen's Association. Ireland owes an eternal debt of gratitude to the Reverend J. M. Hayes, parish priest of Bansha, Tipperary, founder of Muintir na Tire, who has done more than any dozen men in the entire nation to make Ireland in these days more agriculture-conscious. Father Hayes's organization first saw the light of day in May, 1931.

The purpose of Muintir na Tire, in the words of its founder, is "to unite in one body the rural workers of the country, master and man, not for the purpose of attacking any section, but to give the agricultural community in Ireland its due and proper position in the life of the nation. We wish to raise the status of the country worker, be he farmer or laborer. . . . Those who work the land must have a decent living on the land, otherwise they will not remain; we must look to no party, within or without the country, to enable us to do this: we must look to ourselves." There are many signs that this great and modern agricultural organization will be one of the chief answers to Eire's critical problem of emigration.

Ireland is essentially an agricultural nation with well over half a million people engaged in dairy and farming production. But since some of the people, young and middle-aged, will insist upon industrial work as their means of livelihood, the Department of Commerce and Industry has gone ahead in the past year to increase the number of small industries which it is hoped will keep the young Irishman at home in the Republic. The industrialists are being encouraged to use more native and less imported raw materials and to open up new avenues of industry in the towns and cities. Since 1951 both farmers and industrialists have worked hand in hand to bring this end about.

With the extension of the Shannon scheme and new developments under the Lee River project the waters of Ireland are being harnessed to fulfill the necessary needs for light, heat, and power to run these industries. New factories have already sprung up in dozens of towns, and there is evidence of a determination all over Ireland not only to further Irish self-sufficiency but also to keep the people at home by the lure of an eight-hour working day and a just wage. With the farmers increasing production on the land, thereby supplying the industrialists with more home-produced raw materials and by-products, heretofore imported at exorbitant prices, and with the private manufacturers planning to process more and more home-furnished and locally manufactured goods, it could be that Ireland's depopulation problems are on the way to being solved.

There is one thing, however, that could cause Ireland's present industrial and agricultural plans to stem emigration to bog down. It is the nation's lack of necessary capital to develop either farming or industry on a wide scale. Eire never was a rich nation except in its culture and

Christian traditions. It could easily become one of the wealthiest countries in the world because its wealth has hardly been tapped. No matter how much land a nation may have or how arable it is and no matter how determined the individuals in that nation may be in their will to develop the nation's potential, there can be little lasting progress without proper capitalization.

Because foreign bankers across the Channel control the currency and because of other reasons the Irish Republic has not had the chance fully to develop its resources. And here is where interested and enterprising Americans can and should make their contributions. They can do it because the United States has distributed a little less than 10 billion dollars in military and economic aid to foreign nations since 1951—and most of this money has gone to countries which are ungrateful, if not inimical, to the gracious hand that has thus fed them.

By far the most insignificant grant went to the Irish Republic. And recently Eire, the most friendly nation in the world toward America, was cut off from further economic assistance because her government refused to join the Mutual Security Pact on the principle that she could not consistently do so while still demanding the full freedom of her thirty-two counties.

Ireland today is an excellent market for American products, having imported almost 60 million dollars' worth of goods from the United States in 1950 and over 71 million dollars' worth in 1951. Yet the United States imports from Eire during those two years came to a little more than 12 million dollars.

It would be a generous gesture as well as a sound investment for American capitalists to put some of their money into the Irish industries that will be springing up within the next year or two all over the island and that could be started in still greater numbers if the Irish had American capital to begin them. There are innumerable possibilities for a furthering of Irish-American relations through industrial activities being realized from a variety of potentials, for example, beet sugar, which is a thriving business even now in Eire, leather, gypsum, textiles, peat by-products (such as petroleum), cement, processed meats, vegetables, and fruits.

What wonders could be realized were a dozen American capitalists to venture a few hundred thousand dollars on Ireland's stagnant fishing industry, which could net millions of dollars for Americans and millions of pounds for the enterprising Irish fishermen, who know so well the waters surrounding this island and the wealth that is hidden off the four coasts of Ireland! What great good we Americans could effect for ourselves, for Ireland's economic and emigration problems, and for the furthering of the already strong ties of friendship between the United States and our cousins across the Atlantic were we to release some of our surplus capital in the interests of Ireland's agricultural, industrial, and social needs.[1]

In a nutshell, Ireland's depopulation crisis is critical. Its causes are varied: economical, sociological, psychological. The people of Ireland are at long last beginning to recognize the state of affairs, and responsible people in the Church and in the government are anxious to obviate the manifest danger to Ireland's future and are taking definite steps to remedy the situation. The people of the United States, who have such close ties with the Irish people, can lend their assistance to the Irish people during these critical times. The most practical form of assistance is in the form of capitalization and investment in Irish production. An increase of Irish-made imports will allow the people of Eire to earn the dollars for their imports from the United States, which since 1951 have been a hundred times more in dollar value than Irish exports to America.

Much can be done and is being done by the Church, by the government, and by other responsible agencies to encourage more industry, more widespread farming, greater love for the rural way of life, more and earlier marriages. But in the final analysis who's going to force Erin's stubborn bachelors to be less miss-informed and less marriage-shy? Aye! That's the key to the problem!

[1] Editor's note: We heartily endorse this suggestion and suggest that readers interested in making an investment write for further information to the Consulate of Ireland, New York, N. Y.

ROMANCE FROWNED UPON

7 ──────────────────────────────

Shane Leslie

An associate of the Irish Academy of Letters, Sir Shane Leslie was born in 1885 in London, the eldest son of an Irish baronet of Glaslough, County Monaghan, to whose title he succeeded in 1944. After graduating from Eton he studied at the University of Paris and at King's College, Cambridge, where he received his M.A. degree.

In 1911 he visited America, where he met his future wife, Marjorie Ide, daughter of the United States Minister to Spain. Two sons and a daughter were born of this union. Shane Leslie served in both world wars and was invalided in the first. He has made repeated lecture tours in the United States and lectured for two terms at the University of Notre Dame.

His first book was a volume of verse, "Songs of Oriel," which he followed with several others. "The Oxford Movement," "Henry Edward Manning," "The Celt and the World," "The Skull of Swift," and his autobiography "The Film of Memory" are but a few of his many books of poetry and prose.

In 1921 he was made a Privy Chamberlain of the Sword and Cape to His Holiness Pius XI. His hobbies are bird sanctuaries and Irish archeology, and his home is at Castle Lesley, Glaslough, Eire.

I HAVE LIVED IN IRELAND SINCE 1885 AND SEEN THE POPULATION SINK. AT present the Southern Ireland population is under 3 million, and yet Dublin sends out ambassadors and consuls over the world and appears to line up as a third-class power with the potentials of a fifth-class one, rapidly sinking even lower in the materialist scale. It is only by her ideals that her nationality survives.

84

The present desire to leave the country is due to the drab country life and the lack of opportunity for a generation which is educated to leave rather than work the land. The young are well educated as doctors, lawyers, priests, teachers, traders, but gardeners and agriculturalists are despised by the careerists. The latter stay at home, while every other boy or girl who could get a ticket to America or Europe would sail at ten hours' notice.

They leave Ireland to get married, for marriage is dreary on Irish farms, where the old folk cling on and expect sons and daughters-in-law to act as unpaid servants.

The late Bishop Brown, inspecting a camp of Irish girl workers during the last war, congratulated them on their fine behavior in face of temptation. Their reward would come, he pointed out, when they returned to their beautiful homes in Mayo and Sligo. There was a dead silence. Further inquiry elicited the fact that they hoped to find English husbands and return home only for occasional holidays.

They had been treated by the soldiers for the first time in their lives, taken dancing or to the pictures. They had worn pretty clothes and had their pretty hair waved for the first time. They had been admired for the first time in their lives. At home Irish girls receive a treatment just the opposite from that gladly and gallantly bestowed by Catholic countries like Italy and Spain upon their women.

There are many economic reasons why Irish boys and girls avoid marrying at home. The shadow of the Great Famine of the 1840's is still upon the memory and imagination of the land. The larger the family in the forties, the more acute was the starvation. Men practice the only birth control permitted by the Church. They abstain from marriage until such years as they are unlikely to have more than two or three children. Thousands of young men abstain all through life; hence the abnormal bachelordom.

Irish climate and its soft relaxing atmosphere favor celibacy. The passionate crimes of Latin countries are quite unknown. The illegitimate are scarce, and the Irish prostitute is practically unknown except in English cities. This would be a matter of national pride if only the percentage who do not become priests, nuns, and missionaries took up reproducing with hope and vigor.

They are not helped by economic or social circumstances. Marriage is always a joke, and romance is wickedness. Sunday in all other Catholic countries is courting time. In Ireland, however, the men and women are kept carefully on different sides of the church. If any couples walked out together, they would be ridiculed and chaffed. It is no consolation that the Protestants in Ireland reproduce even less than the Catholics. They too seek other countries.

The attitude of the clergy is not encouraging to marriage. Any love affairs or romances are frowned upon, and it is only in that atmosphere that marriages sprout like flowers. Priests have told me with pride that married couples had come to them after a year to ask why God sent them no children. Inquiry disclosed that they were ignorant of the facts of life!

But they intermarry gladly with any other people. There seems to be no changing this. The Irish seem doomed to make perfect grafting for other stock. They make fine families with Scotch or English husbands. America knows this well, for it abounds in families of Irish-Welsh, Irish-Germans, Irish-Bohemians, Irish-French, and Irish-Slavs.

The pure Irish stock is already at vanishing point. Irish clan names remain, and generally the Faith. But, as things are, the Irish of Ireland have resigned themselves to marry and intermarry chiefly in other countries.

When they do reproduce the good old stock, the best and most adventurous rush into swollen cities like Dublin, Glasgow, Liverpool, Birmingham, and London. They add to the wealth and health of other lands. They leave their weakest specimens at home.

The result is that economic adventurers arrive. Jews (and can you blame them?) have bought up many urban properties and leading stores and shops. The English and Scotch follow them. A crowd of the English middle class and English sportsmen buy up old places and hunting grounds in the South.

The Irish of the Gaelic counties, when questioned, have two general desires: (1) to forget Irish and to get rid of its compulsory teaching; (2) to get their children off the land and into jobs in the cities.

Economic politics never worries the government, which is concerned about votes and ambassadors and medical questions, with an ineffective running protest against Partition. Horace Plunkett, Adam Smith, John Maynard Keynes are not the names that inspire interest or study.

The country relies on the cattle trade, on sweepstakes and remittances from America and Great Britain, and on tourists in search of food or scenery or sport.

The fact is there are no national leaders like Father Mathew or Archbishop Walsh in the past, no laymen like Horace Plunkett and Charles Parnell. Politicians can see only the day after tomorrow. The condition of Ireland in 1960 or 1980 is of no concern. After the exodus will come the deluge!

I propose the following constructive measures to halt the depopulation of Ireland.

1. Derate the farms—take away the rates which are levied on all agricultural life, making it impossible to employ additional labor.

2. Make rural life as lively and happy as possible by encouraging athletic sports, dancing, and drama in every parish.

3. Develop an immense national system of forestry planting—a national park in each county on a scale proportionate to what is being done in England and Scotland. Employ 10,000 foresters instead of an army.

4. Build laborers' hamlets instead of suburbs to the swollen city of Dublin.

8

John A. O'Brien

THE COMMON IMPRESSION AMONG THE AMERICAN PEOPLE IS THAT THE IRISH in this country are a prolific people, noted for their large families. They are not merely reproducing themselves but are adding considerably to our population. The national bird of the Irish, as the humorist Thomas Daly was fond of saying, is the stork.

When these facts are challenged and the statement is made that of all the racial groups making up America the Irish are among the least prolific, have by far the largest proportion of bachelors and spinsters, and present the greatest evidence of dying out, people are both shocked and incredulous. They think that the person making such observations is either "off the beam" or has some peculiar and wild-eyed theory to promote.

Among their first reactions is to cite a large Irish family as clinching their point. But when they are asked to mention additional families of comparable size, they usually find their list stopping unexpectedly short. Indeed, when they enumerate their adult friends of Irish extraction, they find themselves suddenly confronted with the names of more bachelors and spinsters than they had realized.

There are indeed some Irish families of unusual size. Not infrequently news editors seeking for a story with a human-interest slant pounce upon such families and feature their pictures. Our good friends, Mr. and Mrs. Thomas Brennan of Chicago, are the proud parents of eleven rather young children. Pictures of the parents and the children stretching between them in stepladder sequence, as they march in the traditional Easter parade, have appeared year after year in the metropolitan papers.

Pictures of them in the last Easter parade, Thomas Brennan informed us, appeared in hundreds of newspapers from coast to coast, and he was besieged on the phone by news reporters seeking additional human-interest slants. Millions of readers were thus unwittingly led to think of the Brennan family as typical of the Irish families in America.

Another instance: After writing an article last year on "The Vanishing Irish," focusing attention chiefly upon the disproportionately large number of single men and women in Eire, we were flooded with letters, many of which contained a news clipping about an Irish priest who was made a prelate. The news item played up the fact that he was one of a very large family. Upon many of the clippings were scrawled phrases such as "This looks like the Irish are vanishing, doesn't it?"

Upon investigating, we found that, although all the members of the estimable family had reached the stage of adulthood and most of them were well beyond it, not less than eleven had passed up marriage—apparently for life. Here then was the irony of the situation: the very family, cited to disprove my thesis, actually proved it to the hilt. One could probably search all Italy, Germany, Poland, Lithuania, France, England, and all the other countries of Europe except Ireland and not find a single family in which eleven of its adult members had chosen celibacy instead of marriage as their state in life. Only among the Irish and their descendants will such extensive celibacy be found.

There is considerable evidence that the nonmarrying mores of the Irish in Eire are being perpetuated among the Irish in America. We touched briefly upon this in an earlier chapter, and our collaborators Mrs. Banning, Mrs. Norris, and Mrs. Rooney will add the results of their own observations. It will be well to present here the findings of earlier investigators, whose conclusions stirred a few ripples of passing interest years ago but failed, unfortunately, to lead to the launching of remedial measures, and to present some additional evidence of significance as well.

This will show that the vanishing character of the Irish in America has been observed for years and has been the cause of great concern to many members of the Hierarchy and indeed to all scholars familiar with the facts. Particularly will it show that the strange phenomenon with which this book deals is not peculiar to the present generation but has been operative among the Irish both at home and abroad for a full century.

Beginning as far back as the 1920's three great American scholars, Dr. James J. Walsh of Fordham University, Dr. Austin O'Malley of Notre Dame University, and Father M. V. Kelly, in a series of articles in *America* called attention to the strange failure of the Irish to reproduce themselves in numbers comparable with other immigrants. Despite the tidal waves of Irish immigration to our shores these keen observers of social life and custom noticed the tendency of the Irish strain to disappear. They were disturbed by it, and they sought to find an explanation for it.

Of these three, Dr. Walsh seems to have been the first to sound the warning publicly and to recur to the theme repeatedly. Historian, philosopher, and medical scientist, he recognized in this trait of the Irish a portent of ominous significance, a wound which, if not healed, would not only stunt their growth but lead to their premature demise. It caused him to institute inquiries in various parts of the New World and to journey to Ireland to consult the Registrar General, Sir William J. Thompson, who had charge of the census, to try to track down in its native lair the cause of the strange blight on the Irish character.

The man who first called Dr. Walsh's attention to this phenomenon and kindled his lasting interest in it was Archbishop Neil McNeil of Toronto, Canada. From our survey of the literature on this subject it appears that the Archbishop was one of the first to note this trait among the Irish settlers of Canada and to express, privately, grave concern over it. We were fortunate enough to know the Archbishop fairly well, and we were impressed by his keen perceptive powers and by his unusual talents in the field of higher mathematics.

"The Irish families," remarked the Archbishop to Dr. Walsh in 1917, "have an enormously disproportionate number of bachelors and spinsters. The Irish are disappearing, not only in the cities, but also in the country districts. The chief cause of their disappearance is not so much small families as it is the failure of so many of them to marry at all. Therein lies their weakness, and I have seen it thin out their numbers in settlement after settlement in Canada. Unless that trait is eradicated, it may bring about their extinction."

"Why," replied Dr. Walsh, "I'm startled to hear you say that. Like most others, I have thought of the Irish as a prolific race and in no danger of dying out."

The Archbishop cited instance after instance to back up his statement. Dr. Walsh recognized that he was in the presence not only of a keen observer but also of a man who refused to accept impressions in place of facts. It was this conversation which got Dr. Walsh started on a line of investigation which he pursued for years and which remained as one of his chief interests until his death.

Five years later Dr. Walsh published a series of three articles in *America,* presenting the evidence he had collected in the interim. In the first article, "Are Irish Catholics Dying Out in This Country?" in the August 5, 1922, issue, he begins by saying rather apologetically that, although everybody imagines the Irish to be a prolific race, his investigations have led him to the conclusion that it is actually dying out in this country. He studied numerous cases of families through four generations and was shocked to find about half the members remaining bachelors and spinsters, causing the families to thin out and ultimately disappear.

"The outlook," he observes, "is alarming. The Irish Catholic families are not only failing to reproduce themselves in our generation but they are disappearing rapidly. It is not an unusual thing to find that a family of six or seven children, born as the first generation in this country, is represented by fifteen to twenty-five children in the third generation, but present no more than four or five, sometimes less, in the fourth generation . . . to keep up the family stock."

His investigation gave him an insight into the almost unbelievable number of bachelors and spinsters among the descendants of Irish immigrants. Thus he cites a grandfather who had 6 children of whom but 2 married and had 9 children. But of these 9 children in the third generation only 2 are married and have a total of but 2 offspring.

Another typical case he cites is that of a grandfather with 7 children. Four of them married and all had children—a total of 15. But of these 15, though all are past thirty, only 1 married and there are no children. Occasionally he would find a happy exception where most of the offspring would marry, but he was appalled at the incidence of celibacy among people living not in a convent or monastery but in the world.

"From what I have found," he reports, "if the Church is to depend on the reproductive increase of the Irish Catholics in this country for its membership the future looks blank indeed. . . . After looking over the data that I have already I am forced to the conclusion that while the fewness of children in the families represents a very prominent factor in the unfortunate situation that is evidently developing, it is by no means the only factor, and I doubt whether it is even the most serious factor. That is, to my mind, the very large number of old maids and old bachelors who are to be found in Irish families in this country."

He mentions that he is well aware that in Ireland there is usually at least one example of these two anomalies, and sometimes one of each in the family. He is shocked to discover, however, that here in America "it is not unusual to have half the children of the family remain unmarried. Sometimes it is actually more than that."

In "Catholic Bachelors and Old Maids" in the following issue of *America,* Dr. Walsh piled up impressive evidence that the blight of excessive bachelorhood and spinsterhood was causing great numbers of Irish immigrant families to disappear in the third and fourth generations. He had conducted an investigation of 50 families in the smaller towns and cities of an industrial region and found that the grandparents had an average of 5 children—a total of slightly more than 250. If this ratio were to be maintained, there would be 1,250 in the next generation.

What number did he actually find? He reports that the number was so much less than would normally have been expected that persons, when they first heard it, would scarcely believe it. "Most people would be ready to feel," he remarks, "that there might be little reason for surprise if there were half that number, say 600, and a few would be willing to concede that owing to the growing habit of later marriages in this country there might even be only one-third, say 400, or even one-fourth, a little more than 300. But, as a matter of fact, there are fewer than 200 children! And that group is not in one of our very large cities, and is not very different from other groups of the same kind but, on the contrary, it is representative of the successful Irish Catholic families in other parts of the country."

So shocked was he by his findings that he thought it was time to sound a nationwide alarm. As his warning would be running directly contrary to a widely held belief, he thought it advisable to associate other scholars with himself in the task. He wrote to Archbishop McNeil to see whether or not he was still of the opinion he had expressed five years ago and if he would be willing to be quoted. The Archbishop replied that all his subsequent study had deepened his conviction and he felt that it was of the utmost importance to call emphatic attention to the unfortunate state of affairs.

Shortly afterward the Archbishop sent Dr. Walsh a clipping from the *Toronto Globe* of June 2, 1922, in which the secretary of a social-service council in Ontario reported the surprising results of a survey of the rural communities in Canada. The survey disclosed that the decrease in the number of children in school sections in Ontario, peopled largely by Irish and Scotch immigrants, was so marked that there was a serious question of closing many of the rural schools. In schools which had 100 pupils forty years ago now but 20 to 12 children were enrolled. In one school section where in 1884 there were 160 children in the families, in 1922, with six more farmhouses occupied, there were only 29 children.

What was the cause of this strange anomaly? The failure of so many of the Irish to marry. Instead of homes filled with children in 1884, the investigators chiefly found houses each occupied by a bachelor and his spinster sister. In 1884, in six of these houses where old maids and old bachelors now live, reports the secretary, there were 49 children. In 1884 in two of these farm homes there were 13 children, in one 12, in three 11, in one 10, in one 9, in one 8, in two 7, and in one 5. "And today [1922]," the report runs, "in these same houses two have four children, one has three, three have one and the rest are occupied by childless couples or old bachelors."

It was no wonder that the Archbishop of Toronto was concerned and urged Dr. Walsh to sound the alarm. Communities where homes full of children once constituted thriving and populous settlements were now marked by the presence chiefly of bachelors and spinsters with their inevitable portents of social decay and death. In Canada with all its boundless land and opportunity was being written anew the strange story of racial decline which the Irish have spelled out for more than a century in their homeland. Scholar, philosopher, and mathematician that Archbishop McNeil was, here was a conundrum that he couldn't quite figure out: why a Catholic people in a land of boundless opportunity should persist in unwittingly committing racial suicide through their refusal to marry.

Dr. Walsh reports an amusing experience that illustrates perfectly the reaction of people to whom one mentions the tendency of the Irish to die out. While taking lunch with Mr. Horan, a prominent Irish politician in the Middle West, he remarked, "I'm surprised to find the Irish, more than any other racial group in America, thinning out in the third and fourth generations."

"Oh, you must be mistaken, Dr. Walsh," replied Mr. Horan. "The Irish are a prolific race, noted for their large families."

"All right," said Dr. Walsh, "let's look at the facts. Suppose you tell me about your own family's record."

"Well, let's see," began Mr. Horan. "My grandparents had 11 children, 7 of whom lived to be adults. One of them was killed in early manhood, 1 is a priest, and 1 is a nun. Of the 4 remaining, the 2 girls have never married and are too old to think of it now. The 2 boys married, one had but 1 son—myself—and the other had 3 daughters, the youngest is past twenty, and none of them is married."

"That means then," pointed out Dr. Walsh, "that instead of the 60 children that might have been expected from the 11 offspring if they were even half as prolific as their parents, there are but 4 descendants in the third generation and only 1 left to perpetuate the name. That is what I mean by thinning out, virtually disappearing, and your own family record is a perfect example of what I'm talking about."

"I'm beginning," said Mr. Horan, "to see what you mean, and I find it disturbing. We've too precious a heritage to let it die out like that."

Dr. Walsh's research brought out another interesting fact which we, too, have often observed. It is this: In the family which produces a priest or religious the number of bachelors and spinsters is generally unusually high. Celibacy seems to be accepted as the ideal even for the others remaining in the world. He cites as typical the following case from western New York: The parents had 8 children, 7 of whom survived. Two sons became priests, and 1 daughter entered the convent. The 3 other sons remained bachelors, and the spinster sister keeps house for them. Not even a single descendant in the third generation!

Another typical case from the vicinity of Philadelphia: The parents have 6 children, 5 of whom lived to adulthood. One son became a priest. The other son remained a bachelor, the 3 daughters are spinsters, and all are well past forty and unlikely to marry.

After finding this pattern recurring time and time again, Dr. Walsh concludes: "I am sorry to say that apparently the more priests and religious there are in the family, the less tendency does there seem to be for other members of the family to get married. . . . The more nearly they are related to the Hierarchy the less of marrying and of giving in marriage there seems to be."

He cites as typical the case of a family in the Middle West in which 1 son became a priest and was made a bishop. One of his brothers married and has 1 son. The other brother remained a bachelor, and his 3 sisters remained spinsters—1 lone descendant in the second generation.

Dr. Walsh's observations coincide with our own. One of the cases which first attracted our attention to the curious tendency of which the doctor speaks occurred in our own parish nearly forty years ago. An Irish immigrant couple had acquired through years of labor extensive landholdings and left their fortune to their 8 children—6 sons and 2 daughters. One son became a priest, 1 son married, the other 6 remained single. When we came to know them, they were all past thirty. Occasionally we would speak to the various sons about the desirability and importance of founding a family of their own.

"You are sufficiently well fixed," we said to Michael, "to get married and start raising your own family. Your parents left their home in Ireland and were adventurous enough to come to the New World and raise a fine family. This is God's plan for those not called to the religious life—'increase and multiply.' Your parents in Heaven would smile down upon you and your little ones. You would bring happiness to some good woman, and together you would pass on the priceless heritage of human life. That's a holy calling too, Michael, and in bringing happiness to others you will find it will come back to you."

"No," Michael replied, "I got a good home now, and I know when I'm well off."

Then, lighting his corncob pipe, he would point at it and snicker, "This is my only wife."

Obdurate bachelors and spinsters they remained till the bitter end. That experience in early priesthood helped us to get at least a glimmering of the strange resistance which the Irish had built up to the voice of God whispering within them: "It is not good for man to be alone. . . . Wherefore a man shall leave father and mother and shall cleave to his wife and they shall be two in one flesh. . . . Increase and multiply and fill the earth."

People of other races heard that voice and gladly obeyed. Why do so many Irish fail to do so? Don't they hear that voice? If they do, what strange mental road block prevents them from following it? These were the questionings which baffled us then, and while forty years of observation have confirmed the facts, much of the mystery still remains to taunt us.

If there are any readers who doubt that there are more bachelors and spinsters among the Irish in America than among those of any other racial extraction, we would suggest that they make a list of a dozen families of different racial groups and compare the number of unmarried adults with those found in a similar list of Irish families. Check, too, upon the unusually large number of celibates found in the family which has given a member to the religious life. These are matters of simple observation, and the conditions which Dr. Walsh described thirty years ago have undergone, as far as we can see, no perceptible change. The Irish have two or three times their share of unmarried adults.

Dr. Walsh once mentioned the results of his findings along these lines to a distinguished American prelate. The latter agreed and remarked that the proneness to be old bachelors and old maids is due to "an inherent love of celibacy that reigns in every true Irish heart." Whereupon the doctor commented, "If that is so, it is a very unfortunate thing for the race and for the Church in this country."

Dr. Walsh's scientific turn of mind prompted him to make some inquiries concerning the situation among the Irish in Australia and New Zealand, and he found much the same conditions prevailing there. Here too were vast countries clamoring for population, for large families and more marriages. Yet despite these favorable circumstances the tendency of the Irish to marry late or not at all persisted. "The Irish families that have gone to Australia are," reports Dr. Walsh, "particularly noted for the number of old maids and old bachelors to be found among them."

Obviously then the factor holding back so many of the Irish from marriage was traceable not to the conditions of the country to which they had migrated but to a factor rooted deep within them. It is doubtless such an internal factor which is responsible for their similar showing in Canada and in the United States. Like his friend Archbishop McNeil,

Dr. Walsh found himself at a loss to account for this strange trait in the Irish ethos or to suggest proper therapeutic treatment for it.

"What," he asked, "is to be done about it all? That I do not know. I am pointing out a condition that exists and not exploiting any theory of my own."

The problem was often on his mind, however, and it continued to disturb him. He had written a book, *The World's Debt to the Irish,* and he thought it was a pity that a people with a great inheritance should be so unconcerned about their failure to pass it on to posterity. So three years later he journeyed to Ireland and with Sir W. J. Thompson, Director of the Census, went over the figures for the censuses of 1911 and 1921. He was shocked to find the appallingly large number of bachelors and spinsters disclosed in each census. Then, as now, Ireland led the world in the fewness and the lateness of its marriages, in the number of its unmarried, and in the number of people who were fleeing from her shores.

A year later he published in the May 1, 1926, issue of *America* an article, "The Disappearing Irish in America," in which he portrays the pattern he discovered in Ireland. The picture which he draws of conditions in Ireland in 1911 and 1921 is substantially the same picture as that which obtains today and which is presented in an early chapter in this book. Though the signs everywhere were then pointing to extinction, little seems to have been accomplished by the leaders of Church or State in the long interim to halt the grim march toward national extinction.

One of the few voices which spoke out a warning in those days was that of C. H. Oldham, professor of national economics at University College, Dublin. "The celibacy of our people," he said, "the lateness of the few marriages that do take place are without parallel anywhere . . . and our emigration has features unlike the emigration that goes on elsewhere." Why did not these strange phenomena stir any commotion or cause at least a few ripples on the placid surface of Irish national life?

Professor Oldham suggests the best answer that I have yet seen. He points out that "nobody knows Ireland who only Ireland knows" and adds a little later in his article, "But nobody in Ireland is aware how anomalous the Irish are unless he has been at the trouble (and it is a very great trouble) to compare Irish statistics with comparable statistics of other countries." Because few Irish took the pains to compare their national record with others, few of them realized that Ireland had then, as it has now, the worst record in the matter of few and late marriages in the civilized world.

Acting on the principle enunciated by Professor Oldham, Dr. Walsh was busily comparing the pattern of few and late marriages in Ireland with the pattern which he and Archbishop McNeil had traced out in America. The patterns, he discovered, were essentially the same: the Irish were perpetuating in the New World the mores which characterized their life in Ireland and which were largely responsible for its decline.

Dr. Walsh points out that the unfortunate persistence of the tendency toward few and late marriages could lead only to the serious diminution of the Irish as a racial factor in American life. "The old maids and the old bachelors who perhaps think that they are exercising their divine right of freedom in this question of late marriages or entirely missed marriages, are not quite so free as they think. They are being influenced by racial custom, established for years among the Irish at home in Ireland, and descending not by heredity but by environment."

What could be done to correct the weakness he had uncovered? "Perhaps calling attention to this situation," he concludes, "may serve to awaken some serious thought on the subject and pave the way for reform. Such a social reform, however, cannot be expected to happen rapidly. In the meantime there is serious danger of the Irish element in the Catholic Church in the United States becoming so vanishing a factor as to be almost negligible. This is not a Brocken phantom of the imagination. It is a definite reality demanding thorough attention."

Four years later Dr. Walsh sounded another warning to the Irish both in the homeland and in America that the failure of so many of them was threatening the race with extinction. He had continued to collect evidence of the disproportionately large number of old bachelors and old maids among the Irish in this country and felt they were doing an injustice to themselves, to the Church, and to America. Hence when the census of population in the Irish Free State was published in 1930, he published in *America,* March 29, 1930, an article, "Shy Irish Bachelors," calling attention to the persistence of the disastrous pattern of excessive bachelorhood.

The census figures show that this trait is not something peculiar to the Irish in America but is even more conspicuous among the Irish in the homeland. Since the Famine in the mid-forties the pathology seems to be endemic to the Irish race wherever they are. But like a fungus it grows to especially lush proportions in its original native habitat. Hence he uses the census in Eire as an effective sounding board for his warning, particularly to the Irish in his own country.

Looking at those census figures, Dr. Walsh observed, "There are more unmarried men proportionately in Ireland than anywhere else in the world. . . . The worst of it is that the number of unmarried, both males and females, is increasing every decade. There are many thousands of eligible young men, but still more thousands of eligible young women, most of whom would surely not require very much urging to marry, but they do not marry. . . . Whosesoever fault it may be is a question, but there is no doubt at all about the almost incredible tendency to celibacy of the Irish race."

Most of the blame rests on the bachelors, as there is no country, points out Dr. Walsh, in which a woman feels her unmarried state so poignantly as in Ireland. He tells of visiting an old Irish lady who had been kind to the younger members of his family many years ago and whom he wished to help in her old age.

"Are you a widow?" asked the doctor.

"Oh," she replied, "I'm the worst kind of a wudda, I'm an ould maid. There are entirely too many of us in Ireland of that same kind of wuddas. I wish there were fewer."

He was deeply touched by the old woman's utter candor in bemoaning the plight in which she and so many other women of Eire were involuntarily plunged. It brought vividly to his mind the comment of the editor of the *Irish Independent* when this census was published, "Ireland is the island of bachelors." The unfortunate consequence of the men's shyness toward marriage, however, was that women were made to share not a similar choice but a similar fate.

What Dr. Walsh finds startling is that the rural districts in Ireland are particularly the brooding places of unmarried men and women. "Up to the age of thirty," he points out, "the percentage of women unmarried in the Free State at the present time is sixty-five per cent in the rural areas and fifty-seven per cent in the towns. At the same age for men, the percentage unmarried in the rural areas is eighty-seven, and in the urban areas, sixty-eight. . . . Compared with other countries in Europe,

Ireland has on the average twice as many unmarried men at various ages as the average in the other countries."

Apparently Dr. Walsh felt that he had tracked down the cause of the pronounced celibacy of the Irish in America at least to its native lair—Ireland. Here the number of old bachelors and old maids reached staggering and incredible proportions: here were formed the nonmarrying mores which the Irish in America were but perpetuating, though in a somewhat diminished degree. The purpose of his article was to warn not only the natives of Eire but also their descendants in America that measures must be taken to heal this strange and malignant trauma in the Irish ethos or the race was doomed.

"Now that Ireland," he says, "has become a nation—if we may say that, *pace* those Irish who are not inclined to admit such a development —it is extremely important that the race shall perpetuate itself. The custom of remaining unmarried until the forties and fifties is birth control not in the accepted usage of the words in our time and without any stigma attached to it, but in very reality *actual birth control*. . . . If we Irish feel that we are in possession of elements for the benefit of the human race that are important, and this our history would seem to demonstrate amply, it would seem to be incumbent on us to safeguard their perpetuation. Unless," he concludes, "the marriage rate in Ireland itself increases and also the marriage rate among the Irish here in the United States, for as I have shown in previous papers it is very low, the Irish are inevitably destined to extinction."

Dr. Walsh was, however, a voice crying in the wilderness. His stern and urgent warning went largely unheeded. No organized effort was made among the Irish either at home or abroad to eradicate the blight of excessive bachelorhood which was dooming them to near extinction everywhere. The decline of the Irish in America continued until it became painfully conspicuous also to Father M. V. Kelly, C.S.B., who has long been interested in rural sociology. Two years after Dr. Walsh had published his memorable series of three articles on the disappearing Irish in America, Father Kelly authored in *America* in November, 1928, a series of three which he boldly and challengingly entitled "The Suicide of the Irish Race."

He explained that the title was chosen not for any sensational effect but simply because it best described the conditions with which his series would deal. At the outset he disclaimed any intention of indicting the Irish at home or abroad of the crime of intentional suicide or of the charge ordinarily associated with the term "race suicide," namely, unethical contraception methods. But populations and peoples, he explains, through other processes have approached and can approach utter extinction.

He then shows how other racial groups settling in a new country, where the climate, land, food, housing, and living conditions are favorable, have doubled their numbers every 30 years. He instances the case of the French Canadians, who numbered 60,000 in 1763, when Canada became a British dependency and immigration from France came to an abrupt halt. In 1923, just 160 years later, the descendants of the 60,000 French Canadians reached the astonishing total of 3,500,000—a ratio of 1 to 60!

During that period of 160 years, Father Kelly points out, at least 5,000,000 Irish Catholics immigrated to the United States. "Today [1923] there are," he says, "possibly 7,000,000 Catholics of Irish origin in the United States. There are certainly not 8,000,000." He contrasts the small increase of the Irish with the enormous increase of the French Canadians. "How," he asks, "are we to account for this astounding difference?"

He attributes the failure of the Irish to achieve anything approaching the increase which would normally be expected to one exclusive factor: the settling of almost all the Irish in the cities, which are not only unfavorable to natural increase but which, like parasites, live upon the accretions from the country. Wall up a city, give its inhabitants abundant food, allow no outsiders to enter, and in four generations that city will be a desert. This is the line of reasoning he advances to explain the strange phenomenon of the vanishing Irish in the United States.

He has put his finger, we think, upon one important factor in the tendency of the Irish to die out in this country. Unfortunately they turned their backs upon the great stretches of farm land, among the most fertile in the world, and flocked chiefly to the great urban centers, with New York, Boston, Philadelphia, and Chicago attracting enormous numbers.

The factor cited explains part but not all of the gnarled difficulty we are seeking to unravel. It does not explain the dwindling of the numerous rural settlements of the Irish in Canada or the United States. Both

Archbishop McNeil and Dr. Walsh call attention specifically to the
decline in the rural settlements, and the careful survey of such communities conducted by the Social Service Council of Ontario corrobo-
rates them with ample and convincing evidence. Friends in the Hierarchy in both Canada and the United States have told us of once
flourishing Irish rural settlements which dwindled to such an extent
that the parishes had to be reduced to outmissions. Neither does it explain—and this is most important—the population decline in the rural
districts of Ireland itself, where the decline is worst of all.

In a Lenten Pastoral Archbishop Kinane of Cashel calls attention
particularly to this disturbing fact. "The decline in the number of children, especially in the country districts," he declares, "is alarming.
Parishes in which there were almost a couple hundred for Confirmation
can now muster scarcely fifty. Already a position of great seriousness
confronts both Church and State and, unless the decline is quickly arrested, the situation will soon be catastrophic."

The abundance of bachelors and spinsters in the Irish countryside is
in sharp contrast to the paucity of children. In traveling on foot and on
bicycle through rural districts we could not help noticing the decrease
in the number of children on each of our visits to Ireland over the last
thirty odd years. Alice Curtayne gives a graphic picture of this in an
article, "Decay of Rural Ireland," in *America*.

"The children are vanishing as rapidly as though they were being
lured away by the music of some fatalistic Pied Piper. If plague or
famine had taken them from us in such devastating numbers, what an
outcry would have been raised, and how the sympathy of the world
would have been invoked on our behalf! But it is worse when children
are not even there to be stricken. . . . Figures from little individual country districts are still more alarming, because they show that the decline
is progressive everywhere, and more marked in the country than the
town."

She can look out from her country home and count home after home
occupied by bachelors and spinster sisters. "Children have always been
such an unvarying feature of Irish life," she continues, "such an in-
separable part of the rural landscape, that it is well-nigh impossible to
imagine Mother Ireland as a sort of Rachel 'mourning for her children
that are not.' Such a concept is like a nightmare from which one would

be glad to be awakened. Yet it has come upon us almost insensibly and we are now in the midst of the catastrophe."

Like Archbishop McNeil and Dr. Walsh, Father Kelly rendered a real service by calling attention to the failure of the Irish to reproduce themselves in numbers comparable with other racial elements in the New World. His interest prompted him to institute inquiries concerning Irish settlers in other countries, and the reports received were equally disturbing. "What every lover of the race," he concludes, "must chiefly deplore in the history of the Irish abroad is their failure to multiply at the rate we might reasonably have expected. This disappointing record is reported from England and Scotland, from the United States, from Canada and from Australia."

The endeavor to account for this strange phenomenon on the sole grounds of urban life, while revealing and partially valid, especially for the Irish of the Diaspora, is, as we have shown, an oversimplification. The decay of Irish rural settlements in the New World, to say nothing of the catastrophic decay of such areas at home, shows the perverse tendency of the Irish everywhere to practice what Father Kelly termed "racial suicide." Regardless of geography, favorable climate, boundless land, abundant food, and every other environmental condition conducive to procreation and child rearing, they stubbornly persist in this suicidal practice.

Dr. Austin O'Malley often called attention to the curious failure of the Irish in the United States to reproduce themselves at anything approaching a normal rate. He ventured the theory that the change from the cooler and darker atmosphere of Ireland to the warmer and brighter regions of this country might be responsible for their lessened reproduction. But the theory totally fails to square with the facts, for the phenomenon occurs in the cooler and darker climate of Canada as well as in the sunnier regions of the United States. The factor at work transcends all differences of geography or climate. Hence we must look elsewhere and search deeper for the hidden abnormality within the Irish ethos, heading the race toward comparative extinction everywhere.

Despite the warnings sounded thirty years ago by Archbishop McNeil, Dr. Walsh, Dr. O'Malley, and Father Kelly, the title of whose series was thunderous with alarm, the Irish *modus vivendi* continued unchanged. All the articles appeared in a periodical read chiefly by a somewhat limited elite, and their cumulative message seems never to have penetrated to the masses of the Irish in this country and certainly never reached the masses in Ireland. The theme at virtually every St. Patrick's Day banquet or meeting continued to be a glorification of the Irish race at home and abroad, usually abounding in extravagant rhetoric and fulsome praise.

The result has been to create the psychic atmosphere of a dreamworld in which the Irish revel in the thought that they are the greatest race in the world and that Ireland is the best of all possible countries. Any suggestion that everything isn't simply wonderful with Erin and with her children at home and abroad is regarded as hostility bordering on treason and sacrilege. Shillelaghs laden with sulfur and dynamite come flying at the head of the person who has the temerity to suggest that the Irish may have an Achilles heel and that Eire seems well on the road to extinction. The slightest dose of the cold water of reality causes many of them to fly into a rage and to strike back with wrathful epithets instead of reasoned argument.

That is why the article by Father J. J. Murphy of Denver, "St. Patrick's Day Reflections: 1949," in *America* came as a welcome relief from the traditional pattern. He pointed out that we Irish-Americans are fully conscious of the undoubted merits of our ancestors and of their contribution to America and to the world and that the time has come for us to look profitably on the other side and examine our consciences on several points.

"First," he says, "what about the Irish attitude toward Christian marriage? In the Irish love of the priesthood and the religious life is there not too often a concomitant lack of full appreciation of the sacrament of matrimony? It is true that when some modern secular periodical wants to show how many gadgets a family needs today, it will probably show Kathy and Tom Mulloy and their nine children. It is equally probable, however, that the Mulloys are the only Irish-American youngsters with many brothers and sisters in Annunciation School in any big city in America. Check the Irish families in a number of metropolitan parochial schools, and you will find that large families are the exception."

As a result of this failure to inculcate a practical appreciation of the importance of marriage and of the fact that it is intended by God as the normal state for the overwhelming majority, the Irish, he points out, suffer from unduly late marriages and an abnormal number of bachelors and spinsters. He cites the record of his own family as typical of what he and other priests of wide experience have observed as the common pattern.

Four of the children of his Irish-born grandparents never married; 3 of the other 4 married late in life. Of the 10 children in the second generation (after 8 in the first), 4 are past fifty and unmarried; 2 married when over forty; 2 when almost thirty; only 1 at a reasonably early age; and 1 (Father Murphy) entered the priesthood. "These personal figures would not be at all significant," he points out, "were it not for the fact that they formed a pattern found in all Irish-Americans in the seminary with me, and quite in contrast with the record of those of other ancestry."

In common with many other Irish priests, Father Murphy wonders if there may not be an underlying touch of Jansenism in the Irish attitude toward marriage. "This shows itself," he continues, "in the reluctance of Irish parents to prepare the minds of their daughters for motherhood, as other Catholic peoples, such as some Slavic-American groups, do so well. It shows itself in an attitude toward the religious state that carries with it an undervaluing of the sacrament of matrimony, an attitude revealed on occasion even by some teaching Sisters. In short, Irish-Americans seem to be committing race suicide."

Here Father Murphy has singled out a factor of enormous importance in explaining the grotesque proportion of bachelors and spinsters among the Irish: the typical Irish attitude toward marriage, which, as he and many other priests have suggested, would seem to have an underlying touch of Jansenism. That attitude looks upon marriage and sex as rather regrettable necessities in the propagation of the race: it would have been much better if God had arranged for offspring in some other way. Irish parents shy away from the distasteful task of lifting the veil upon this earthy, unappetizing, and somewhat unclean subject.

Recall the observation of the American prelate about the "inherent love of celibacy that reigns in every true Irish heart." That observation throws a flood of light upon the tremendous emphasis upon the nobility, dignity, and transcendental character of the religious life, a celibate state, which prevails among the Irish people. This concept runs through the whole education of the child, in the home, in the church, in the

school, and in the whole social milieu in which he lives. It is the basic
principle establishing his scale of values. At the shining peak is the celibate religious state; at the earth-stained bottom is marriage.

As a result, more young men and women in Ireland enter the religious
state than in any other country, and fewer young men and women enter
the married state than in any other country. Indeed, it is probably truer
to say that in Eire more than five times as many embrace the religious
life and several times as many of those who stay in the world remain
bachelors and spinsters as in any other country.

Ireland has provided and is still providing enormous numbers of
priests and nuns to America, Australia, New Zealand, and the mission
lands as well. In large sections of the United States, especially in the
West, Irish-born clergy constitute the great majority of the diocesan
priests. For that tremendous contribution of consecrated vocations the
Church in America can never adequately express her indebtedness and
gratitude. No single word in this context is intended to mute her note
of thanksgiving.

The point is simply that in our rightful stressing of the dignity of the
religious life of the consecrated celibate we have unwittingly under-
valued, as Father Murphy points out, the dignity, importance, and necessity of the vocation to the family life. It is not that anything is consciously said to disparage marriage, for the teaching of the Church concerning its dignity and holiness is unmistakable, but rather that there is
an unconscious depreciation of it as a result of the tremendous, lifelong
emphasis upon the celibate religious state, the like of which is found in
no country in the world.

For almost forty years we have ministered to young men and women
of university age, counseling them on problems of courtship and marriage. We have introduced thousands to one another, married great
numbers, and followed them in their expanding family lives. We have
not been able to escape noticing the difference in attitude toward marriage characterizing so many Irish-American young people and in that
common to those of other extractions.

The latter look upon marriage and the family life as their normal,
natural goal; they are frankly eager to meet young people of the other
sex; they mingle together with ease and, before long, have found their
mates. Indeed, if they haven't, they get rather clear-cut directives from

their elders that it is high time for them to do so. The result is that they are practically all married at an early age. The home training has predisposed them for family life, and they take to it, as the saying goes, "like ducks to water."

In contrast, the Irish are much more shy and aloof, to the point of being impractical. They hide their natural interest in the other sex under a mask of jaunty nonchalance and seem to lack the clear-cut perception of the others that marriage is the natural, normal goal to head for, the goal designed by God and nature for some 95 per cent of the race. Many of them, of course, reach the goal, but frequently by a casual, circuitous route, which takes them much longer. And not a few miss it altogether—more than those of any other race.

This defect is traceable, we think, to a failure on the part of many Irish families to give their children the training that would dispose them, if they have no religious vocation, toward marriage as their goal and prompt them to take the practical steps to achieve it. We have known great numbers who, when they were old enough to look back appraisingly on their home training, have told us this. Instead of pushing the fledglings from the nest when they are able to fly, Irish parents not infrequently hold on to them until they have long passed maturity and indeed not infrequently until death.

Some years ago we wrote an article for a magazine of national circulation on marriage as the vocation for the overwhelming majority of young people not called to the religious life. Letters from all parts of the country flooded our desk, many coming from those of Irish descent who were past the normal age for marriage. Running through the latter was the note of regret that their parents had done little or nothing to prepare or dispose them for that vocation but in many cases had, perhaps unwittingly, turned their thoughts from it and even prejudiced them against it. We quote a portion from a revealing letter of Irene Scanlan, which might be read with profit by every Irish-American family.

"Having read your article," she writes, "I hasten to volunteer some information about why our young people feign such indifference, if not reluctance, at meeting those of the opposite gender [this was the question we had raised]: I believe this attitude can be traced directly to teachings received by young people of Irish descent from parents and other misguided grown-ups; I know that in my own case this is true. . . . If at the age, let us say, of eighteen, I had admitted that I had what you describe as 'a hunger for the love and companionship of a helpmate who will lessen the sorrows of life and increase its joys,' my Irish mother would have been thunderstruck. She would have sorrowfully considered herself a rank failure as a Christian mother to have brought up a daughter so lacking in delicacy.

"If now at the age of thirty-one I should express such an opinion she would most certainly consider me lacking in daughterly charity. That I should feel any dissatisfaction with my life of loneliness in supporting her would be unbelievable. Have I not a good position, a good education, a salary sufficient to maintain a pleasant home? What more could I wish? So I continue to 'feign indifference to the opposite sex.' Mother takes great pride in the fact that I am a 'ladylike person,' that I have the respect of her aged relatives and friends, that I stay at home evenings with her instead of 'galavanting' with the men as some other young women do.

"From my earliest childhood I can remember, on the occasions of weddings or engagements among our relatives or friends, such remarks as these: 'She would be much better off if she would stay single.' 'She doesn't know when she is happy.' 'The idea of a girl with her education throwing it all away for marriage.' And when it was observed that a girl was trying to catch a husband, the remarks were of this type: 'Brazen huzzy,' or 'Running after the boys!'

"So I grew up with the idea that indifference to men is a positive virtue. I felt that I was being very noble when I studied hard, kept my eye on a good, salaried position, and acted accordingly. I had the idea, not put into words even in my thoughts, that to wish to marry would somehow be shameful. Quite logically then, I was unable to act naturally in the presence of men.

"Nor did I notice that I was letting the worth-while things slip by until a very few years ago. Then I began to feel that perhaps the ability to be spontaneously friendly with the few Catholic men I ever met might be more valuable than the ability to integrate an expression in calculus or to translate a bit of German prose.

"It is true, as you say, that social life is not sufficiently fostered in schools and parishes; but I believe a more fundamental cause of mixed marriages and of no marriages at all is that idea, almost amounting to a heresy perhaps, that has crept into our Irish-American consciousness, that marriage is somehow a bit shameful and, at any rate, a low estate.

"That is the real reason why so many of us are bachelors and spinsters and why the Irish-Americans are dying out. It is surely high time that something be done to remove the false conception of marriage, which is responsible for the frustration of God's plan for so many of us—a truth we sadly glimpse only when marriage has passed us by."

That is the refrain which is echoed and reechoed in thousands of letters which have come to us over the years. In that letter there is depicted with remarkable accuracy and even vividness the attitude of so many Irish parents, especially mothers, toward marriage that lies back of the grotesque number of old bachelors and old maids in our ranks. Not much progress will be made to stem the tendency of the Irish to die out until that attitude is changed. While lip homage may be paid to the abstract ideal of marriage, as the Church demands, little is done in a practical way to implement that ideal and much is done to frustrate its attainment.

The far-reaching consequences of the differences in attitude toward marriage prevailing among the Irish and those of other racial extractions in America is illustrated in the case of two families within our acquaintance. Some thirty years ago at the University of Illinois we had in class at various times a half dozen members of a German family in which there were 14 children. All married, and now the elder couple have children, grandchildren, and great-grandchildren totaling 142. In the same classes we had members of an Irish family likewise counting 14 offspring. Recent inquiry disclosed that only 4 have married, and they have 7 children and 3 grandchildren.

Thus the elderly Irish-American couple have a total of 24 descendants as compared with the 142 descendants of the German-American family. The former are thinning out in each generation, the latter are multiplying rapidly. In these two families there is illustrated strikingly and dramatically the tendency of the Irish in America to disappear through the failure of so many of their members either to marry late or not at all.

Dr. James J. Walsh concluded the series of three articles which he ran in *America* over thirty years ago with an earnest appeal to the Irish in America to face the fact that they are dying out and to do something to halt their march to extinction. "Let us find the reason, as far as we can," he said, "and if we are worth preserving, let us see what can be done in that direction. A dear friend who knows this subject better than I do has said, 'The one thing that the Irish do very well in this country is to fill the graveyards.' I am optimistic enough to think we can do better than that." We join Dr. Walsh, Archbishop McNeil, Dr. Austin O'Malley, Father M. V. Kelly, C.S.B., and the other scholars of the preceding generation in uttering that same appeal to the Irish-Americans of today. We add merely the note of urgency, for the sand in the hourglass is running out on us.

LOVE AMONG THE IRISH

9

Seán O'Faolain

Seán O'Faolain (*pronounced Shawn O'Fwhaylawn*), *novelist and biographer, was born of Denis and Bridget Murphy Whelan in Dublin, February 22, 1900. Since that was the period of reborn pride in things Gaelic, his name, John Whelan, became cast at an early date into its Gaelic form.*

He was educated at the National University of Ireland and at Harvard, from both of which he received an M.A. degree. He was a Commonwealth fellow at Harvard from 1926 to 1928 and lingered on the following year as a John Harvard fellow. While teaching Gaelic at Harvard, he lectured on Anglo-Irish literature at Boston College.

In 1929 he went to England, where he taught English at St. Mary's College, Strawberry Hill, Middlesex, from 1929 to 1933. It was here that he found himself as a writer. His book of stories, "Midsummer Night Madness," dealing with Irish life, particularly in the days of the "troubles," 1916 to 1924, attracted wide attention. It was one of three works nominated for the English Femina prize and brought him a charter membership in the Irish Academy of Letters.

His first novel, "A Nest of Simple Folk," is the most widely acclaimed of all his novels. In his fiction he undertakes to depict chiefly the simple people of Ireland. "We may dream of romance," he says. "But we know that it must be made out of what we have—rags and bones, moonlight, limed cabins, struggle, the passion of our people, a bitter history, great folly, a sense of eternity in all things, a courage never to submit or yield."

O'Faolain is gradually becoming better known as a biographer than as a novelist. His biography of Daniel O'Connell, published under the title "King of the Beggars," was especially well received. Other works

111

are "There's a Birdie in the Cage," "A Purse of Coppers," "Come Back
to Erin," "She Had to Do Something," "The Life Story of De Valera,"
and more recently the life of Cardinal Newman as a young man, "New-
man's Way; the Odyssey of John Henry Newman." O'Faolain and his
wife Eileen, who has published stories for children, reside with their
one daughter in Dublin.

EVER SINCE THE BLACK FORTIES OF THE NINETEENTH CENTURY WE IRISH
have been flying from our homeland. And I am using the right word, for
the wholesale Irish Diaspora of the nineteenth century was nothing but
a wild, terrified flight from hunger, even if it ended all too often in the
exchange of one kind of hardship for another.

We always maintained in Ireland that this national loss of blood—I
might call it a racial hemophilia—was entirely due to foreign misrule.
We promised ourselves and the world that once we got a native government we would soon put a stop to all that.

In 1946, after a quarter of a century of native rule, we looked at the
ledger, and we got a bad shock. Census figures showed that we were
still on the downgrade. We had to face the bitter truth that something
more than foreign misrule is involved. We had to pick rock salt out of
our sores when we discovered simultaneously that while our own people
were vanishing from Ireland the English were coming back to it in
droves: in full flight from the austerities of socialist England, they were
buying up houses and farms in every part of the country. To discourage
what became known as England's reconquest by checkbook we promptly
clapped a tax on all alien purchasers of land and property. But, seven
years after, we are still ruefully scratching our heads over the essential
problem of our own racial decay.

It is a poor consolation to tell ourselves that we are never likely to
disappear from the earth. That is merely to say that we are performing a
graceful and gradual diminuendo into insignificance. It would give us
even less consolation to observe that at the rate of recent years our population will not drop below the 2 million mark for at least five generations, if then. A land so underpopulated could neither feed itself, clothe
itself, nor defend itself. We would be like a scattering of chaste rabbits
nibbling around the coast line of Australia. In the black forties of the
nineteenth century we were hungry because we were so many. In the

black forties of the next century will we be hungry because we are too few?

What explanations do we usually offer for this persistent withering away of the Celt?

Emigration is the first explanation. Now it is chiefly to Great Britain. It is a convenient safety valve for unemployment at home. But should there be, at any time, serious unemployment in Great Britain, the thousands we have been sending over there for years past will come stampeding back to us to queue at our labor exchanges for a weekly dole. A bottling-up like that could easily produce a social explosion and shake our economy to its foundations.

The second explanation is a brutal one. It is that old Irishmen never die, they just fade away at ages of such fantastic antiquity that their off-spring are by then too old to start fruitful lives of their own. The commonest example of this adamantine refusal to surrender is the aging farmer who will not hand over his farm to his sons. When one of these old Irish farmers refers to his "boy," it is 10 to 1 that the boy is hitting fifty. A while ago when two brothers, aged about sixty and sixty-five, came before the courts for riotous and wanton behavior, it developed that they were two "boys" who had been having their first taste of liberty and liquor on the night of their father's unlooked-for demise at the early age of ninety-two.

The results of this old vs. young tussle are late marriages, a low birth rate, and a declining population, not to mention poor productivity from the older age groups.

This is where we bump up against the most disturbing explanation of all. For the surprising fact is that even in our towns and cities, where the boys and girls can earn enough money to be independent of the old, they still refuse to marry young. The state appeals to them to wed. The Church appeals to them to multiply. In the blunt language of Shaw's Miss Eliza Doolittle they reply with one voice, "Not bloody likely!" This is the core of the whole thing. It is a human resistance that defies statesmen, churchmen, and statisticians. "Why," we all ask, "why, ye young divils, why in the name of God and nature won't ye marry one another?"

Well, here are their own replies, chosen from scores which came to me through the mail some time ago when I happened to be writing articles for a popular newspaper about this very question of late marriages in Ireland.

To begin with, let us see what the young men have to say about the girls. Two plaints are made by the young men. The first: What they want from their girls is not love, not romance, not passion, not beauty, not companionship, not charm, not wit, not intelligence—but simply the plain, homespun qualities of housekeeper and mother. The second: They are extremely skeptical about the capacity of the modern young Irishwoman to fill either of these two very simple requirements.

Here is how one young Irishman approaches wedlock. One might think that he is not so much approaching woman as stalking her.

"I am a bachelor, aged 38. I am in no hurry to get married. Next September, or the September after, I will take a holiday with an object at Lisdoonvarna, County Clare. I will inform some of the priests on holiday that I am on the lookout, and that I am a bachelor of some substance who requires a wife with a dowry of a certain minimum figure. The good priests will pass the word around. In due course a girl will be selected and the wooing will proceed on a sane plane. At Christmas [this eager lover continues] my people will visit her people, and her people will investigate my background, credentials and relatives. I will meet the young lady again on some such occasion as the Rugby International in Dublin during the following Easter. In due course the nuptials will take place. If I marry at 40 on the lines I have indicated I will guarantee that at 60 my wife and myself will be fonder of one another than any couple of the same age who married in their youth for what Hollywood miscalls love, but which is in fact *lustful infatuation. . . .*"

There are, in this letter, two points of some anthropological interest to anybody investigating the problem of love among the Irish. This man wants his bride to bring him a dowry. He also considers that he is young enough to marry at forty but does not mention the desirable age for his bride. If he is prepared to allow her the same slow-motion approach to marriage as himself, it is evident that there could not be a very large family—if any! But in practice our hairy old Irish bachelors seek out young brides—and they seem to get them. It is to be remembered that there are more men than women in Ireland, one of the very few countries in the world of which this is true. Besides, as one of them shrewdly remarked to me, "A young woman can take a chance on marriage. She must, because she cannot wait. If she waits her good looks will fade. But we men *can* wait!"

But there is often an implicit objection to young wives. Harken, ye tender virgins of Eire, to another of your potential husbands:

"The average, modern Irish girl is a painted, powdered, padded, puffed parrot, except for her nails which are hawk's claws. Their adoration of film actors has reached a STATE OF IMBECILITY! It is often said that slow horses and fast women would ruin any man, but we don't need the horses, the women do it alone. How could any man in his sane senses, for whom marriage means a family and responsibility, contemplate a life spent with one of these lassies?

"The sight alone of one of them swigging expensive liquors in lounge bars at a rate that would knock out a navvy in half the time is enough to deter any man from taking the plunge. Marriage is a hell of a serious business. It is not a business for flighty flibbertigibbets like these. It is a business for grown men and women with their eyes open. The modern Irish girl seems to be quite unaware of this fact. I will not jump headlong into matrimony. I will look carefully around me. I will wait and bide my time, and choose with careful circumspection. Marriage is for ever. It is a sobering thought for any man. . . ."

Unreliable, extravagant, spoiled: such, according to the men, are modern Irish girls. They say it over and over again, in various ways:

"I am a bachelor, and so far as I can see I am likely to remain so for some years to come unless God is especially kind to me. How could any man expect the girls that are going nowadays to cook and wash for him, to rear his children and to keep his home, with their heads full of all sorts of nonsense from morning to night? And they have no more sense of the value of money than if they were John D. Rockefeller himself.

"Recently I was rather inclined to be interested in a young woman. I went out with her one night, accompanied by another lady. The first thing was I found myself in a lounge bar, and I felt it was up to me to invite the two ladies to have some refreshment, with no thought in my head but that they would ask for a soft drink, or at the most a sherry. I was much astonished when the young woman I was attracted to asked for a 'gin and it,' and her friend demanded nothing less if you please than a Pimms Number One. Now, I am a mechanic by trade, earning around 7.10.0 pounds [$21] per week. How could I keep up that rate of going? And it is a poor preparation for matrimony. If the girls are not married it is their own fault by the example they give beforehand. . . ."

What pleases me most about these letters is their splendidly hoary smell. That last chap is not a modern Irishman at all, except in the sense that every modern Irishman is a medieval European. All these attacks on women are part of that ancient and undying battle of the sexes on which we come with such glee in the scabrous, antifeminist pages of Rabelais or Jean de Meung.

When we turn to the girls' opinions of the men, we find almost precisely the same charges. In their belief the men are cagey, spiritless, selfish, and spoiled by their mothers.

"I have been reading what the men are alleged to think of the women. In my experience modern Irishmen are nothing but a race of male cuckoos, beer sharks and boogie-woogie fanatics. This is a land made for the male—card playing, horse racing, coursing, fishing. It is a paradise for the male. It is not that the young man in modern Ireland cannot afford to get married. It is that he cannot get married and still afford his car, his club, his betting, his poker, his golf and his holidays. So the young man remains single. . . ."

On the overmothered Irishman:

"The men of today are mammy's darlings. They have everything at home so why should they leave it? Their mothers slave for them and they expect that their wives will slave for them in the same way. Gosh! Haven't men got away with a lot! It is no wonder they used to marry early long ago when they even expected their wives to polish their boots for them. But we women now want marriage on a 50–50 basis, so the darlings have slowed up. Look at the way a man can drink Lough Erne dry and it is not called a binge, but if a poor woman gets a cold she is told to cure it with buttermilk boiled with onions. There is no doubt either that parents do influence their sons to wait a little longer, and you know what that means—10 or 15 years maybe. The odd thing is that these mothers are more than anxious to find other mothers' sons to marry their own daughters. The sum of it all is, mother is an Irishman's landlady—without pay."

What has happened to the legendary Irish lover? Another letter:

"I used to think Irishmen ideal. After meeting Englishmen and men of other nationalities I soon found that he has feet of clay. He may be brave on the battlefield but when it comes to love he is the greatest coward in the world. And the conceit of the creatures! Quite laughable to the Latin races who are so busy adoring women they can sometimes forget themselves. I used to think of all Irishmen as dashing, romantic fellows. . . .

"But now? Did you ever read the 'get-together' columns in the newspapers? *Young man, teetotaller, no means, wishes to meet girl, same, with means.* Emphasis on the means. How blooming romantic! It should read, *Young man, adventurous and enterprising, wishes to meet beautiful girl and have a whale of a time.* Instead, how often do we hear, 'He's after marrying 5,000 pounds.' The truth is our eligible bachelors are quaking bundles of inhibitions. You will find the answer to the whole thing in Arland Ussher's *The Face and Mind of Ireland.* He states that Irishmen have hardly enough sex to perpetuate their own cantankerous species. . . ."

After reading such outbursts as these—however we may laugh at them, whatever may lie behind them—we can hardly be surprised to discover that, according to the last census, only 1 person out of 100 marries each year.

How do they manage it? How can any normally sexed man (for I refuse to believe that Arland Ussher's opinion is the right one) wait as patiently and as dangerously as these Irish near celibates do for the joys of love and marriage? And we must remember that there are no irregular safety valves in Catholic Ireland. In the whole country there is not one brothel. Prostitution is exceedingly rare, sordid, and furtive. There is a certain amount of illegitimacy, but no reliable statistics are available because there are so many loopholes—emigration before the birth, marriage after conception, and so on. Some believe that homosexuality is on the increase. There are no proper figures for venereal disease, but its incidence is large enough to be taken seriously by Church and state. If there were an atmosphere of free and frank discussion, as there is not, we might get a better general picture.

I have heard only four plausible explanations for Irish continence: that sexual desire is sublimated by religion, exhausted by sport, drugged by drink, or deflected by either an innate or an inculcated puritanism. The fact stands that Irishmen can and do wait longer than any other race in the world for the joys of love.

What lies behind those angry letters I have quoted? How seriously should we take all such sparrings between young Irishmen and young Irishwomen? I think that we have to take them quite seriously, but it would be a mistake to take them quite literally.

Irishmen, for example, are undoubtedly much more calculating in love than a foreigner might think if he based his notions on the reckless and dashing characters of Anglo-Irish fiction. Those gallant rakes were bred in the big houses of a minority landlord class. The mass of the people were hard-pressed peasants for whom love had to take a second place before the essential tie of blood and economy. Today this basic, rural class is dominant in Ireland, and they have brought into the towns and cities the traditions and techniques of the country. Furthermore, matriarchal power still counts for a good deal. Prudence and respect for family authority can easily become misinterpreted as caginess and "Momism." When the girls, grown wiser in their generation, respond to what they consider caginess with a bit of dash—and Irishwomen have far more "go" in them than Irishmen—the boys react by calling them extravagant, spoiled, unreliable. Mutual irritation has set in.

The young people are angry: there is no denying that. But it is a transferred anger. I am satisfied that these young people are dying to throw their arms around one another, human nature being the same the world over. But because, for one reason or another, they cannot make the grade they foolishly turn on one another all the anger and frustration that—if they had more courage—they would turn on the conditions that are denying them a natural sex life.

What are the conditions that keep them apart? Poverty? Nonsense! And here is the proof of it: when most of our people were living on the lowest subsistence level, a hundred years ago, 57 per cent of the younger people normally got married between the ages of twenty-three and thirty-four. Today, when the standard of living is incomparably higher —though by no means as yet high enough—only 25 per cent marry before the age of thirty-four.

What is creating the psychological block here is something far nearer to the opposite of poverty. All our young people are developing a proper concept of what constitutes decent living conditions, and until they get them, they are on strike against marriage. We are rearing generations in Ireland that have ten times more pride and ambition than their parents ever had, and good luck to them for it. As one young woman put it to me in two sentences: "I saw what my mother went through. Not for me, thank you!"

Naturally the young folk do not fully realize what they are doing: theirs is an instinctive reaction. For the first time in our history they have begun to taste, though still only to taste, the rewards of a full life, and they very naturally want more of them. Nor is it likely that our young celibates will be any more objective when, at last, no longer quite so young, they cease to be celibates. Then they will tell us that they are entering the happiest years of their lives, forgetting that they waited for them—dangerously, painfully, and prudently—until they had first collected every possible cushion against their hardships and risks. And no doubt when they become fathers themselves they will, in their turn, wonder why their children do not marry young and proceed simultaneously to excuse, uphold, and consolidate all these discouraging living conditions which had been responsible for their own procrastination.

What are the conditions which cause them to hesitate before assuming the heavy responsibilities of marriage?

Social services are not generous in Ireland. A children's allowance grants 17s. 6d. (about $2.44) per month for every child after the second. There is no comprehensive maternity-grant system. The children of the destitute are delivered free of charge, the poor pay whatever they can afford to pay. Nursing homes for middle-class mothers are expensive. There are no comprehensive state schemes for prenatal or postnatal advice.

In 1951, when the then Minister for Health, Dr. Noel Browne, wished to introduce a mother-and-child scheme of a comprehensive nature, with pre- and postnatal advice, free medical attention without a means test, and other such benefits, the Catholic Hierarchy condemned the scheme, the government obeyed without question, and the scheme fell through. It is only proper to add that the Irish medical profession opposed the scheme root and branch.

The fact stands that marriage can be a costly business in Ireland, and our provident young men foresee this.

Housing is dear and often difficult to come by. An average worker, say a bus driver or a garage mechanic, who will draw a pay packet of between £7 and £8 (about $21) a week will pay about a third of his wages for a couple of rooms and may have to wait for years before he can rent a small house or an apartment worthy of the name. For those couple of rooms are not what any American wife would call an apartment; they are simply a couple of rooms in a house, with a makeshift kitchenette and with one shared lavatory and bathroom for a whole houseful of families. Why should any young man be expected to take his young bride into a couple of rooms of this type? It is right to say that our government has done a great deal of work to provide housing for the workers, but the leeway yet to be made up is great.

Rural living conditions are enough to drive any young man of spirit to emigration or to drink. All the small towns and villages are dwindling for this reason. Before the cinema came, these places offered virtually no means of entertainment in the winter other than the public house or the free pleasure of standing with one's back to a damp wall surveying the falling rain. And those of us who visit and revel in the Irish countryside during the brief summer months must not forget that our winter lasts long, that the high spirits which are turned on for social occasions die down as quickly as they flare up and remain down for a long solstice. The natural instinct of any young man or woman born into such places cannot be to marry and sink deeper into their Nile mud but to get out and marry elsewhere; and so they do, via the larger centers to England.

But the term "living conditions" involves far more than physical limitations. The whole question of sex in Ireland is dominated also by profound psychological repressions. To explain this, I have kept to this point one extract from a letter by a young man who has been very honest and percipient about these limitations. He writes: "We Irishmen have been conditioned into a state of sexual frigidity and repression because for generations we have clothed the sublimity of love in shrouds of taboo, false prudery and an attitude of Victorian Puritanism that has given to the act of sexual union the blasphemous nature of something offensive."

If this attitude has been—and I am afraid it has been—fostered by the Church in Ireland in our time, it has not been fostered consciously and deliberately. How could it be? It is the doctrine of the Catholic Church that to seek satisfaction of bodily desire in sexual union, that is, in marriage, is one of the most virtuous functions of mankind, a holy act in which God and man must take constant joy and delight. It has been fostered, most unhappily, because the young people will not marry young and the clergy fear that the result must be a relaxation of sexual morality. The stage is set for conflict and an impasse. The Church thunders against the dangers of sex. The young men, obedient up to the point of marriage, at which they balk, are inevitably conditioned into a frustrated terror of woman.

I am an Irishman and a Catholic. I live in Ireland. I am bringing up my children in Ireland as Catholics. I fully acknowledge the right of the Catholic clergy in Ireland to adopt any attitude they think fit toward the problems of young love. I am simply objecting that the position I see adopted by the state and by some of the clergy in Ireland is shortsighted, inhuman, unwise and may be fatal to both.

Since my boyhood I have heard my elders fulminating about keeping company, night courting, dancing at the crossroads, V necks, silk stockings, late dances, drinking at dances, mixed bathing, advertisements for feminine underwear, jitterbugging, girls who take part in immodest sports (such as jumping or hurdling), English and American books and magazines, short frocks, Bikinis, cycling shorts, and even waltzing, which I have heard elegantly described as "belly-to-belly dancing." Perhaps the most extreme example of this kind of thing was to hear woman described from a pulpit to a mixed congregation as the "unclean vessel."

Enough. What we need, surely, is the lifting of an unclean cloud. For a picture of a saner attitude to woman go into any southern city of Europe. There the God-given beauty of woman is almost adored. Courtship is frank and fair. The youths discuss the charms of their girls openly and with enthusiasm. Their songs are of love; their thoughts are of love; their blood is at natural blood heat. They marry young. While the population of Ireland is dwindling, the population of Italy, a much poorer country, is soaring.

Is this change of attitude likely to occur in Holy Ireland? If it does not, what is happening will go on happening. The more cautious will marry late in life. The more spirited will go on emigrating to get out from under the cloud. And the saddest fact of all is denied by nobody: that when the Irish do emigrate they fall away from their religion in large numbers, so that both the nation and the Church lose them. If some such revolution does not takes place, it can mean only that that impalpable thing we know as the Irish nature is shriveling and hardening into selfishness, is growing less and less attractive in its smug blindness to the unhappiness of this generation and the threat to the generations of the future. In that sense the Irish whom the world has known, and admired, may indeed vanish from the earth; and I am still proud enough of my race to think that their disappearance would be the world's loss.

THERE IS STILL HOPE

10

Margaret Culkin Banning

Born in Buffalo, Minnesota, Margaret Culkin Banning was educated at Vassar College and at the Chicago School of Civics and Philanthropy. Deeply interested in civic affairs and social questions, she has written and lectured extensively on topics in these fields.

Widely traveled, Mrs. Banning has been active in the work of business and professional women's clubs and has been a national officer in a number of these. During the war she participated in all the war-loan campaigns and made extensive tours in their behalf throughout the Middle West and on the West Coast, receiving the special commendation of the government for her services.

She is a prolific writer of articles, short stories, serials, and novels and has contributed to "The Saturday Evening Post," "Reader's Digest," "Colliers," and other leading periodicals. Her articles "The Case for Chastity" and "Savings of a Lifetime" in the "Reader's Digest" have attracted especially wide attention. She writes with insight and wit, and her deep interest in social problems gives substance to her novels.

Among her better-known novels are "The Women of the Family," "Mixed Marriage," "The Iron Will," "The Clever Sister," and "Fallen Away." Prominent among her nonfiction works are "Letters to Susan," "Salud! A South American Journal," "Letters from England," and "Conduct Yourself Accordingly." The list of all her books runs to the staggering total of twenty-three—averaging almost a book a year for the last twenty-five years!

In private life she is Mrs. LeRoy Salsich and lives with her husband in Duluth, Minnesota. She has two children by an earlier marriage: Dr.

*Mary Banning Friedlander, a research physicist, and Lt. Comdr. A.
Tanner Banning, who was on active duty with the United States Navy
from 1941 to 1945. Her writing studio is one which most authors would
envy, for from it she can look out over majestic Lake Superior.*

THERE SEEMS TO BE A RATHER DISINTERESTED AWARENESS AMONG INFORMED
Americans that the population of Ireland is waning. But because they
take for granted that this decline is largely due to migration and that
what is Ireland's loss is surely America's gain, most people in this country are not greatly disturbed by what they regard as a probably inevitable population shift. It is only when you suggest in any group of
Americans of Irish descent that the Irish in this country are not carrying on their racial strain as strongly or as successfully as the descendants
of other races that you usually are met with disbelief or flat contradiction.

"It's absurd," you will be told; "look at the Harrigan family. It's the
biggest one in the neighborhood. The Harrigans certainly aren't dying
out!"

There is nearly always more than one large Harrigan, or Dugan, or
Maloney family to be looked at in any community in the United States.
There are families with Irish surnames which stand out for both size
and vitality. It is only when you begin to count the number of such
families in any neighborhood and cannot use the fingers of both hands
or when you begin to consider the unmarried or late-married mature
Irishmen and -women in an average American parish and keep on
thinking of more to add to the list that disbelief becomes surprise and
concern.

Recently I asked two young men, both of Irish-American families, if
they thought the Irish were vanishing in America. They lived in different cities, but their reaction was identical. Each laughed, said, "I
should say not," instanced a large family with an Irish surname, and
spoke of the Catholic resistance to birth control. But each young man
came back to the subject later and said, again almost in identical words,
"I've been thinking more about that. First or second generation Irish in
the United States aren't so numerous as they used to be in the industrial
and political fields. Nor so powerful an influence."

One of them went on, "My great-grandfather was an emigrant from
Ireland who began as a bricklayer and became a prosperous contractor.

He employed a good many Poles and Italians in the early days. But in the city where I live now, it is usually the Irish who are working for Poles and Italians."

The other young man had been thinking about his family tree. He told me, "My grandfather was one of ten children. Four of them did not marry. Three married rather late in life and had no living children. That may be the answer."

This problem of late marriages or none at all plagues Ireland itself. The visitor sees evidence of it throughout the countryside.

In 1946 I traveled through most of Germany. The cities were horribly wrecked and devastated. But all through the country districts it was astonishing to see the great number of healthy and vigorous children. Some of these undoubtedly had been bred because of war propaganda or even edict, but there they were, the hope of the nation.

In that same year, and more recently, when I have traveled in rural areas in Ireland, I have been impressed more by the presence of old people than by the presence of children. It is a tender and gratifying thing to observe that the aging have a respected place in a village. But where are all the children? They have been vanishing, wrote Alice Curtayne in September, 1939, as if a Pied Piper were luring them away. If plague or famine took the children of Ireland, what an outcry there would be! But the children are not even there to be stricken.

A surprising proportion of Irishmen and -women pass their whole lives not only celibate but usually chaste. An Irishman does not seem to regard getting married as the normal, almost inevitable thing to do, nor do Irish girls consider the unmarried state too pitiable or embarrassing an unfulfillment. It is also a vocation in life. So they have been taught, and so they have observed.

If this situation presents a modern predicament for Ireland, it is one which that country alone can solve. Any exhortation or even advice would be presumptuous, especially if it came from those in a nation which is better off economically and is not tempted by the possibilities of emigration. The Irish leaders know very well what is happening to their nation. Some have said bitterly that the chief export of Ireland is its own people.

But outsiders, even those who love Ireland deeply, must leave the application of social and economic remedies to the discretion of Irish leaders in their homeland. What properly concerns those to whose countries the Irish emigrate or who themselves are of Irish descent is whether this reproductive slackening and failure to carry on the Irish strain has been transferred to other countries and is presently existent here in America.

The inquiry into this is certainly worth the consideration of everyone whose forebears were Irish, and it is important to all American citizens. For the Irish contribution to this country has been very great. If today in the United States we have less wit and more coarse talk, less poetry and more pornography, less oratory and more speeches, less belief in chastity and more women under psychiatric care, it may be due at least partially to the fact that there are fewer people of Irish descent in the American melting pot than there used to be.

My paternal grandfather came to the United States from Ireland at the time of the Great Famine in the middle of the last century, known as the "potato rot." The photograph of his completed family, taken when his eldest son wore a moustache and his youngest was in his mother's lap, is of twelve handsome and apparently intelligent people. It was made about seventy years ago, and there has been no such family photograph in any branch of our family since that time. My mother's family was a small one, pinched off in numbers by the Civil War and the early death of my maternal grandmother. Recently we counted up the living children of those in the photograph, and ground had been lost numerically. It is the same story as in Ireland. Too many of my uncles and aunts did not marry or married late and had few or no living children.

The influences which play upon the life of a person of Irish descent who is a Catholic are three: the influence of the Church; the influence of his family; the influence of his own inherited temperament. These are the forces which should be analyzed to see whether they have worked for or against, or can be encouraged to work for, perpetuation of the Irish strain in America.

For the Catholic Irish, religion is the central reality of life. The Church exerts authority over many of the practices of ordinary living, including marriage. Consistently, it stands against artificial birth control. Its influence therefore should militate for constant increase of the Irish strain in the American mixture. Yet that increase is not apparent.

The fact that many of the healthy young men and women in every

parish are drawn into celibate vocations, as priests or nuns, is not sufficient explanation. It is perfectly true that, in order to supply the growing
needs of modern parishes, expanding parochial schools, and the numerous Catholic convents and colleges in America, there is constant pressure upon pastors and parents to discover and to encourage vocations for
holy orders. It is equally natural and right that the vocations of the
priest or nun should be rated as high and noble, when the personal choice
of vocations is explained to young people. But it is unfortunate that
many Catholics seem to have received the impression that marriage is
a secondary and often imperfect state of life.

There is a constant effort by the Catholic Church in America to make
Catholic married people resist birth control. This is uphill work in a
country in which non-Catholics as a rule regard such limitation as normal and sensible. It means that a large proportion of sermons in Catholic churches are devoted to exhortation against this practice. These sermons usually stress the sins of marriage far more than its happiness and
blessings, and though this emphasis may be the only way of getting
points across to a congregation dulled to the subject and though harsh
language may be the most apt to excite attention, there are results which
defeat other Catholic ideals.

A young mother told me not long ago that she heard such a sermon at
a Mass which was predominantly attended by children, and she was
greatly distressed because she did not want her nine-year-old son to get
the impression that marriage was "wicked." From what the child had
said to her, he had begun to believe that marriage was an occasion of
sin. This young mother was thoughtful and wise enough to be able to
straighten out the tangle in the boy's mind. But many other children
have less guidance or might store away the idea without mentioning it
to a parent out of sheer embarrassment.

If many Catholic women have become marriage-shy, and the fact
that so many marry late or not at all is pretty good evidence of this, it
may be because so much emphasis has been laid on the temptations and
sins of marriage. A long engagement is a fairly safe environment for
virtue. I know of one such engagement between two Irish-American
Catholics that went on for fifteen years. The soul of a bachelor or unmarried woman is not in the jeopardy spoken of so constantly from so
many pulpits.

It is also true that the Catholic always has an outlet for his emotions in the practice of his religion. He has protection from loneliness, reassurance, uplift. He is never without an object of love or without the consciousness that he as an individual is greatly loved and sought by God. Having supernatural love, he is less at the mercy of human desire. Delay in marriage or forgoing it altogether results in far more frustration for a non-Catholic person than for a Catholic, unless the affections and passions of the Catholic are deeply involved.

No one who understands the deep values of Catholicism would wish that any of this supernatural love be lessened or lost. But the teaching of the Church is that grace and devotion can coexist with human love and marriage. It can be unfortunate for any person, who has no religious vocation, to use emotional piety as a compensation for the natural love between man and woman which is basic for continuance of any race or any religion. In priest or nun celibacy is fruitful of good works. In the lay person it leads too often to selfishness or abnormality.

Why did neither of the Casey girls marry? They must have been beautiful, desirable young women. They are good workers in the parish, but how much better if they could have offered it six children!

If there is fault, it is in the wording and accents of some sermons, in overemphasis, and in things left unsaid. This is not a question of doctrine. For it is only the Irish we have under consideration, not the multinational body of the Church. In American parishes whose congregations derive from French, Italian, Polish sources, there is no departure from the basic doctrine of the Church concerning marriage, and yet in such parishes marriage seems often to be a more desirable, natural, gayer, less fearsome state of life than when it is expounded by the Irish Catholic clergy. It is the Irish themselves, in their home country, and also in the countries of their adoption, who too often diminish the joys of marriage.

Some of the responsibility for decrease in fertility among the Irish in this country must also certainly be laid at the door of the Irish-American family of the generation which is immediately past, or almost past. This was often an outgoing hospitable group, at ease in a mixed American community. But even more often it was a close, jealous, deeply affectionate and just as quarrelsome, vain and humble closed corporation. It usually felt at a social disadvantage. Nonetheless, it had a conviction that it was cleverer, wittier, and more interesting than any other family. The members could be mercilessly critical of one another, but they were in permanent alliance against outsiders.

They were likely to resist the attraction of one of their members for any stranger. This was done by mockery as a rule. I knew one Irish-American man who married a Canadian girl who had very little sense of humor. His unmarried brothers and sisters made fun of his Canadian wife for twenty years, though they admitted it was a good match. They never let her into the family even when she was there. Nor did they let the brother out of it.

Such families made and endured trouble enough, but they had a very good time among themselves and built up a great reserve of jokes, good memories, ridiculous accidents, and deep griefs. They were sustained by a warmth of intimacy which slowly burned to ashes as the members became very old or died. Of course these same things are true of many other large families which have no Irish blood at all. But the Irish, even in America, perhaps because history has left them on guard and suspicious, weave their family ties close.

The members of such families in the last generation, and sometimes today, were slow to leave the nest. Often they never did. The Irish mother did not push her children over the edge and rarely insisted that they learn the independence of solitary flight. It is characteristic of Irish maternity to relinquish children reluctantly and to whisper secretly to them that they can always come back. The Irish mother is a forgiving mother and by the same token is not likely to be a generous mother-in-law.

The Irish mother's own life, as her children saw it, may have been another factor creating marriage shyness in them. She was usually overworked. She had no respite from maternal duties or any prospect of release from marital ties even if her husband drank, abused her, or did not support her properly, and all three things were often simultaneously true. She aged early. She had few if any interests outside her home and Church. The average man of Irish blood did not sustain a romantic attitude toward his wife or idealize her to his children. She was often shrewish as far as he was concerned, developing and showing contempt for the faulty male even though she endured him.

The family example and talk were not encouraging to early marriage in many big Irish-American families in this country, and many a young man and woman put it off. When the parents died, the unmarried brothers and sisters often lived on together, adding to the household a widowed sister or unsuccessful brother who had drifted back. There are old cities in this country which were largely settled by Irish emigrants a hundred and more years ago and which today repeat the pattern that is frightening Ireland, of childless bachelors and spinsters living together and coming rather to like it that way.

What is it in a person of Irish descent which makes him or her accept life without marriage more willingly than would a man or woman of almost any other racial strain in the Western world? Have the Irish for a long time been suffering from some depletion of sex or vitality? Are they more selfish than others? Are they better fitted to endure loneliness? Have they special compensations in a bachelor or spinster life? How far is the Irish temperament, that indestructible thing, responsible for the reproductive lag of the Irish people?

Arland Ussher speaks of the "ferocious chastity of Irish lower-class women" and with more elaboration of the lack of passion in Irishmen, which he traces back to Gaelic mythology. There is truth in this, as no one with any knowledge of Irish people would deny. As a rule, any person with Irish blood in him takes the matter of his personal chastity very seriously. He is instinctively modest. It took the combined efforts of all his brother officers to break down the chastity of one Irish-American of the fourth generation during the last war. And it took them six months and a great deal of whisky to do it.

Catholic girls of Irish descent, even when the Irish blood is considerably diluted, have the same instinct of modesty. Before them always, and from childhood, is the ideal of the Virgin Mary, and so both their training and their temperaments work together to curb passions before marriage or without it. It is also against the instinct of these girls to seek men. They may have the "comether" in their eyes, but today other girls use more direct methods of attraction, which are both forbidden and repugnant to an Irish-American Catholic girl. It is not that the Irish do not like sex, but they have always disciplined sex. They have found and they have seen, in their admired priests and nuns, that life can be lived without it.

At this point it must be set down humbly but definitely that the Irish are an intellectual people. Their poverty has prevented proper development and expression of their intellect both in their home country and elsewhere. But the average Irish person has always found compensations in the mind for what the body might need or lack. Perhaps he had to, but certainly he was able to. The Irish love of words, of argument, of any mental exercise is genuine, traditional, and inextinguishable. An Irish person has great mental curiosity, and when personal relationships disappoint or fail him, he can find compensation in the pursuits of the mind.

This may lead him only to the tavern or bar. It may take the woman only to the back fence with her gossip. But they find a delight and release in talk. It is a pleasure for the Irish to probe the condition of the world and its problems. They may take only a short step in the direction of philosophy, but to them it seems a stride, and they enjoy it as others might enjoy human relations.

In addition to the compensations of the mind in an unmarried life, the Irish have spiritual compensations. They are fitted to endure loneliness, because a Catholic's belief in the actuality of immortality always keeps the dead whom he has cared for close to him. The imaginative Irish temperament can almost project itself into the next world for conference or comfort or bring at will those he loves back into this one until he feels their spirits near him.

It is because the Irish have these gifts of intellect and spirit, these virtues of modesty and devotion that we cannot spare them from the mixture of races that combines to make up this country. Nor is that going to be necessary, for the forces in America which tend toward diminution of the Irish strain have begun to be corrected.

There is a great effort going on in many American Catholic parishes to educate young people for marriage, to encourage them to undertake it. This effort needs all the scientific aid it can secure and extension into every corner of the country. It should present the married state as natural, desirable, happy, and fruitful, as well as highly responsible.

The present mood of American young people is toward marriage and plenty of children. This is the non-Catholic as well as the Catholic attitude. The trend is also toward the individual home, the small, functional, one-story house, which will have no room for bachelor brothers and unmarried sisters; in another generation those family houses where unmarried adults grew old together will be a thing of the past.

There will always be men and women who do not marry, and for excellent reasons. But the waste of good mothers and fathers, and the loss of children who should be born, can be increasingly corrected in a society which is better adjusted. The usefulness and the happiness of the unmarried vocation can be increased, especially if even those who do not marry look to the future of the next generation with as much interest as do parents.

It is encouraging that in the United States Irish-American families are not so clannish or so inbred as they used to be. In my own city they mingle so freely that it is hard to distinguish them. The false pride and false humility that used to characterize so many of them is vanishing. That is what should vanish, not the valuable Irish strain.

But it is very important to call attention to this danger. The ones who should be informed are those with Irish blood in their veins. It is their responsibility to pass on the mysticism, the wit, the endurance, the intellect of the Irish race and to eliminate the faults which a painful history has left clinging to the Irish temperament. I think that young people of Irish ancestry would take great pride in doing this. But they must hear that it is necessary and that the numbers of a great people are rapidly shrinking.

STEMMING THE FLIGHT FROM THE LAND

Making Farm Life Attractive

11

John M. Hayes

The Rev. John M. Hayes, pastor of the parish at Bansha, Tipperary, Ireland, is the founder of "Muintir na Tire" (The People of the Land), an organization to improve the social and economic conditions of the people of rural Ireland and thus help to keep them on the land. Instead of merely bewailing the flight from the land and the steady stream of emigration, Father Hayes decided to do something about it. His work has attracted the attention of the people not only of Ireland but of other countries as well.

Born on November 11, 1888, in County Limerick, of Michael and Honora McCormack Hayes, John studied at St. Patrick's College, Thurles, and at the Collège des Irlandais in Paris, where he was ordained in 1913. For the following nine years he was on the mission in Liverpool, serving as a lecturer for the Catholic Evidence Guild.

During this time the fight for Irish freedom took place, and the young priest took an active part in that struggle. He was a leader at the meeting held outside Wormwood Scrubs Prison in London, where his brother, among others, was on hunger strike. Upon returning to Ireland he endeavored to improve the miserable lot of the people on the land. While an assistant priest in Tipperary Town, with the help of a few others he founded "Muintir na Tire."

He has an admirable background for such work. In the struggle of the Land League to obtain ownership for the tenant farmers his parents participated and, like many other such families, were evicted by the

133

greedy landlord—the bane of Ireland for centuries. His father and mother and three little children lived for thirteen years in one of the wretched huts erected by the Land League. There seven children, including John, were born, and five of them died in it.

"Those little brothers and sisters of mine," Father Hayes often remarks, "died as martyrs in the struggle of the Irish to wrest ownership of the land from the absentee British landlords. Hence I often say that I was suffering for rural Ireland even before I was born."

His heart is set upon improving the drab, dreary life of rural Ireland, which causes so many thousands of young people each year to flee from it as from a plague. With genuine insight and social vision he is endeavoring through "Muintir na Tire" to provide the farmers with the most efficient methods of scientific agriculture, dairying, and cattle husbandry and to brighten their lives with wholesome recreation and entertainment. Dances, concerts, games, lectures, demonstrations, dramatic performances are but part of a well-organized program to enable them to enjoy richer, fuller, and happier lives.

Instead of prowling with a shillelagh along country lanes, intent upon scaring the daylights out of a young couple keeping company, Father Hayes with understanding heart and warm human sympathy does everything possible to promote social acquaintance and to foster early marriage among the youth of Ireland. His ideal is to triple the productivity of the land so that rural Ireland will be filled with homes of people living a happy and abundant life, close to nature and to nature's God. His goal is to enable every young man and woman who wishes to marry to do so and to remain on the land instead of fleeing to the cities and even to foreign countries.

In spending himself to lift up the submerged social, economic, and cultural life of his people, Father Hayes is living up to the finest traditions of that priesthood whose Founder declared: "I am come that you may have life and have it more abundantly." If Ireland had a thousand priests like Father Hayes, it would speedily be transformed from a dwindling nation teetering perilously on the brink of near extinction into a thriving and prosperous land filled with happy homes echoing with laughter and cheer and gladness.

Indeed, other lands, such as America, Great Britain, and Australia, would likewise profit from that transformation. Irishmen and -women *would then bring with them the mind set and the heart set which would prompt them not to bury their talent in the ground like the misguided servant in the Scriptures but with generosity and a true sense of stewardship to pass on to others the precious and divine heritage of life—the greatest gift within the power of human beings to bestow.*

Father Hayes was chosen to represent Ireland at the National Catholic Rural Life Congress at Columbus, Ohio, in 1949, at the International Rural Life Congress at Rome in 1951, and at the recent International Catholic Migration Commission meeting at Barcelona, Spain. He has written and lectured extensively on behalf of the people of rural Ireland, and it is no wonder that he is one of the most beloved priests of the Emerald Isle.

THE THEORY THAT THE IRISH ARE A VANISHING RACE HAS CREATED QUITE A storm on both sides of the Atlantic. Many have sighed, "Alas, only too true." They are quite prepared to assist at the funeral service and thus feel they at least have done their duty by the old country. Others have sprung to arms, saying there is not an iota of truth in it. They feel it a duty to defend the fatherland rightly or wrongly. They too seem to be prepared to die for Ireland. In this magnificent unity of death, exiles and patriots have found a common field.

The truth is that statistics are terrible things and if cleverly used can prove anything. One cannot, for instance, take the figures from 1840 to 1946 as if nothing terrible had happened to this country during that period. The Famine of 1847 which wrecked this country is ignored. Death and emigration then joined hands in the loss of our people. From 1841 to 1851 our population fell from 6,529,000 to 5,112,000, and in the next ten years we lost 750,000 more.

Thus in twenty years we lost 2¼ million from a population of 6½ million. Now this was a catastrophe. This period should find no place in normal statistics.

However, excessive emigration has gone on without catastrophes and if continued could become a catastrophe itself. We realize the seriousness of the situation and are doing something about it, but we need time.

It must be remembered that we have had political freedom for only thirty years; that we had a civil war and a world war; that the British had destroyed our industries except in the northeast separated corner.

It must be recalled that our money had gone to England and our people followed it; that a very poor Ireland was handed over to us, poor in its land, poor in its industries, poor in its civics for reasons beyond our control. Thirty years is a short period, and in the circumstances we have made great efforts. Every native government since 1921 has been active in improving the economic conditions of the country.

Industries have sprung up, unfortunately most of them in the cities, but still our own. Much has been done to improve agriculture. Rural electrification has brought power and light to the countryside. There have been big schemes for turf and afforestation. Practically speaking we have no coal; now water, of which we have plenty, is producing power. In 1948 the government set up a special Commission of Inquiry into Emigration and other population problems. The findings are not yet published.

I am offering no apologies for our position, but I think it quite wrong to accuse the leaders of the nation of *complete* apathy while Ireland bleeds to death. I wonder whether or not we are bleeding to death after all. Admittedly we are ill, admittedly we are losing more than we can afford, admittedly if we go on as we are there may be grave danger of death, but after all the patient is showing some vitality, and there is at least some hope. We know of our extreme illness, and that is a big step forward.

To realize our weakness is the first step on the road to recovery. Statistics have shown how serious is our state, but the latest statistics show that there is a turn for the better. The most recent census of population in 1951 showed a slight gain in the total population, an over-all increase of 3,771, or 0.1 per cent. For a century of racial suicide the plus sign was completely missing. Now in 1951, thank God, we can cross the minus and make a plus.

I am far from boasting that this is a great achievement, but we cannot be exactly vanishing if we are increasing even a wee bit. Perhaps after all we have turned the corner and this is the very time when we must concentrate on a complete recovery.

Now I come to the important, disturbing, and distressing aspect of our population. While our total population had shown a slight increase in the latest census, our rural population showed a decline of almost 60,000 in the five years since 1946. Our town population has increased to a point to maintain the total population at a slight increase, while our rural population shows a big loss. Therefore the whole question of depopulation must be viewed from a rural standpoint.

This is more serious for us than for other countries, as practically speaking all our wealth comes from the land. We have no great mineral deposits, and the wealth of the nation will be in accordance with the production of the land. Herein, then, lies our problem.

There is little doubt that the chief causes are economic. Flight from bad land is much greater than flight from good land. In 1948 our national income was estimated at 310 million pounds; yet half the population, that is, the agricultural population, received less than one-third, although at that period agriculture was supposed to be prosperous. People will not stay on the land unless conditions give a reasonable hope of economic security. The same reason holds for late marriages and no marriages.

Today many farmers find a difficulty in paying wages to the agricultural laborer. No man is more worthy of a decent wage than the rural laborer, and no man is more worthy of the means to pay than the farmer. Many of the young laborers leave the country. The old rural industries have, to a great extent, disappeared. Their modern successors are in the cities, and the people are gone with them. The arts and crafts of other days are fast disappearing. The village blacksmith is becoming rare; he is going out with the horse. These are some of the economic reasons why the countryside is becoming depopulated.

There is no doubt that the tendency of the old folk to hold on to the farm is a deterrent to early marriages. The old people cling to security, and the young people, lacking it, marry often too late if at all. There has been the drabness of country life, lack of recreation, lack of conveniences, and lack of comfort in the home. It is very nice for the ultra-patriot to glory in the old boreens, but I can assure him if on a dark night he was tramping up one of these old roads he would prefer to be on a good highway. "The Old Bog Road" may sound nice in a song, but is the devil on a winter's night.

Many of the old amusements associated with seasonal farm work are going. The hay shed has killed the days when the neighbors had to combine to bring home the hay, after which a dance was held. The modern threshing machine has killed the harvest gatherings. We must put something in their places.

Finally there is an urge to go. I think this is psychological. We can counteract it by an urge to stay. This urge to stay cannot be made by loud talk. It is more subtle. It must be understood that years of alien government have denuded our country of civics. With the Americans' long history of freedom, it may be difficult for them to understand this serious want of a sense of duty to our country. A creation of a healthy community in every parish in Ireland will bring back what years of slavery have destroyed.

Then many go to England because it is near. Higher wages attract them, and perhaps a feeling of a free leg, too. They keep in touch with their families and are usually home twice a year. There are signs that conditions may alter in England as regards employment. If this should happen, the Irish will return to a home they feel they have never left. There are a number coming back, and some day their example may influence others.

I am not going to put our missionaries on the list of ordinary emigrants. They are going as never before, but we do not look upon them as Ireland's loss. We regard them as Ireland's gain and Ireland's glory. We hope to continue to give spiritual transfusions to many countries, but we realize that these transfusions must come from a healthy body and not one ill and weakened by depopulation. We have no illusions; we realize the depopulation that is going on even in the very place where it is most disastrous, that is, in rural Ireland. If it continues, the nation is in grave danger. If we want our population to expand, we must create conditions under which they can live with a decent standard of livelihood.

Cures must be found. We have got to face up to the position, and our first effort must be in the economic field. Prosperity in any country is achieved by increasing production, which might of course be either industrial or agricultural. The prospects of increasing industrial production in this country are limited by the lack of raw materials and the scarcity of skilled industrial workers. Therefore we have to rely mainly on the development of our agriculture for increasing our prosperity.

The agricultural possibilities of the country have been surveyed and commented on by home and foreign experts. They agree that production could be increased by 50 per cent, with comparatively small effort and expense, and that an increase of 100 per cent is well within the realms of possibility. Many big economic problems must be solved if the nation is determined to maintain its rural population and consequently its total population. I do not attempt to determine what the figure of rural population should be. I realize that the quality of the land varies greatly from point to point, and possibly some transference of rural population may be necessary.

But I do feel that the rural population should not be allowed to fall below its present figure and that a big effort should be made to develop fully the resources of the country. If the agricultural industry was prosperous, if regular employment was available for the workers, I believe that the people would remain on the land and that the social amenities would then be provided by common effort. While government action might be needed in a number of the larger activities, no real results could be obtained without the building up of the community spirit and co-operative action.

Much agricultural employment is of a seasonal nature, and to provide regular employment in any area, there would need to be coordination so that work on roads, drainage schemes, afforestation, or minor village industries would be fitted to some plan to give regularity of employment. The shape that the drive should take has been indicated by various agricultural experts. The Committee of Enquiry on Post Emergency Agricultural Policy, which reported in 1945, gave very valuable suggestions in the Majority and Minority Reports, and I feel sure that an agreed program could be hammered out by experts.

I am not hopeful, however, that it will be possible to carry the farmers into a big technical advance by the usual methods of a government department. The task will be an enormous one and must be approached in a new way. Conditions vary from county to county, even from parish to parish, and a variety of technical changes must be made to meet those altered conditions. Our farming methods and practices are, to a great extent, traditional. Our farming implements are better than they were at the beginning of the century, but our farming systems have changed little, and our agricultural output has increased little, if at all.

The contrast between our progress and that of some other small countries depending mainly on agriculture, notably New Zealand and

Denmark, is great. These countries have doubled and trebled their agricultural output in the last twenty-five years and have increased their agricultural exports to an even greater extent. They have paid great attention to increasing their output per acre and per man employed, and in this way they have decreased their costs of production so that they can farm profitably even when agricultural prices are low. We have given little attention to those important matters.

Much of the agricultural backwardness of this country can be put down to the farmers' lack of interest in agricultural education and to their failure to keep in touch with the scientific literature and to attend agricultural lectures and demonstrations. Put in another way, the farmers of this country, or at least many of them, do not look out for information which would help their advancement. For over forty years, the Department of Agriculture has been endeavoring to advance our schemes for agricultural instruction and for livestock improvement. Yet these have changed little over that time and have not achieved any notable measure of success.

Some of the schemes are administered directly by the Department and some through the county committees of agriculture. In either case, their administration is widespread and diffuse, and the great majority of farmers have failed to become familiar with them. They are therefore availed of by only a small percentage of the usually more progressive farmers and I suspect these farmers would be progressive anyway.

Increased agricultural production will not be attained unless a new approach is made to the matter. Parish experiments in agriculture should be tried. A parish council could arrange for the cooperation in the scheme of all the farmers in the parish. An agricultural adviser could be sent by the Department to survey the area, to get soil testing carried out, and to submit to the parish council his suggestions for the improvement of production in the area. He would bring to the notice of the farmers the government schemes which would be appropriate to the area and encourage them to apply for the facilities offered.

Veterinary advice should be made available freely so that animal diseases in the area could be checked. The parish council would be encouraged to provide any necessary machinery on a cooperative basis. Advice would also be given to individual farmers on the purchase of implements, fertilizers, and seeds. Cow testing would be a feature of the dairy areas and the improvement of herds aimed at by provision of good sires.

A parish experiment of the kind suggested would get all, or the great majority, of the people of the parish interested in increasing production, and it would provide a more intensive education in agriculture than would be possible under the present arrangements for occasional classes. It would in time create a rivalry in agricultural matters between parishes, which would in itself be of great value. It would prove the extent by which agricultural production could be increased by greater effort and improved methods. It would bring the force of public opinion to bear on farmers refusing to cooperate.

Eventually, it will be necessary to establish in each county a county agricultural institute, as recommended by our Commission on Vocational Organization. As suggested by the Commission, the institute should include administrative offices, an agricultural college, a demonstration farm, and certain statistical general information and research departments. It should appoint a county director of agriculture. Unless the agricultural colleges and demonstration farms are linked up with the ordinary farmers in each county through a county scheme, much of their value will be lost.

There is great need for increased capital in the agricultural industry. An estimate of the amount required has been made by one of our most distinguished experts in agriculture in an Appendix to the Reports on Agricultural Policy 1945.

He gives the figures needed under the following headings:

Land (fertilizers and improvement)	58	million pounds
Housing (for stock)	98.5	million pounds
Equipment	23	million pounds
Stock	22.5	million pounds
Water supplies	15	million pounds
	217	million pounds

This looks like a huge sum, but it is no use tilling a garden with a broken spade. It will not be a financial loss to the country but will be ultimately a financial gain apart altogether from its social repercussions.

The increased production will greatly increase the income of the farming population and enable them to pay back the large capital required. The program for better farming is, however, of such urgency as to justify a very great expenditure in this way. The size of the rural population is the key to the question of population for the whole country. If the rural population continues to decline, a serious situation must arise which will in turn affect the cities and towns. I do not believe that an immediate crisis is likely to occur. I believe, however, that many years of hard work lie ahead of the nation before we arrest the decline in rural population and possibly turn the tide in the opposite direction.

There has been no significant increase in the agricultural output of this country for over a hundred years. Let me say right away that unless there are reasonable guaranteed agricultural prices there can be no security, and security is necessary for the retention of the people. I have dealt a good deal with economic remedies as regards the land, for I feel that the right use and capitalization of our land will go a long way toward solving the problem of depopulation. I mentioned previously that our arts and crafts and our local mills are going or gone. Now they must be replaced by rural industries, especially now that there is electricity for power. If possible, these industries should use local materials, such as milk, meat, fruit, and timber. Our Department of Industry is moving in this direction.

Another great help to stem the tide of emigration is good housing. Great progress has been made in this respect. Over a quarter of the homes in my parish are the work of the local authority. Each house has an acre of ground, and the rent is about half a dollar a week. This program must expand to provide more homes, for a good house is an excellent inducement to remain.

Often the failure to marry or late marriages are caused by the tendency of the old people to hold on to the home. I suspect this is in order to have security. Increased old-age pensions given without too many conditions are helping to remove this difficulty. In 1937 at a Rural Week, De Valera suggested that dower houses should be built into which the old people could go. As far as I remember, the idea was that the eldest boy would go into the dower house, get married, and act as a working steward on the farm until the rest of the family were settled. Then the old people, probably with their old-age pension, would go to the dower house. This idea was never carried out, probably for economic reasons, but it would be worth a trial.

Rural electrification has increased and is fast spreading through the country. Over 18 per cent of the rural homes now have electricity, and 25 per cent of the countryside is covered. Board of Health cottages for rural laborers have been wired free. The material used to half its value has been made and processed in Ireland. It is hoped at the present rate of progress that the whole country will be covered in twelve to fourteen years. This will relieve the drabness of country life.

My own parish is a rural one, about 60 square miles with 400 homes. Virtually every home in this parish of farmers and laborers has electricity. The homes are brighter, and the womenfolk have those simple conveniences which mean a lot, such as the electric kettle and iron. It means much to be able to turn on the switch. The cattle and pig houses are lighted, milking machines are installed, and the little village, the capital of the parish, has its public lighting. I believe that rural electrification has been the greatest help to brighten, in every sense of the word, the countryside.

Our road conditions are improving and the old bog road is fast passing, to be remembered only in Gramophone records. I mentioned that the old amusements are gone beyond recall, and we must put something in their place. The parish hall must take their place. It will serve for education and amusement. Useful lectures will be given in it on the subjects close to the people's lives. It will have its own 16-mm projector; dances, dramas, and concerts will be held in it. Our own local dramatic society performed one of Shaw's plays last year, and this year it is going on to pantomime. Do not think for a moment I am lowering the standard of Shaw.

These things bring healthy amusement to rural life. Perhaps I hear some exile saying, "Where is the fun of the old days?" It is gone, my friend, and we have to make the best of it, and the little hall is doing it. There are playing fields for hurling and football, tennis courts, swimming pools; many of them on the rivers' banks are also bringing necessary recreation to rural parts. The community ideal in work and play will help to conquer the urge to go.

I have tried to deal with the facts of depopulation. I have tried to analyze the reasons for it, and I have suggested some of the preventatives. Now I shall tell you of a movement of which I happen to be the chairman. It is called Muintir na Tire (The People of the Land). It was started fifteen years ago in Tipperary and is now making good progress. Its chief aim is to save the rural people. It is based on the parish community. The spirit of Christian charity is its guiding force. All the people of the parish without distinction of class, politics, or creed are called to an annual meeting. This meeting is called the Parish Guild. The Guild consists of all of good will who are willing to cooperate for the common good of the parish community.

At the annual meeting, a Parish Council is elected by a vocational method, as recommended by the Papal Social Encyclicals. Each vocation, or section, of the people of the parish chooses its own representatives. The number of sections, or vocations, will depend on their number in the parish. Irrespective of numbers, each vocation, adjudged by the general meeting to be big enough to be recognized as a section, elects equal numbers to the parish council. This is important, for it creates a better spirit of cooperation in the council and when elected the whole council is concerned with the whole parish.

Take my own parish. We have five sections: (1) farmers; (2) laborers; (3) business and professional; (4) women; (5) youth. To a desk man these may not look like vocations, but I assure you they are in practice. We found out by experience that women are a vocation in themselves. The general meeting elects five to seven representatives as arranged by the general meeting. You have then a parish vocational parliament on which all sections of the parish are represented. The general body, or Guild, meet a few times during the year to see how things are going and to make suggestions.

There is no more suitable basis on which to organize the rural people and agricultural efforts than that of the parish because:

1. The parish is a defined geographical unit and a successful basis for the organization of many other activities.

2. The people of the parish know each other because they were educated usually in the same primary school, go to the same church, and are followers of the same hurling or football team.

3. People generally have a pride in their parish and its institutions, and this can be utilized to spur them on to greater effort in demonstrating the progressiveness of their parish in agricultural matters.

4. The clergy and teachers of a parish can act as leaders and unifying agents among its people, and this is an advantage not possessed by an

area lacking geographical recognition and without historical background.

The fact of including all sections in the parish council gives a strength and unity that would not be possible if confined to agriculturists only. Saving rural Ireland is a work for all, especially those who live in the country. The work of the parish council is under four headings: social, educational, economic, and recreational. In other words, it caters to the whole life of the parish. It is worth noting that if you develop only one portion of the social body, you produce, as you have produced in many great countries, monstrosities.

The objectives just mentioned are put in the order of their value. We put "social" first. It is time for the whole world to realize that you cannot build a good economic order on a bad social order. Forgetting this truth has given the chaotic state of today's world. The work of the Council, in this respect, is to assure good relations between employers and employees, good relations between families—in other words, to assure peace.

Unless this is assured the other works are in vain. The very fact that employers and employees sit in the same Council assures cooperation and peace. The Council's next object is education, and it is necessary to put this also before economics. The Council provides education by lectures, films, and libraries. It gives scholarships to poor boys and girls for agricultural and domestic science courses. Muintir na Tire runs its own summer schools for both.

We come now to a very important object, namely, economics. We realize its importance, but we believe it will be poor economics without a good social order and education. Our approach to agricultural economics is our Parish Plan. A plan has been formulated for the advancement of farming and the increase of agricultural production on a parish basis. First the Parish Council acquires an Enquiry Office. A parish map indicating the different characteristics of the land and sometimes the characters of the owners is hung on the wall. A register is kept of the farms and plots and gives area and production. Books and leaflets of agricultural information are kept in it.

The Office will give and get all information that will be useful to the people. It will cooperate with public officers and organize group action where necessary. This means that the distant Department of Agriculture is brought right down to the parish. Our Parish Council is now, in conjunction with the Department, organizing the first area Tuberculosis Testing Cattle Scheme in Ireland. Soils have been tested, cattle have been examined, and trees have been provided. A list of all the Department's schemes and services are kept. Parish Councils have reorganized fairs, opened markets, and started rural industries. It is much better to build upward than impose.

All these economic efforts of Parish Councils also unite the people. A number of experts under the OEEC, traveling recently through Europe, paid a visit to Ireland. They had many complaints to make of our agricultural progress, but they ended their report with a ray of hope by stating, "The new Parish Plan is a most forward step in the improvement of agricultural advisory work in *Europe*; it should greatly improve the economic conditions of farmers as well as the social conditions in the several communities." This is high praise for Muintir na Tire's Parish Plan from such experts. Note it is the most forward of its kind in *Europe*.

We come to the last objective—recreation. Halls have been built, projectors installed, dramatic classes formed, dances under proper control arranged, playing fields acquired, and swimming pools provided. There are now 375 such Parish Guilds and Councils in Ireland. They are not all doing all the things I have mentioned, but they are doing some of them and aim at doing all.

Our youth section is being trained to give, not get. Sacrifice has always given us the highlights of our history. We give our youths responsibility. They take care of the hall, the cinema, the parish Office, the graveyards, the library, and the poor. They are responding splendidly. We appeal to them to stay in Ireland, and we endeavor to get them employment. Their efforts will produce that civic spirit so lacking in the country. With them lie the hopes of the future. The Parish Council must meet at least monthly and as often as occasion requires.

This is the parish community life we are now building in rural Ireland. There are about 1,100 parishes in Ireland, the vast majority of which are rural. Most of these parishes, in the rural parts, are a combination of two parishes. This was brought about by the great loss of population after the Famine. These parishes still preserve their individuality although both have only one parish priest. We respect their historic independence and have a Guild and Parish Council for each.

Thus it will be seen that for the purpose of Muintir na Tire there are about 2,000 parishes; so we have yet a long way to go. When I speak of Ireland in this case, I mean the whole of Ireland. We have no Guilds yet in the divided portion of the country. We expect to start these next year. We believe our method can do much to remove in time the boundary and reunite our nation in peace and harmony.

In this community life lies the greatest hope to kill the urge to go. I can hear someone say, "How parochial." Yes, the movement is based on the parish, and let me say here that the hope of all big communities depends on the quality of the small communities. However, with the parish as our foundation, we go higher. The neighboring Parish Guilds and Councils form Regional Councils for matters concerning a wider area. County Federations are the next step, then Provincial Conventions, and finally a National Executive. The National Executive consists of thirty-two members with officers. They are elected annually by the Guilds. Each Guild is entitled to two voting members. They exercise their votes through the Provincial Conventions.

The work of the National Executive is to organize new Guilds and help weak ones. The headquarters are in Tipperary. The National Office will provide all information and will issue suggestions to Parish Councils. It arranges summer schools and the annual Rural Weeks. It has three publications: one monthly and two annuals. It has now started a Social Credit Society. This is all voluntary work, but all the time we look for the state advice and cooperation to which we are entitled. I must say in this respect we have received abundant courtesy and help from all departments. The officials know we are not looking for anything to benefit only one section of the community, but the entire community, for what we seek is for all.

The Archbishop of Armagh and Primate of All Ireland, the Most Rev. Dr. D'Alton, and the Archbishop of Cashel, the Most Rev. Dr. Kinane, are our patrons, and our National President is the Bishop of Cork, the Most Rev. Dr. Lucey. The priests of Ireland are giving us excellent support and are working hard in their Parish Councils. I may have painted a paradise but we aim at getting one. Muintir na Tire is only fifteen years old. During these years we had a world war when almost all organizing had to be stopped. In fifteen years, 375 Parish Guilds is no mean progress.

I am going to say something now, and I appeal to the editor to let me say it. For our progress we need funds. We want the movement to be voluntary; if it be state-controlled and -financed it will die. We can afford only one paid organizer for the whole country, and our office expenses are heavy. We depend completely on subscriptions from the Guilds, and many of them are in debt as a result of building halls. Many sectional organizations have received money from abroad, especially from England.

We have received nothing. I must correct that statement for there is one glorious exception. We received $5,000 through the Archbishop of Boston, the Most Rev. Dr. Cushing. Without his splendid gift our paid organizer would have to go, and it was the Archbishop's gift that enabled us to form our Social Credit Society. Friends of Ireland in America, you realize the dangerous state of the old land today. I have not exaggerated, I have given you plain facts. There is no doubt our country is in danger, but not so badly that she cannot be saved. We in Muintir na Tíre are doing all we can to save her. Some of us are sacrificing all we have, time, money, and health, in this work. We badly need financial aid. We know we have your sympathy. We would be grateful if you could make it practical. Every dollar will be used to its limit, and it will give you a chance to save Ireland.[1]

I believe, then, that if we are to keep our people we must concentrate on rural Ireland. Our cities are big enough, if not too big, for a small country. In rural Ireland lies the danger of the "vanishing Irish," and in rural Ireland lie our hopes. Our community method is, I believe, the only hope to retain our rural people and so retain a living, strong Ireland.

---

[1] Funds may be sent directly to the Rev. J. M. Hayes, Bansha, County Tipperary, Ireland, who will see that all donations are used to the best advantage.

MUTED WEDDING BELLS

12 ————————————————————————

Kathleen Norris

Kathleen Norris, second in a line of three brothers and three sisters, was born in San Francisco. Daughter of a country banker, she was orphaned suddenly in 1900, her twenty-year-old brother and she taking over the support of the other children, the youngest then eight. She worked in shops, in a private library, and finally on a newspaper.

In 1909 she married Charles Gilman Norris, brother of the well-known novelist Frank Norris, and moved to New York, where the only surviving son of their several children, Frank, was born. Her first book, "Mother," published in 1910, was an instant success. She is probably the most prolific living author, having written the staggering total of eighty-eight books.

Among some of her better known works besides "Mother" are "Treehaven," "Lost Sunrise," "Little Ships," "Belle Mere," "Burned Fingers." Despite the enormous number of her novels the reading public is always clamoring for more, and Mrs. Norris is endeavoring to meet that demand with "Shadow Marriage," which will soon appear in bookshops throughout the nation. She is a gifted and polished writer with a knack of reaching the hearts of the millions of her readers.

After World War I, Major and Mrs. Norris moved to California, where they had a large ranch, on which the children of a deceased sister were raised with their own son. Frank Norris, their son, is a doctor in San Francisco, father of three children. Mrs. Norris was widowed in 1945 and now lives and writes in a small house in Palo Alto. To the twenty-eight grandchildren of the original six, she is "Granny."

IRELAND WITHOUT SONS AND DAUGHTERS? IRELAND SLOWLY DYING, AND BY
her own hand? To read that this is so, to have to believe it, is to feel one's
heart grow strangely heavy.

No, I am not Irish-born. But I was named for a great-grandmother in
Cork, and my loved mother's name was Josephine Moroney. As children,
raised in faraway California, we came to love what we were told of Ireland, of the sweet green place where the countryfolk walked to Mass
while the bells were ringing and the crooked little streets ran down to
dancing waters where the little fishing smacks jostled together.

We loved it all. We read Charles Lever and Jane Barlow, we sang
"Silent, O'Moyle" and " 'Twas Dying They Thought Her." We envied
the big families of sons and daughters, cousins, aunts, grandmothers, in
the big country houses of the quiet Irish towns.

So it is staggering to learn, these long years later, that the old country
is reduced to "a crop chiefly of bachelors and spinsters." Her men and
women, if they marry at all, marry late. And even in marriage the
nurseries are no longer the big nurseries of yesterday. The Dark Rosa-
leen, so long beset by enemies from without, is now perishing from the
apathy and coldness of her own people within.

If there are biological causes for this state of affairs, they are beyond
my comprehension. They lie so deep that even the trueborn Irish, the
students and scientists who pore over her great story, are at a loss. But
here in America we have a somewhat similar situation, in which there
are several quite obvious elements. I mean that we have many families
of Irish descent, in which groups of sisters, five, six, or seven, will fill
good positions in the educational or business world, and maintain a comfortable home, without marriage, and indeed with an amused pity for
married friends.

If they do marry, it is some familiar old beau of many years' standing:
"Annie's old John, of course," or "the Martin she's been going with
twenty years." These are often dignified and happy unions, but blessed
with only one child, or no children at all.

Of the several causes of this state of affairs one is basic, and they all
contribute to that. It is this: that Catholic women take marriage far
more gravely than other women do, and Catholic Irish-Americans and
Irishwomen themselves assume marital responsibilities more seriously
than all others. They know marriage is a lifework; they solemnly ac-

cept the great vows involved, and they realize that their burdens as wives cannot be lightened either by contraception or by divorce.

Here in America, therefore, the position of the young wife is in sharp contrast to that of her non-Catholic friends. Many of these elect to have many carefree years before having a child; many break away, in divorces, without apparently losing either the general respect or their own spiritual peace. The young Catholic girl, her eyes wide open to the situation, naturally balances what she expects her own cares as a wife must be against that state so long known as blessed: "single blessedness."

Perhaps this girl has grown up in a household crowded with younger members. To her the constant arrival of little brothers and sisters means merely added care and annoyance. She has none of her mother's ecstatic love of her babies, none of her father's pride in his rising family. She sees only the disorder, the accumulating washing of small clothes and dishes, the cramped quarters growing even more cramped, the coughs and colds and disorder and racket.

Perhaps poverty is added to the picture. The girls have no social opportunities, no room to which they can ask boy friends for evenings of games and singing. Denied in the early years these innocent affairs, the girls get their first jobs. They are independent now for the first time; dignified and comfortable living is within their grasp.

Perhaps intemperance colors the early picture, too. To many children thoughts of Dad and drink are forever united. If he comes home Saturday night with a heavy breath, a heavy hand, a bad temper, the frightened, quiet children perfectly appreciate the situation and their hearts harden against the circumstances that are so unjust to the family saint—Mother.

One of a household of four unmarried sisters and one bachelor brother said proudly to me one day, "We've given Mother everything she wants, after those hard years of work for all of us and care of my father. She has her own little home, her car and radio and TV and dishwasher."

The mother smiled at me patiently. She knew what she wanted, and I knew what she wanted: grandchildren. She was hungry for the touch of a soft little peachy face against her own, a soft little flannelly weight against her shoulder. And all the dishwashers in the world don't compensate.

Lastly, there is the immense influence of happy communities of nuns, to contrast sharply, in our girls' school days, with the confusion and uncertainty of home affairs. A nun with a true vocation, and most of them have that, is the one person in a troubled world who tastes the security and bliss of Heaven in this life. She has given her life to God, once and for all; nothing now can go wrong. Humiliations and disappointments are all a part of her pattern; she accepts them courageously, if she does not actually welcome them.

The wife and mother has no such security. She must consider the spiritual values of what her husband and children want, as opposed to what is right and safe for them. She must watch books, amusements, associates; she must be the one to insist that Mass must come first, before the summer Sunday plans; that Friday abstinence is observed. She must choose, over and over again, the harder course.

It is not, therefore, astonishing, that the more thoughtful element among our young people hesitate at matrimony—and are lost. Most girls would marry confidently enough, in the teens, but each later year adds to increasing satisfaction in independence and self-respect, increasing misgivings as to the married state.

Protestant churches in America handle this situation with encouragement of social activities among the young people. They have sales, movies, jolly-ups, picnics, theatricals, not just at long intervals, but every week. Each Wednesday night Church Street in our college town boils with these festivities. Every boy and girl is drawn in. While still in an impressionable stage, they meet each other casually and unself-consciously, and a crop of healthy young marriages is the result.

On our side, we have for our young Catholic collegians the recently established Newman Hall, a club that already rates 400 enthusiastic members. An old home with spacious grounds and with a big outdoor kitchen and grill was secured for the club, and an exquisite chapel was added by Clare Boothe Luce in memory of her daughter Ann, whose death in a motor accident took place here some years ago. Already many young marriages have taken place in this chapel, and already the club has an enviable reputation with the students.

It might pay Irish fathers and mothers to maintain such clubs. Ours has a young priest in residence and two or three college boys as workers. With only a little help in getting started the young people will carry on by themselves, and Mother Nature will step in to convince them of the glory and beauty—even on quite natural human grounds—of a good and fruitful marriage and the incomparable opportunity for service to God and country.

It should be done! For we must have the Irish! We must have their laughter, their divinely simple philosophy and faith, their understatement that is more forceful than any exaggeration, their mystical poetry that rises triumphant over poverty and drudgery, over crowded nurseries and disorderly kitchens and sees in the smallest scrap of babyhood the glow of the eternal soul that makes it a child of God. We cannot lose them. We cannot afford to answer in the affirmative Tom Moore's plaintive query:

> Are Ireland's sons so good or so cold
> As not to be tempted by women or gold?

THE INHERITANCE

A Tragedy in One Act

13

Paul Jones

CAST   MALACHY MAC AOSTA *A farmer*
        SEAMUS *His eldest son*

SCENE: *The parlor of a substantial farmhouse, anywhere in Ireland.*
TIME: *The present.*

When the curtain rises, Malachy is sitting in an old-fashioned easy chair by the fire. His dog Tray is sleeping at his feet. Seamus enters.

MALACHY: Sit down, Seamus. It's time I had a talk with you.

SEAMUS *(seating himself)*: Yes, father?

MALACHY: You've been a good son, Seamus. All the others went away, and I hope prospered. But you stayed . . . you stayed . . . What age would you think I am, Seamus?

SEAMUS: Ninety-three?

MALACHY *(proudly)*: Ninety-four last Wednesday . . . What age are you, Seamus?

SEAMUS: Sixty-nine, father. Just rising sixty-nine.

MALACHY: Do you know what I've been thinking, Seamus?

SEAMUS: No, father.

MALACHY: I've been thinking, and I sitting here, that it's time you settled down and got married and made a home for yourself. What happened to that nice girl of the Dalys you used to have an eye for? Annie Daly, wasn't that her name? The dark-haired one that used to wear a red ribbon in her hair.

154

SEAMUS: She went to England ten years ago to be a nurse.

MALACHY: And that little Sweeney girl, that won the prize for the dancing at the Feis in Gortnatubber?

SEAMUS: She went to Swansea and married a Welsh miner.

MALACHY: Did she, did she? They do say there's a lot of them gone. Right enough, I haven't seen many young girls in this part of the world in the last few years or so.

(*The dog stirs uneasily in his sleep.*)

MALACHY (*patting the dog's head gently*): Poor Tray, he's thirteen years old now. He's dreaming of the times he used to be out after rabbits . . . Do you know, Seamus, I'm beginning to think I'm getting past my work. I think you ought to be looking out for a good wife for yourself and settling down. I've only at most about another three or four years to go, and then the farm will be yours.

(*Seamus bites the dog.*)

CURTAIN

THE BOUNDARY BETWEEN
THE SEXES

14 ───────────────────────────

Arland Ussher

     Born in London on September 9, 1899, Arland Ussher is the son of Beverley Grant Ussher and Emily Jebb Ussher. He is a Protestant, a member of the Church of Ireland, and a descendant of the famous Archbishop Ussher of Armagh. He went to school at Abbotsholme, Derbyshire, where the cold was of such intensity that he says he is hardened against all the Irish climate can do to him.

    In 1918 he enrolled at Trinity College, Dublin, and the following year at Cambridge, but remained for but a term at each institution. "I was," he says, "in a state of intellectual ferment, brought on largely by a manuscript work of D. H. Lawrence lent me by a friend."

    Ussher spent the next twenty years chiefly in County Waterford, engaged partly in farming and partly in building up a private philosophy, with occasional trips to the Continent, above all to Germany, which he says was then his spiritual home. During this time Ussher produced two volumes of Gaelic phrases and witty sayings taken down from the lips of his plowman Thomas Murray, a translation of Merriman's "The Midnight Court," and the burlesque epic of a Waterford bard, "The Adventures of a Luckless Fellow."

    In World War II, Ussher came to Dublin where he has lived ever since at Sandymount. In these latter years he has given us two volumes of philosophical essays, "Postscript of Existentialism" and "The Twilight of the Ideas," and also two books of a more popular nature, "The Face and Mind of Ireland" and "The Magic People," a book about the Jews.

*Art critic, philosopher, and Gaelic scholar, Ussher describes himself
as "Irish by birth and choice with a good quarter of English blood." He
writes in a sprightly style and has done much to interpret the Irish to
the English and the English to the Irish, serving as a bridge of understanding between the two races.*

*"He has, as befits an Irish philosopher," observes Harold Nicolson, "a
gift of phantasy." Writing in the "Catholic Herald," the Earl of Wick-
low says of him, "Though he comes of one of the oldest Ascendency
families, his viewpoint is very different and he uses the Anglo-Irish
Colonels among whom he spent his childhood as Aunt Sallies for his
wit."*

It all began with the Famine. In the hundred years previous to the
catastrophe, the Irish population had steadily mounted. During the hundred years which have followed, it has uninterruptedly declined. We
live in the trough of a great tide, and there are still no signs of it turning. It is recognized that quantitative differences at a certain level become qualitative ones, and the principle holds good in regard to populations.

We can at once distinguish the man or woman who has grown up in a
large household or community from the person who has been reared
in a small one. The Irishman of literature, the Irishman whom the world
loved well, belongs to the century before the debacle, to those years before, in the acrid and unfair phrase of H. G. Wells, "the weary potato
gave way under its burden."

It is, of course, not merely a question of numbers. Very great density
of population is not perhaps compatible with all that we mean by civilization. But the Famine of the forties inflicted a wound on the Irish
psyche which has not yet healed. *An droch-Shaoghal!* "The Bad Times."
At almost every fireside for three generations the same stories have been
told.

In my own childhood I was shown the pits into which the dead and
dying were hurried higgledy-piggledy—the shells of the granaries where
speculators hoarded grain. The rumors of the tragedy reached the ends
of the world, so that even the Sultan of Turkey and the Negroes of Ja-
maica were moved to send relief. But owing to hopeless inefficiency
and preposterous governmental red tape little of it reached the victims.

All this is well known, and there have been enough horrors in the world since to make us forget it.

The Irishman is not, in spite of the legend to the contrary, excessively vindictive; and he is only too prone to attribute every shocking misfortune to the will of God. Though a son of the landlord class, I was never in youth made to feel the responsibility of my class—or of a part of it. But the Famine did something to the Irish, as the phrase is, which will not soon be undone.

The Irish of those pre-Famine days would seem to have been a gay people, almost Latin in expressiveness and expansiveness, warm-blooded and inclined to gallantry. Wolfe Tone could suggest, as a plan for winning over the Irish prisoners in France, that a troop of engaging damsels should be introduced among them (*Diary*).

It would not be too much to say that the Irish of today are just the opposite of all this: somber, likely to be suspicious and reserved, puritanical to the point of regarding marriage itself for any other motive but worldly betterment as an almost reprehensible weakness.[1] And the symbol of the change is that the modern Irishman is, and will almost certainly remain, English-speaking. It is possible that the Irish of that old Ireland were aping in a certain degree the manners of an irresponsible aristocracy. But if so it cannot be said that in discarding them we have developed the energetic and realist virtues of a *bourgeoisie*.

The stage Irishman, laughed off the stage by Bernard Shaw, was unattractive because he was a fake: exploiting the traditional Irish qualities to flatter the master race. But he has been succeeded by what may be called the "Abbey Theatre Irishman," familiar in a hundred skits on matchmaking or county-council rigging. This Irishman unfortunately is far from unknown in real life, and he is scarcely an improvement. His weaknesses are not very amiable ones, and a warm heart for the colleens is certainly nowhere in the list.

Nevertheless there is a very great deal to praise in Irish social life— ways of thought and behavior which carry on the primitive health of the world in our fevered and rather vulgar age. I need only mention

[1] It is however worthy of note that in the greatest modern Irish poem, *The Midnight Court*, written in the late eighteenth century, an inquiry is held by the queen of the fairies upon the very same problem which here concerns us and that most of the grievances therein advanced would apply in the identical way at the present day.

the respect for leisure, good conversation and sane ideals and the almost complete absence of class and racial strife.

It is these things which will often cause the tourist to exclaim (I have heard him over and over), "This is the country I would choose to live in *if there were employment for me.*" And the emigrant will admit these things are all very nice, but he or she will usually add, "*There is no employment for me.*" It all seems to come back to the lack of employment; and whatever may be the complex causes of that phenomenon in the world at large, in Ireland the main cause is a thin and contracting population.

Lack of employment with us means lack of employers, and the lack of employers is a consequence of the dearth of consumers. Even our carefully sheltered infant industries have to face a stationary, or even a falling, demand. Thirty years of a vigorous tariff policy and of government aid to industry verging on the dreaded "socialism" itself have failed to create an Ireland which all Irish-born men and women of a goodly majority can live in. And the reason, in my belief, is that all is not well in the relations between the Irishwoman and the Irishman.

The attitude of Irishmen to the females of their species, to put it shortly and, as we shall see, not quite fairly, is that of a very primitive peasant community. But this comment, which has often been made, needs much qualification: for the Irishman is not primitive or boorish *except in this one point.* The Irish land worker is on the whole more intelligent and refined than the typical peasant of Europe or than the English rustic. He instinctively prefers mental to manual occupations, and he has a natural thirst for elegance of living. One might almost indeed say that he is the natural townsman, despite the odd fact that the old Irish never built a town.

How few among the millions who have left our shores have taken to agriculture! The Irishman is a highly civilizable person, and one has known the sons of Irish peasant farmers to turn into mathematicians or art critics within a few years of leaving the potato patch. The reason may be that the old Gaelic civilization was slow in dying and that the dispossessed native aristocracy mingled its blood with the mass.

All this, of course, is as true of the Irishwoman as of the Irishman; in some respects it is even more true of her, only that, by some baneful perversity, these two do not face the problem of civilization as partners.

Rather they are apt to see in each other and in their natural mutual attraction the destiny that holds them back, the curse of Adam and Eve. *Irishmen and -women regard sex instinctively as they regard mud*—that mud which symbolizes to them their ancestral thraldom to the land. In the moments when they (the girls at least) dream of "romance," it is always the world overseas they dream of: that world of freedom and movement brought to them by the films.

This is, of course, not always conscious, and I anticipate that many will contradict me with vehemence. But it is plain enough to any unprejudiced student of Irish life. The Irishman is convinced that the woman's place is the home—and nothing but that; yet he himself is a far from home-loving creature. He escapes from it as often as possible to foregather with the "boys," which term covers unattached men of all ages. If married, he seldom thinks of bringing home presents or giving his house any grace of decoration. He does not go out walking with his wife or often take her to amusements; in the summer he does not generally take his family with him on tours, even when he can afford it. Frequent days at the races with male "buddies" are more to his taste.

All this goes with a rough male camaraderie and gaiety which I, as an Irishman, find not unattractive. But the Irish wife, at grips with a numerous family in a rather comfortless home, with a not-too-generous housekeeping allowance, comes off less well. The Irishman likes to spend his money "like a gentleman." It is the one perennial Irish quality, but it is not part of the conception that he should provide his spouse with any of the amenities of a lady. The word "lady" indeed, in his mouth, has usually a rather ironic and resentful sound. "I don't want to marry a lady," he says, "with newfangled grand notions."

The "home" represents to him what his instinctive idealism fears and wants to forget: the material side of life. The wife is not merely, as in most peasant communities, the rather oppressed "adjunct"; she could bear that more easily. She is the suppressed half of his divided personality—the symbol of his hated bondage to blood and soil.

So much for the Irishman in marriage. But this attitude of his to the sex he scarcely thinks of as "fair" extends, of course, through all his social life. One is tempted to say that Ireland is intersected by an even more pernicious Boundary than that between South and North: the Boundary between the sexes. Irishmen do not treat women coarsely or brutally. They simply try to ignore and forget them.

At any social gathering, the men and the women will invariably segregate themselves in compact groups at opposite ends of the room, if possible with the table or buffet in between; and the daring individual who seeks to stray from one group to the other can provoke titters and embarrassment. Hostesses who deplore this oil-and-water-like behavior of their guests—a constant subject of complaint with our foreign visitors—can do nothing to change it.

Whatever one is told about Irish "blarney," I have almost never heard an Irishman pay a *compliment* to a woman. So unused indeed are the women to such graceful forms of address that they would probably in most cases reply by a rebuff, fancying an intended assault upon their virtue. Irish girls in fact seem often to cultivate, on their side, a defensive —and entirely unnecessary—ungraciousness and tartness. All this would not perhaps be so surprising were it not that Ireland is, in so many ways, an "Old World country"; here at least, one would imagine, one might expect to find the remains of "gallantry."

Actually the Irishman of the cleverer sort prides himself on his freedom from nonsense, or, as he calls it, "cod." He is not, he thinks, as other men are—romantic and sentimental. If he takes a girl friend to a café, a rare occurrence and a poor substitute in his eyes for tea with her family, it is likely to be the girl who must pay. If he goes with her to a dance, it is she, as often as not, who procures the tickets. And nothing arouses in him a deeper scorn, half ascetic and half "Rabelaisian," than the normal human experience called falling in love.

The Irishman in love feels ridiculous; and to drive the feeling home, an enamored couple in any country parish are exposed to derision and every sort of ill-natured prank. The laughter is not smiling or kindly, as it is in the case of habitual drunkenness; for drunkenness, just because it is gregarious, is altogether respectable.

I do not know how far one should blame the parish clergy and the missioners, for whom "company keeping" is a staple subject of denunciation providing, I am told, one sermon in each of the fairly frequent "missions." Certainly the puritanic bias of the Church in Ireland surprises visitors from other Catholic communities. It is often said that Irish schools and seminaries in the last century were infected with the remnants of Jansenism. I should fancy myself that the lack of a Catholic aristocracy, to set a more humane tone, and the fear, whether justified or not, of Protestant libertinism had rather more to do with it. But the causes are certainly complex, and speculation about them would lead us too far from our subject.

The dismal fact remains that Irishmen tend to regard procreation as a shameful necessity, and Irish girls grow up to think of sex as something dark, cold, and forbidding. Statistics are scarcely available, but it seems to me that the word "dirty" is used in modern Ireland in one sense only, namely, to cover every manifestation, even the most natural, of sex passion. It is forgotten that what is too often called dirty has a tendency to become so, and to be shunned as such. Irish married couples seldom give the impression of being biologically satisfied or even awakened; and if they are not, it may partly account for the slovenly, listless, don't care rather than devil-may-care quality of Irish life—the "spit" but never the "polish."

I have heard of mothers of large families who confessed, not without a certain sense of virtue, that they had never at any time enjoyed a satisfying physical relationship with their husbands; and I believe their case is not untypical even today. The theories of modern psychology should be accepted perhaps only with great reserve. But the fact that so many Irish youths are "mama's boys," the objects of a jealous and monopolizing affection, may have some such cause; and it is a fact which certainly helps in postponing marriages.

There would be little use in attacking the system of dowries and "made marriages," common to most peasant communities, or in stressing the well-known fact that a country couple very frequently obtain their first viewing of each other before the altar rails. This is a subject incidentally of many amusing and probably true stories, such as the following:

"THE SON: You didn't tell me she was lame.

"THE FATHER: Get along with you! Sure it's not for racing you want her!"

This, after all, is part of the old social pattern of Europe. But the marriage of the eldest means of course that the younger sons and daughters, if they are a bit enterprising, must quit the farm; and for these outgoers Eire is not a land of opportunity. In the bad old days of land-lordism, a younger son could at least stay on the land, *rent* a farm, and be thus enabled to marry; or he could become a workman on a large estate. Long-term land leases are not given today, however, owing to the odium and uncertainty attaching to rent; and the social gap between the farmer class and the laborer class has become fixed and almost impassable.

A farmer's son who marries a poor girl, a farmer's daughter who marries a workman, even one earning a good wage, must be prepared in most districts to be thrust out from their own family and class. Therefore if not personally ambitious, they will prefer to "hang on" in an almost menial, and of course wholly celibate condition upon the home farm. But if they are ambitious, they will go to the towns; and, by a malefic dispensation, most Irish towns are situated on the other side of the Border.

Eire, more than any modern civilized state, is a nation without towns; it is also a nation without any large-scale scientific agriculture, forestry, or fisheries. I am here considering these things only from the point of view of *employment*. Still, no doubt some Irish young men and women will find employment in Eire, which generally means in Dublin. Let us see what the possibilities are for them.

A boy, let us say, wants to become a schoolmaster or a girl to go in for nursing. In these professions the key jobs, generally speaking, are held by "religious": priests and Christian Brothers in education, nuns in the nursing profession. In most Irish hospitals the "theater" sisters and senior sisters are nuns. Therefore girls will find that promotion for them beyond a certain point is likely to be barred.

It is not for me, as a Protestant, to criticize this system, which may have much to be said for it from a Catholic point of view. I would only point out that it has the effect of discouraging lay professionals. I have heard of cases of lay teachers, especially women, with many years of service and experience being passed over for promotion in favor of clerics who had much less to show of both. A teacher in a rural primary school will be forever in fear of any tittle-tattle about his, or her, private life reaching the ears of the clerical manager; and we have noticed what the attitude of the country clergy to company keeping, that is to say, normal courtship and wooing, is. If the teacher is an enthusiast for the

Gaelic language, and it is an enthusiasm which has kept many gifted young people in the country, he or she will generally meet with discouragement and opposition from the parish priest.

In this attitude there may be much justification for the priesthood since the policy of reviving the Gaelic is of dubious wisdom. But seeing that that policy seems to express the wishes of the nation, since so large an amount of money and teaching time is bestowed on it, the lukewarm attitude of many of the clergy is apt to produce a very dreary deadlock. And one suspects that their coldness toward the language springs from a distrust of Gaelic socials, *céilidhthe* and feiseanna, and of any of those attempts to brighten rural existence in which both the sexes can participate. Irish country life, as I shall try to show, is often extremely somber and depressing; and a large part of the success of the Gaelic League in the early days was due to its social side: its dances, games, and festivals.

Let us look again at prospects in the nursing profession. In English hospitals today the girls as well as male nurses get free uniforms and a fairly good salary while training. In Eire fees are charged, and there is no real salary until the final year. This of course means that, while nursing in England is open to any girl of fair education, in Eire it is reserved for girls from secondary schools and fairly comfortable families.

The point about wages during the period of training is important for others than nurses. Typists in Dublin firms begin at a wage which is mere pocket money; for they are expected to be "nice" girls, which is to say that they are living at home or under the care of elder relatives. In England there are now county council hostels for such business girls, where two of them can share a bed-sitting room at a reasonable rate. The result is that they feel themselves, when work is over, to be free. It is possible that these conditions may, as the cautious phrase is, "lend themselves to abuse," though I have not heard of it. But girls who have to work under modern competitive conditions feel they have a right to such freedom, and they will not stay in Ireland if it is denied to them there.

Finally Eire is, and will doubtless remain, largely agricultural; and Irish agriculture is in the condition described by St. Thomas More when he said, "Sheep are eating men." But for "sheep" substitute "bullocks." This of course has for long been the case; but the process has been accelerated and not arrested by the policy—up to a point perhaps inevitable but carried much too far with us—of carving estates into small holdings. Again and again one has seen a large estate employing much labor divided among "landless men" without capital or instruction. The immediate result is the dispersal of the working population, some of whom, such as foresters and gardeners, may have been highly skilled operatives, while the new landlords either work their farms with the unpaid, much sweated, labor of their families or, very commonly, let their land on short term for grazing.

It would appear that about 60 per cent of Irish farms are below 30 acres in size, while some 40 per cent are actually between 15 and 5 acres; in other words, they are uneconomic. Peasant holdings as small as these may be common in Holland, Scandinavia, and elsewhere, but in these cases the urban markets are usually nearer at hand. If they are not, the producers are enabled to reach them by highly developed systems of cooperative marketing to which the individualism of our people seems hopelessly opposed.

Certainly no one would defend the old-style absentee landlord. It is sufficiently recognized, however, that we are creating a new class of absentee tenants, townsmen who lease land for grazing from poor or incapable owners on the system known as the "eleven months," year after year, and putting back nothing into the soil, till it will no longer support anything but snipe. The many Irish land-distribution schemes have had a definitely "pauperizing" effect on the nation, and much Irish land remains as useless and undercultivated as if it were put in pawn with a usurer. Of this anyone can convince himself by looking about him on a long train journey through the country.

Where petty landlords accumulate, the land decays and men decay with it. It has been computed that the area of our twenty-six counties covered by hedges and walls is actually equal to the six alienated counties of Northern Ireland. A country which has come to take the Chestertonian view of ownership as the cure for all ills must of necessity enjoy a small population; for it is clear that there is a natural limit to the number who can be possessed of those twin Irish desiderata: the "bit of land" and the "bit in the bank."

A further result of the breaking up of estates and large farms is that Eire is a country almost without villages. The rural population live for the most part in isolated dwellings, reached often only with extraordinary difficulty by passing over rain-sodden fields or down muddy boreens (lanes) which in winter become lakes. Nothing, I think, contributes more to making Irish life dismal, soggy, and ungracious; for the small towns, scattered at distances often of 10 or 15 miles, do not take the place of thickly spread and cheerful rural centers.

It is possible that this dispersion of dwellings, each standing amid its own fields like an ancestral fort, corresponds to something independent, fierce, and fine in the Irish mentality (I have maintained this view elsewhere); and no doubt the suspicions and hostilities engendered by Irish history have much to do with it. But it is scarcely surprising if the modern youth and girl prefer lighted streets to lonely mud-moated farmsteads, where even the postman very often calls but twice or thrice a week. And it should be remembered that the dispersal of dwellings renders difficult the provision of all conveniences and amenities.

It was revealed by the 1946 census that only 5 per cent of farm dwellings had a piped water supply. In other cases water is carried laboriously from wells; and water rights constitute another kind of inexhaustible well—an abounding source of friction and litigation between neighbors. I am told that a scheme for rural electrification is now at last in hand; the wheels of bureaucracy revolve slowly in Ireland as elsewhere, and one can only hope that such a scheme will soon be implemented. At present the towns alone are lighted. All over the countryside the veils of night hang damply, during the autumn and winter from 4 or 6 o'clock onward. For the men there is perhaps a "pub"; for neither sex is there, or scarcely ever, such a thing as a parish hall or reading room.

There are occasional dances held, when the clerical manager permits, in the schoolroom. When he withholds permission, the back parlor of the pub is likely to be used, with greater danger to morals. Usually the clergy are strong in condemnation of dances, and, with most domiciles distant and scattered and to be reached only on foot, one can readily appreciate their reasons. But in a rural existence so gray, so monotonous and cheerless, with, above all, so complete a dissociation between the ideas of marriage and romantic love, it is hardly surprising if the normal social amusement of dancing leads to "incidents."

And then the pub. Heaven knows I am no enemy of the cup that cheers, but surely Eire's drink bill per annum and per man must be the biggest of any country in the world. Nor is Irish drinking on the whole marked by much cheerfulness. I speak of the Irishman, for Irishwomen do not in general, as in England and other European countries, make use of the public houses. The typical Irish pub is, alas, no pleasant inn or café. In other words, drinking is a pastime in which the women suffer from most of the ills but enjoy little of the refreshment and social recreation. It serves once again as a means of sex exaggeration and is, I think, leniently regarded for that reason.

The Irishman's liquor consumption would matter little, or at any rate less, if it were not so largely a substitute for nutrition; for our Irish dietary is another dreadful subject on which I must touch. It is the astounding fact that we Irish in a fertile land among "mackerel-crowded seas" must be the world's poorest consumers of fish, cheese, fruit, and most sorts of vegetables; and that no Irishwoman, it would seem, has any suspicion that cookery is an art worthy of her attention.

There are, I am aware, the cookery classes in our technical schools, but our teachers apparently specialize in the making of cakes and not very imaginative cakes at that: seedcakes, scones, and what have you? The crown of every girl pupil's ambition is the wedding cake which, ill equipped as she is for captivating a husband, she may never be called upon to make.

Irish diet in all classes consists for about half the total number of meals chiefly of bread, tea, and some sort of manufactured preserve—"bread and spread" as it is aptly enough described. For breakfast, Father, but generally no one else, may have in addition an egg, or "fry." For the evening high tea even Father does not get this, except in well-to-do homes, and not always then. At most schools there is some sort of mid-morning snack, usually milk (not enough of it) and, again, bread and spread. The midday meal consists of potatoes, perhaps meat (too often something tossed out of a pan), and some stodgy pudding. Of what is possible in the way of soups, salads, omelettes, ragouts, the hundred and one tasty mixed meat dishes which French housewives can conjure from the scantiest materials, little is known or taught. Calves' heads are cheap and easy to come by in Ireland, but where is the cook among us who has heard of *tête de veau vinaigrette?*

In a land flowing with milk, we eat on an average 0.46 ounce of cheese per head per week[1] (cheese, for the most part, of standardized types,

---

[1] See Irish Statistical Survey 1950–1951.

fitter for the mousetrap than the table); amid waters chock-full of fish
the figure for fish eating is 2.58 ounces per head per week (this chiefly,
in a penitential way, on Fridays!). The result of it all is that we are, as a
people, irritable and neurotic, rickety and tuberculosis-ridden; and Irish
faces, though often possessing the "spiritual" beauty which fascinated
Mr. Broadbend, are more often than not ill formed: the forehead is apt
to be bulgy, the nose too flat, or the lower jaw falling away—so many
mournful testimonies to a defective dietary.

Lastly I cannot refrain from mentioning the discouraging situation of
that class, surely necessary to the healthy functioning of a nation, called
intellectuals and creative writers. Eire is a country with a vigorous and
not very intelligent Censorship of Books but (partly as a consequence)
no publishers for general literature. The Irish author, if he lives—in the
body—in Ireland, has at the same time to live effectively and for the
professional side of his existence in another country. He must publish
his works, if he is clever or lucky enough, in London and see them
return to the homeland (most often) to be branded as contaminated
goods because they offend the very small-town susceptibilities of some
of his fellow citizens. For in Eire, owing to her smallness and isolation,
there is no escape from Main Street mentality—the type of mind bred
by what in many Irish towns is called simply and for lack of rivals "the
Street."

It is notorious that almost every Irish, indeed every modern, author of
importance (including Catholic writers like Mauriac and Graham
Greene) have come under the ban of our mild inquisitors. It may be
said that this is irrelevant to the present subject, for the Irish are not a
reading, any more than they are a feeding, race; and the few who are
driven to emigration by such conditions would never be missed. This
few, however, exists; and it happens to include most of those richly
gifted spirits which our country in every generation seems to throw up
and unfortunately to throw out.

As with other emigrants, the money spent on their education is a dead
loss to the nation even when that education has been an asset to them
personally and not, as so often, a frustration. It is seldom true of living
organisms that they are improved by having their brains extracted, and
Eire is sorely in need of intellectual life, not excluding a Catholic intellectual life, which seems scarcely to exist among Irish layfolk. Where is

the Irish Chesterton or Maritain? But Ireland will not get them unless the arena be kept open to all.

The removal of Partition might freshen and invigorate the Irish intellectual air. But its abolition is not in sight and, I believe, is secretly feared by many on both sides of the Border for this very reason. As it is, the dispersion of Irish intellect is not the least important part of our present problem of the vanishing Irish: the problem of a people which has concentrated so long, in current philosophic terms, on the *essence* of nationhood that it is in real and terrible danger of throwing away its very *existence*.

15

Mary Frances Keating

One of the best-known among the women journalists of Ireland, Mary Frances Keating was born in 1907 in County Limerick. After graduating from Notre Dame Academy in London, she taught domestic science in a convent school near her home in Dublin.

Finding that employment rather bleak, she went to Italy, where she worked and studied for a number of years. Her brother is a well-known painter, and Miss Keating found Italy an ideal place in which to quicken her own appreciation and love of art.

"I spent many years in Italy," she writes, "and having my share of Irish good looks I was often upbraided for my coolness where men or marriage was concerned. I was shy and lonely, but would never have dared to admit it because of my strict upbringing and the frequent admonitions to 'behave like a lady,' that is, to freeze any one of the male sex who seemed to manifest the idea that I was another human being."

Upon returning to Eire she entered upon a journalistic career, contributing feature articles for "The Irish Times," "The Sunday Independent" and other leading papers. Her marriage, rather late in life to one of her editors, has proved most happy. "We hope," she says, "in our own small way to make life for the youngsters a bit less unhappy and a little more human that that of our own childhood. Meanwhile I have a chance to make my ideas felt in my various columns—and need I say—I never neglect the opportunity."

Mary Keating writes with an engaging frankness and a forthright honesty, which her readers are quick to discern and to appreciate. In addition to her newspaper articles, she has written a book on "Cookery and Homemaking." With her husband and three children she resides in Dublin, where she takes an active part in civic and cultural affairs.

THE IRISHMAN AS A LOVER IS PROBABLY FAMOUS ALL OVER THE CIVILIZED globe. Gay, light-hearted, tender and generous, he can make the girl in whom he is "interested" (note that I don't say whom he loves) feel like a queen! Yes, up to a certain point, the Irishman is a charming lover. But should he be so incautious as to allow the girl whom he is courting to think that he means matrimony even at a remote date, then he can do a disappearing act which would make anything staged by Maskelyne and Devant appear as so much amateur bungling!

No, marriage is for morons. At least that's what about 80 per cent of Irishmen seem to believe. How, they wonder, will that wretched 20 per cent who have so foolishly allowed themselves to be submerged in the matrimonial bog ever have the face to lift up their heads and deny the suggestion?

On rare occasions it will happen that the "courted" young woman shows herself to be of a tough make and that she knows "how to play her cards properly." The phrase, though crude, is one in common use in Ireland in discussing such matters. She will succeed in "inveigling" the man into matrimony, and then, poor girl—could she but know it—her troubles are about to begin.

It were far better, she must often sigh, that she had let him "dilly and dally" and kept alive her hopes and illusions about a happy married state. Once he is "hooked," he will neglect her, returning to his men friends at the "pub," backing horses, and refusing to enter into any real companionship with this woman. Though she is his wife and the mother of his children, she is really a bit of a nuisance, too "demanding," and will "never let a chap be free."

In general, the Irishman hates marriage. He doesn't really like the company of women except inasmuch as they confer some luster on him. He doesn't mind taking a lovely creature out for an evening; he likes to chat with a witty conversationalist and bask in the adoration of a girl who subscribes to the theory of the super-Celtic male. Being reared in the tradition that in Ireland we have the best system of education, the most rational outlook on life, the finest schools, the finest morals, the best butter, bacon, eggs, cows, horses, and men (my eye wanders over the headlines of one of our brighter newspapers as I write), the Irishman feels himself to be not of the common herd but far above the ordinary laws which govern human beings in relation to friendship and love.

The Irishman also loathes responsibility and will evade it when possible. The notion of marriage and of the responsibilities which it entails is utterly repugnant to him. If the circumstances of his life force him into matrimony, he indulges in some form of escapism after recovering from his first panic. The favorite forms are drinking, gambling, politics, and sport. He is not a good husband or a good father, and the blame for the fact that the Irish are a vanishing race must be laid squarely and solely on his shoulders.

"How he got that way" is a story that needs to be told. One must look at the pattern of life as it is lived today in Ireland and scrutinize the influences which are brought to bear on young people. No matter how human and warmhearted the young women are, the young men slight and evade them.

This state of affairs is condoned, if not actually fostered, by the attitude of both parents and educationalists. Mothers would be happier to see all their sons and daughters become priests and nuns than to see any of them mix with their own kind and seek salvation in the world. How has this unnatural state of affairs come about, and how could it be remedied? Why do Irishmen, who are credited with having a gay and confident outlook on life, shrink from the responsibilities of marriage and ignore the first and most elemental of all duties, even where economic conditions make the establishment of a family a state to be enjoyed without anxiety? Why do they regard womanhood as a snare for manhood and not as a complement designed by God Himself?

How do Christian people, who do quite earnestly seek for spiritual guidance in their daily lives, deny by their actions that they believe that God's holy will should be done in all things or that they believe in the humanity of Jesus Christ? Why do they let a cold and materialistic outlook govern their actions and their dealings with one another until malice and frustration come to triumph over love and the fulfillment of a normal life?

As a matter of strict fact, normally sound people would not be so bitterly sex-conscious as we are now in Ireland. It is as bad and humiliating to be undersexed as to be oversexed. Surely sex is inherent in every human being living in a natural and unaffected way, and it is utterly wrong to seek to impose an education which tends to outlaw sex as an indecent and unworthy thing. *Yet that is the general tendency of education both in the home and in the school.*

It is, of course, neither today nor yesterday nor the last generation nor the generation before that nor the generation before that again that Irishmen were being rated for their coldness and disregard for women. So at least we must be fair and not pile all the blame for the fact that the race is at the vanishing point upon the shoulders of those few Irish who are extant today.

The Irishwoman has had to become the "dominant" female, a role which suits her ill and makes her quite frequently dislike herself heartily. It earns for her, too, the dislike of the man. If he would take his proper place in life and accept his share of responsibilities, he could be as dominant as he likes. Then we would give three cheers for his rehabilitation.

In marriage, if it occurs, the woman has to be the driving force, the seeker out of ways and means, the home finder. One knows that the worm turns, and so, from being the slighted and bullied one, she becomes the bully. Often denied the protection, affection, and tenderness of marital love, she placates herself with a strangle hold on her children, refusing to allow them to grow up and accept their share of responsibilities in case they may find that they too have legs and wish to move off.

Her girl children she disposes of, round the place, if she can. They are useful, anyway, even if only as an audience for her laments. But the boys—oh! that's another matter! She wraps them round and ties them up with so many bonds of maternal love that should they ever burst away for any reason they can do so only by wounding their adoring mother almost to death.

As a result of this overwhelming maternal devotion many a young man's outlook on life is warped when it comes to falling in love or making any of the preliminary ventures on the road to matrimony. He may well feel, and indeed he is very often told, that he is "well off enough where he is." He may feel too that it is one thing to be a pampered and petted slave to his mother but quite another thing to start off being a slave to some unknown entity who may want to be petted and pampered in her turn.

Admittedly it must be very hard for a young Irishman to grow up at all, seeing the way his life is regulated by his elders. If it is possible to keep him dependent financially, he is never encouraged to be anything else. He gets practically no freedom and is never allowed to shoulder the smallest amount of responsibility if his parents can prevent it.

If he shows any aptitude for study, he is pushed in for exams which land him in dead-end but secure, pensionable jobs like the Civil Service or the teaching profession. If he is a country lad, he is naturally glad to get away to the cities so that he may build up a private life for himself, free from eternal vigilance and comment.

Considering how hard he has had to struggle for a shred of privacy, it is not surprising that he will scarcely hurry to endanger the whole structure by taking a wife to his bosom. While he knows very little of such a creature, he has been taught to expect the worst.

It will be useful to consider some of the factors which have contributed to give parents such a determination to cling to their children, especially the male ones, and to instill into them a fear of accepting responsibility or of getting themselves involved emotionally with other people.

It is true perhaps that famine times and famine memories have left a bitter taste behind, bidding us be very cautious in all our dealings, scrape and spare and give nothing away. Perhaps our build-up of generosity, or *flaiteamlact,* has about as much foundation in fact as the Frenchman's respect and adoration for *l'amour* or the Italian's for *il corragio* and stems from the same lack and desire to assume a virtue if we have it not.

Famine, plague, coffin ships—who knows what part such national calamities play in shaping the outlook of a race? Might it not be that, as a race, we accept the fact that we are not as tough, psychologically speaking, as other peoples and do not find in ourselves the life urge sufficiently strong to warrant us passing it on?

Longevity is a characteristic of the Irish race. My father lived to be ninety-seven, and his father died at an age a little short of that. As a middle-aged woman, memories of things I was told by my father and grandfather, who came from Limerick County, where the Famine brought the plague in its wake, are still as fresh in my memory as a visit I paid to America three years ago, but not at all as pleasant.

As a young child, I remember my father and grandfather discussing a marriage. My father thought that the pair "ought to wait a few years."

My grandfather very heartily concurred. I was surprised at this, for they rarely agreed about anything.

"He's a great foolah," said my grandfather in Limerick parlance, "to go marrying a girl without means. If he saw what I saw and people dead by the side of the road with green round their mouths, he'd think twice about marrying at all, much less marrying with a girl of no means."

This word "means" often cropped up in the conversation when there was any discussion of marriage. "What means have they?" It was a long time before I had the grasp of what "means" really meant. But how a dead person, lying by the side of the road with a mouth stained green with grass, might look haunted me. It was for me a vivid picture and a terrible glimpse into a life shared by the older people.

Similarly there were the stories of the coffin ships and of how my father, *as a little boy* being put to bed in his home in Bank Place in Limerick, would hear the wailing and crying of the poor emigrants as they left their homes and country, most of them never to return.

Switching my mind back to the present, let me cite a typical case showing why there are such late and such few marriages in Ireland. I think of Mary Boylan as she comes walking home from the village this lovely autumn evening. At thirty-nine she has given up caring for what was at one time very real beauty. It is her birthday, and she is feeling "low." She has been visiting her sister's home, where things are not so good.

Now she is returning home, to her elderly parents, where the atmosphere at the moment is almost unbearable. Why? Because her only brother, still the "boy" in spite of his forty odd years, has his "eye on a girl" and his mother, good Christian lady that she is, "won't hear a word spoken of a marriage."

Poor Mary's ears are assailed all day with her mother's laments about the "ingratitude" of the "young ones."

"To think," says the mother, "of all the work and hardship I've put behind me in this place and the way I'm thwarted with each and every one of you.

"Wasn't it my dearest wish, Mary, that you'd enter [the convent] after your brother, poor Father John, laid his bones to rest for the Faith, away in foreign parts? But not you! Getting yourself 'named' indeed it is you are, and you with your decent family connections and your uncle, the Canon, worrying the life out of himself, the stories he's hearing about you and the way you've been talked about these years past.

"Oh, don't sigh, Mary, sure I hear plenty too, and is it like your sister above in the village you'd be, with your small children driving you crazy, wailing and crying, and your husband always at the dogs or the horses and you scarcely knowing where the next meal is to come from. Aren't you the foolish girl, Mary, scorning your good home and your ease and plenty and the knowledge that you'll have a tidy bit to come when your father and myself are laid to rest?

"And mind you, Mary, I warn you, don't be putting in on the side of your brother James. He was a good lad till that strap from Dublin laid her eyes on him, but I tell you, Mary, she'll never cross the threshold while I'm alive. . . ." And so on and on, harping forever on the same sordid unhappy theme.

"It's true," says Mary. "Mother did have a hard time and a hard fight to make the home, and Father never helped her—drinking and spending all. My sister is badly married, and her husband scarcely knows she's alive. It's the dogs and the horses for him. And maybe mother has the right of it! Maybe I'd be right to put all thoughts of Kevin out of my head, and maybe I'd enter yet if they'd have me at my age now, and if it weren't for him. Sure they'd be pleased and glad at me, at home, anyway, and that would surely be a change for the better!"

Mary is a lovely girl and a kindly girl, with a sense of humor that would charm you, when she is not brooding over her unhappy state. 'Tis true, she didn't "get the vocation," and maybe Kevin was to blame for that. She can't keep her mind away from him. And she is in no way surprised when he joins her, wheeling his bike along the path, ready to ride off at once if the parish priest or the curate looms along the sheltering bend of the road.

For fifteen years Mary and Kevin have met in this casual way. They have never made a rendezvous: that is the solemn truth. They are generally supposed to be "keeping company." Mary knows that she has been "named" with Kevin, though scarcely one intimate word has been spoken between them.

A despairing hope of arriving at some conclusion rises in Mary's bosom and encourages her to speak. "Kevin," she says timidly, "you know people are saying that we are getting on. That 'tis time we were married—the both of us!"

"Well, indeed now," says Kevin, shocked out of his silence, "and is that a fact. But, Mary, sure and who'd have us?"

Well, indeed. Who in Ireland would have either of them? Gentle domesticated souls, they might make a go of it: they would probably make a happy married pair if it weren't for their rearing and education, plus their own vacillating characters, plus the relentless hostility of their elders toward marriage in general.

What can the woman do but timidly suggest what seems to be the logical outcome of their continued association? What can he do but grope for a reason as to who should be married to whom? Or, more probably, why on earth should the problem of marriage arise at all?

Now *she* has spoiled *everything,* and they will meet no more as friends!

Poor Mary, she will feel herself disgraced and humiliated. So he didn't mean anything, didn't want her after all. If she has the courage to break her home ties and brave her mother's laments, she'll get off to England. And maybe . . . off to work and economic freedom, and freedom too from laments and taunts of ingratitude, and from sick loneliness bordering on despair. And maybe . . . !

But in case this sounds as if I was going on in a big way for Kiltartanese[1] or had lifted my characters and diction from the Abbey stage, let me say that I have more than once listened, sickened, at conversations and upbraidings and reflections, all in the same strain. All were concerned with the iniquity of persons whose minds turned to matrimony *even* while their parents were alive!

While having a holiday in a lovely small village in County Cork a few years ago, our stay had been made very pleasant by the cheerful service and bright smile of the maid in the tiny hotel.

Winnie was sweet. Smart, pert, capable, and very, very gay. We teased her about her passion for dancing. Off, every night she was free, to any dance within a long cycle ride of the hotel. But, mind you, back by eleven o'clock! Or her mother would "kick up the devil" and make Winnie's father put her out!

She giggled a lot. We asked if the road wasn't too dark to cycle so

---

[1] Editor's note: "Kiltartanese" is a synonym for speaking English with a Gaelic construction, using the autonomous "I do be" for "I am."

far? Didn't she have her boy to see her home? She got very serious indeed. That was no laughing matter! Indignantly she said, "I've no boy. I go with a girl friend. If I came home with a boy to see me along the road, I'd be 'named.' If I was named, I might as well leave the village. But I'll go to England, anyway, when I'm trained a bit. The boys there will take you out, I'm told. But then their mothers couldn't get after them. There's no life at all in this place, but it's better not to be 'named.'"

What dreadful consequences followed upon being "named" I did not ask. It was obviously a serious and painful business for Winnie, and to be avoided absolutely.

Marriage, indeed! How or where are the young people to meet when everyone seems bent on making them feel that, if they as much as glance at one another, they are doing something darkly wrong? No wonder a 15-mile ride along a cliff road unescorted and uncompanioned except for the sound of the Atlantic crashing on the rocks a few hundred feet below is less terrifying than the possibilities of being "named" for being the kind of girl who would let a boy see her home!

That's the country outlook. Look at what happens in the cities.

I have a friend who spoke to me quite freely from time to time about her sister. The girl was "wearing her heart out" more or less for a number of years. She had been keeping company with a young man of her own class, and it would be a suitable marriage, if it ever came off. They both had "notions." He had been "given" a profession—architecture; she was a teacher.

But their people frowned on marriage. His, because he would be entitled, having a profession, to "look for a girl with money." Hers, because she had really no "fortune," and they weren't going to have *his* family look down on theirs. Not that anyone really wanted a reason. Both families were determined to stop either of them getting married.

One day the young architect's partner decided to sell out his share in the business. The way to matrimony was clear if the partner left could scrape up enough money to buy the business. The girl had worked for years and had saved for just such an opening. Her money was enough to bridge the gap.

All the details were discussed between this cool pair in a very capable fashion. But on the night the final agreement was reached, the girl came home to her sister in a state bordering on hysteria.

"Well," said the sister, "I suppose everything is all right now?"

"I suppose it is," said the bride-to-be. "I suppose we *are* suited. I suppose we'll marry."

The sister was alarmed. "What do you mean," she said, "you 'suppose' it's 'all right.' You 'suppose' you are both suited to each other. You 'suppose' you'll marry. . . ."

The girl burst into tears. "I'm very fond of him," she said. "We've been going together for a long time. I thought he'd kiss me, put his arms about me, or something. But now I don't know. He didn't even call me darling! And I think he must be a cross between St. Joseph and a mouse!"

This somewhat unnatural situation was further complicated by the fact that, the idea of marriage having penetrated into the minds of both the families concerned, the sister of the architect, "at home in the country," avowed her intention of marrying a local "boy" with whom she had been keeping company for about sixteen years. The marriage would be, however, contingent upon the girl "bringing in a fortune" to the bridegroom's family. But since her brother had been "given a profession" with whatever money there was, there was no fortune forthcoming for the girl.

Consternation reigned! Imagine all these hotheaded youngsters (none of them less than thirty years of age and some of them over forty) conspiring together to get married. What were things coming to! Farm yields were discussed, passbooks examined, stock told and retold. Nothing could be done. No fortune could be forthcoming for the girl!

To save her long-postponed marriage, the teacher decided that she would pay the fortune of her sister-in-law-to-be by "keeping on her job" after marriage. She went to her school manager and told him her plight. He refused to keep a married teacher on his staff. As he was quite within his rights in so doing, the marriage failed to materialize after all!

Certainly marriage is not encouraged! Too often those few marriages which do take place have to wait until the "elders" of the courting pair have departed this life and left the persons free to marry without suffering a lot of harsh criticism or even breaking entirely with their parents. It is extraordinary, but the state of matrimony in Ireland is regarded with a certain mixture of scorn and dislike. The man is often spoken of as a "poor fool who has let himself be hooked." The woman is a "silly idiot who does not know what she has let herself in for."

If there is the rare person who marries young, "That one was wild, headstrong, ungovernable," or worse. If the parties are old, "There is no fool like an old fool" as far as the man is concerned. The woman "ought to have more sense . . . making a laughingstock of herself . . . at her age!"

Lamenting the decline of the marriage rate, it is the fashion to assign the cause to economic factors. No doubt there is some truth in the assertion that young people in country areas cannot marry because the young man has no place to bring the young woman. Supposing that the man's mother is willing to allow the girl to share the hearth—which is supposing a lot—the man can't marry until he gets his sisters out of the house and married in their turn. But his sisters can't marry for the reason that their young men cannot bring them into their homes until their sisters can be placed in somebody else's! So the vicious circle goes on and on.

Generally speaking, tuberculosis, the flight to the cities, the intervention of madness brought about by frustration thin out the contestants in this dreadful game, shortening the odds on the few who are left competing for the matrimonial stakes.

In fact, the greater portion of the young women have departed to England. There they find economic freedom and freedom to move about, meet men, and have the possibility of being asked in marriage.

Though the atmosphere is lightened and mothers no longer need fear that matrimony will bereave them of their sons, agricultural problems loom. "The government," say the elders, "must do *something* to keep the young people at home. More rural amenities must be provided, better roads for getting about, more building grants too." De Valera did have a whack at trying to get the elders to build houses on the farmsteads, into which they could move to enable the youngsters to get married and run the farms in their turn. But this idea of his did not cut much ice, in spite of the esteem and love which the people bear him.

If all this were done, it is suggested, people would marry, stay at home, and be economically sound and healthy: just one big happy family with children and grandchildren gathered round the patriarchal knee! No one believes for a moment in this kind of talk, but it serves to shift the blame, which is comforting. Not so comforting, however, is the result of a careful scrutiny as to what is and has been the attitude of the elders toward their children concerning matters of such urgency as the right to grow up, accept responsibility, marry, have children, and live ordinary normal lives.

To what extent have parents implanted in their children's minds a base and un-Christian idea of the iniquity of sex? To what extent have they exalted the idea of the celibate life, and how has this idea reacted upon the minds of young people?

The boarding-school system, which has contributed to a great extent toward relieving parents of the responsibility of rearing their children, has also contributed in no small measure to the idea of the segregation of the sexes. To keep youths disciplined, it is necessary to create bogies for them all during their scholastic lives. True to the ungenerous Celtic tradition, this bogy, more often than not, takes shape as a woman. Youths are led to believe that girls are nothing less than manifestations of Satan. Women are there to entice and destroy them. Should a youth as much as look at a girl, she will ruin his purpose and prevent him from getting exams.

Don't think I trifle. This is a very serious consideration with the young in a country where "book learning" and the pursuit of respectability, with a pensionable white-collar job attached, is still the fetish of a whole nation. The misguided young man, if he persists in frequenting the society of his sister human beings, may find himself further seduced. He may be "hooked" into matrimony: made to sweat and slave to maintain a wife and family, give up his "independence," leave his mother and comfortable home, sell his freedom-loving soul for a woman, a creature who in the Irish vernacular is but the image of Satan.

Given the sort of education which has tended from the beginning to create an illusion of voodoo where sex is concerned, no wonder the Irishman shuns marriage as he has been taught to shun the devil. All this may suggest an almost monastic state of chastity on the part of the menfolk. Regrettably, this is not the case. A 2.46 per cent illegitimate birth rate is not high in comparison with the rate in other countries, but one wonders if the figures can be regarded as reflecting the real situation. In Ireland illegitimate births are frequently concealed, and young unmarried mothers are usually hurried out of the country "with a 10 pound note and the parental injunction not to show their faces at home again."

We talk a lot about the Oedipus complex, the Jansenistic outlook, the ascetic monasticism of the Irish race—and get nowhere. Heaven knows what we really should discuss would be the institution of a saner approach to education, not as a means to "exam cramming," but as a means of preparing human beings for the art of living in a dehumanized and rather crazy world.

Instead of feeding the young with a badly assorted mess of raw materialism and predigested escapism, educationists might be persuaded to study the humanities a little and, seeing the urgency of the case, to encourage young people to mix with each other in a spirit of respect and affection. In the home there might be less moral chastisement from the elders for the faults which they imagine themselves to have committed for bringing youngsters into the world.

In general, there might be less drinking and more laughter, less bragging about our noble inheritance of culture from the dead kings of Erin and much—oh! so much—more concern for the happiness and well-being of the adolescents. Then they would know something of the wider and more gracious life of sharing, especially in such essential matters as good will and love and marriage.

WE'RE NOT DEAD YET

16

John D. Sheridan

John D. Sheridan was born in Glasgow in 1903, of Donegal parents, but grew up in Dublin. A former teacher and an M.A. of the National University of Ireland, he is the editor of the "Irish School Weekly," official organ of the Irish National Teachers' Organization.

He is best known in his own country as a humorous essayist, and it has been said about him that he writes "with the lean line of Swift." His work has a strong Catholic note, and he has been called the apologist of the little man.

His first volume of essays, "I Can't Help Laughing," published in 1944, has already run to seven printings, and he has followed it up with many others: "I Laugh to Think," "It Stance to Reason—the Intelligent Rabbit's Guide to Golf," "Half in Earnest," "My Hat Blew Off," and "The Right Time." All these collections have been best sellers in Ireland, and the two latest were also published in London.

Sheridan has also written four novels, including "Paradise Alley," which was published in Dublin by the Talbot Press and in America by Bruce, and "The Magnificent MacDarney," which was published in Ireland, England, and Holland, while an American edition was issued by Pellegrini and Cudahy. Among his other works are a "Life of James Clarence Mangan" and "Joe's No Saint," a volume of poetry. In addition he has written, compiled, and edited many school texts.

Sheridan is a foundation member of the National Film Institute of Ireland and has written the scripts for three government-sponsored documentaries. One of these, "W. B. Yeats—a Tribute," has been shown in Britain and in the United States and received a special award at the Venice Film Festival in 1950.

He has contributed poems, short stories, and essays to the "Sign,"
"Books on Trial," "Commonweal," "Capuchin Annual," and many
other journals, and his Saturday morning essays in the "Irish Inde-
pendent" are regarded as one of the best things in current Irish journal-
ism.

WHEN I WAS INVITED TO TAKE PART IN THIS SYMPOSIUM, TWO MEMORIES
came back to me—one a very old memory, the other not so old.

The first was about "poor Tom." The whole parish (it was a poor,
mountainy parish) was talking about him; and it was talking in the
past tense. He had been such a nice boy, such a good-looking boy; such
a mannerly boy. But Tom wasn't dead or in jail. He had simply got
married.

He married young—in his early twenties—and he married "into a
house." He hung up his hat in the place where his bride's mother,
brothers, and sisters were still living. And everyone said that he should
have waited until he had "a better way of marrying on him"—especially
the still-hopeful bachelor "boys" of forty and fifty, who crossed off poor
Tom as another good man gone wrong.

Poor Tom is close on fifty now, and he still hasn't much of a way on
him. So he would have been a long time waiting. But he hasn't starved,
and he has reared a family, and all in all he has had a lot more happiness
from life than the cautious bachelors who thumbed over their shoulders
at him thirty years ago.

The more recent memory concerns a search for a child that wasn't
there. Some years ago we spent a holiday on the Irish Atlantic seaboard, and we had things with us that hadn't been seen in the place for
quite a long time: we had children. We had children, and we wanted
holiday playmates for them. We would have settled for even one child,
but there wasn't even one. Nor any chance of one. For all the young
men and women were in Scotland or America, and there hadn't been
a marriage in the village since their parents went to the altar.

These two depressing memories fitted in so well with the gloomy
pictures of Ireland's survival prospects that when I turned them over
in my mind I felt like agreeing that our island will be a vacant lot in
less than a hundred years. But although we have the lowest marriage rate
and the highest marrying age in the world, I don't despair of the chances

of the Irish race and I see no reason for putting the crepe on the door.

Battalions of frightening statistics have been produced to prove that the Irish race is on the way out, but before we panic, it might be well to study some of the statements made by one of our best-known Irish statisticians, Dr. R. C. Geary, in a lecture which he delivered at University College, Dublin, in August, 1951. Here are some of Dr. Geary's conclusions, and they are based on the figures:

"Ireland has a normal birth rate and a normal death rate.

"The natural increase is substantial, but it is *skimmed off regularly by emigration.*

"Ireland's population has remained fairly steady at 4¼ millions for fifty years.[1]

"The total population has remained stable during a period when the marriage rate was the lowest in the world.

"Though a quarter of our population never marry our fertility rate is *one of the highest in the world.*

"The net reproduction rate gives no cause for alarm at its present level."

I know that figures, and names, and prophecies can be cited against Dr. Geary, and I am not enough of a demographer to take sides confidently in a battle of experts. But I feel that some commentators have paid too much attention to the calamitous decrease in population during the post-Famine years (which was due mainly to mass emigration and starvation—abnormal causes) and not enough attention to the fact that when normal conditions were operative (since 1926, for instance) the decrease was so small that the total population remained comparatively stable.

Nevertheless, a decrease, however small, remains a decrease. We may or may not be a disappearing race, but we are certainly acting as if we were content to disappear. One in four of our people never marry, and most of us, when we do marry, are nearer the tombstone than the cradle. We cannot therefore evade the responsibility of examining the factors that have helped to bring about this state of affairs and of thinking out means to improve it.

In fairness to ourselves, however, I must point out that this is a problem

[1] Editor's note: This figure is for the whole of Ireland—the Republic of Ireland and the six Ulster counties.

that has been by no means ignored here in Ireland. On the contrary, it has received and is still receiving the attention of our best brains.

But it is not a simple problem. It is complex and many-sided. It touches our political history, our economic conditions, the balance of population as between urban and rural districts, and our restlessness as a people. It has contacts even with our classrooms and our pulpits.

My contribution is not that of a statistician, a demographer, or a student of social conditions, but merely that of an Irishman who has lived among his own people for well over forty years. I may not be an expert, but I am at least an inmate. And the problem, after all, is not one of black, lifeless figures on white paper, but of a people, a place, a way of life. It is because I know the place, and love the people, and have shared the way of life, that I go willingly into the witness box.

I begin by saying that the main factor in Ireland's population decline is the economic one. There are many other factors, and some of them are very important, but this one shades over into nearly every one of them, and it reaches out into the long past that has influenced the present.

In order to discuss the effect of economic conditions on the marriage rate and marrying age it is necessary to consider certain well-defined regions separately:

1. The infertile western seaboard (much of Mayo, Donegal, and Connemare, and parts of Kerry).

2. The rich farmyards (parts of Cork, Limerick, and Tipperary, with Meath, Westmeath, and the river valleys).

3. The towns and the smaller cities.

4. Dublin, that topheavy, ever-growing city that now houses more than one-sixth of the total population of the twenty-six counties.

In the first of these regions, the highlands of the western coast, we have poor land, hungry fields, and pitifully small farms—so small that in many places 10 to 15 acres of cold soil is the average holding. It was to places like these and to farms like these, that the native Irish fled or were driven at the time of the Plantations. They managed to live there—God alone knows how—and to rear families. Big families often. But they were reared for the emigrant ship. The poor thatched cabins were nurseries for Glasgow and Boston, and their chief source of income was the letters brought by Johnny the Post.

There are few big families in the seaboard districts now, for people are not content to live, as their grandfathers lived, on stirabout and potatoes, and marriages are few and late. In the nineties, a few emigrated from every house so that they could send home as much as would buy flour and meal for the winter and pay the rent on gale day. Now almost everyone goes, and they go to escape economic misery. The boy who is left at home has to wait till his mother is in her dotage before he can bring in a woman of his own, and a sullen courtship may smolder on for a quarter of a century.

What can be done to improve conditions in these rural slums and give the Gael a chance to rear children at home? God knows. Government grants help (a bonus is paid to every Irish-speaking child of school-going age, for instance), and new rural industries (like the industrial alcohol factories at Corroy, in Mayo, and Labadish, in Donegal) have brought a little hope to some of the lonely places. But lonely they remain. The drain of human beings still goes on. The young folk leave home as soon as their shanks are fit for traveling, and the old folk sit by the turf fire and tell their beads. The Highlands of Ireland, like the Highlands of Scotland, are emptying into the cities.

Next we come to the rich farm lands. And the tragedy of the rich farm lands is that in general (for there are some exceptions like Wexford, and Carlow, and parts of Cork) they are not farmed. The plow has given place to the bullock so that one farmer with the help of his young children and a single hired man can tend the rolling acres that supported twenty families before the days of the Famine. Dairying is carried on in many places, but dairying, in comparison with mixed farming, gives little employment to human beings.

Moreover, since beef pays better than milk and butter, our dairying is on the decline. Our number of milch cows is going down, and instead of having surplus butter for export we have to call on Denmark and New Zealand to make up the deficit. This economic pattern tends to a small and shrinking population. One child inherits the farm, one goes for the Church, and the rest leave home with fiber suitcases to drive lorries in Liverpool or make munitions in Coventry.

Strangely enough, even the mixed-farming districts produce their annual quota of emigrants. Stranger still, emigration from these districts remained at a high level during the past six years—although prices for farm produce were higher than they had ever been in living memory and the farming community experienced a belated wave of prosperity.

The explanation would seem to be that emigration is a pull as well as a push. The presence of big Irish communities in certain parts of Britain and the United States seems to acts as a sort of human osmosis on the people at home. John goes and Paddy follows. Mary writes to her cousin, and Larry's uncle sends him his passage money.

This phenomenon is an offshoot of the economic factor. A necessity has hardened into a habit. In many parts of Ireland living conditions are better than they are in the big industrial cities. And we have our share of modern amenities: the bus stop, the cinema, and the electricity pylon are to be found in all but the most remote parts. But the exodus still goes on. When emigration becomes a tradition, and when it works with the force of a magnet, it is hard to break its grip.

It might be thought that, given good economic conditions, the natural attraction of the sexes would result in early marriages and that early marriages, in their turn, would act as a brake on emigration. But in districts where emigration is a tradition many of our young people grow up with the firm intention of leaving home as soon as opportunity offers and steel themselves unconsciously against the danger of making matches locally.

In the towns and smaller cities conditions from the marriage point of view are not so bleak as in the rural districts. But the marriage rate, though relatively good, is lower than it ought to be, and the marriage age is too high. The population is increasing, but the pace is very slow.

The trouble with the towns and small cities is that until very recently most of them were simply distributing centers—places where the surrounding rural population sold its produce and bought its shirts, boots, spades, and fertilizers. The towns produced nothing. They had no factories, no industries. Their prosperity was based on and limited by the prosperity of the surrounding countryside. So again the setup tended to a stable population. Twenty shopkeepers might have a hundred children between them, but the town hadn't the business for a hundred new shops.

But the outlook for the small towns is more hopeful than it was. Factories are springing up everywhere—boot factories, textile factories, small foundries—so that a boy who wants to marry has a chance of a job at home. If the economic factor were the only one involved, the small towns might yet prove our salvation, since the rural districts about them would share in their prosperity; but the pull of emigration is felt even in the towns, and the effects of the social and human factors which have affected our marriage rate, and about which I shall have something to say presently, are by no means confined to the fields.

So far as the reproduction rate is concerned, Dublin does not seem to fall into the general pattern; for Dublin is full of children, and its count of young heads prevents our statistics from being much worse than they are. But Dublin *is* part of the general pattern, and its rapid growth is a bad sign rather than a good one. It amounts to emigration at home, emigration without the emigrant ship.

Father Timothy Corcoran, S.J., who was the first professor of education at University College, Dublin, used to remind his students that Dublin's greatest growth took place during the years immediately after the Famine. And the present spurt of the city is of the same unhealthy character. Dublin is thriving at the expense of the rest of the country. There is plenty of room in the fields, but the people are flocking to the cities, and most of those who come to Dublin may be regarded as emigrants who didn't get as far as the quays.

Dublin is a congested district nowadays, and some of the congestion might be avoided. All our civil-service departments have their headquarters there, and there is no reason why some of them (the Department of Agriculture, for instance) should not be transferred to inland towns. The ratio between the population of Dublin and that of our other cities (it is seven times as big as Cork, our second city) is fantastic, and something could be done, and should be done, to reduce this unhealthy balance.

And even in Dublin the average marriage age is higher than it is in English and American cities. One reason for this is that Dublin has a very high cost of living. But there is another reason. The average Dubliner spends more lavishly than he should on drink and amusements, and thrift is not his strong point. Dublin is a fine city, a friendly city, a beautiful city, but it has a tradition of genial improvidence that derives from the days when it was an aristocratic city. A development of this point would be outside the scope of this chapter, but it is significant that Dublin has more cinemas than any other city of its size in the world and that each of them is filled on seven nights of the week.

As I have already said, my conviction is that Ireland's decline in population is due primarily to economic factors, but I do not believe that these factors work blindly, or inevitably, or of themselves. Man is shaped to some extent by his environment and by the material circumstances in which he lives, but he remains free to choose this rather than that. It is obvious then that in examining the reasons for Ireland's shrinking population we shall have to examine not only the Irish scene but the Irish character and divert some of our attention from the country to the people who live in it.

The late Aodh de Blacam wrote once of "the racial despair that filled our people during the horror years of the Famine." The phrase "racial despair," I suggest, is very significant. Despair of this kind is deeper and more lasting than any personal despair. It is passed on from generation to generation till it becomes a national heritage.

The despair of the Famine years and after was a conviction that the race could not survive. The race *did* survive, and the despair eased in time, but it has not completely disappeared even yet. It has left a stain of pessimism on the national character. For we are not, as is commonly supposed, a light-hearted people. We are a little bit afraid of life.

I do not want to overemphasize our pessimism. National self-respect is strengthening (and it must be remembered that we have been in business for ourselves for a bare thirty years), and the effects of our history are being steadily eradicated. But we are not quite over the shock of the Famine. The memory of it is still somewhere in the whorls of our minds. Without being conscious of it many Irish people are afraid to marry and have children without an assurance of material prosperity which more buoyant peoples do not require. For marriage is a vote of confidence in oneself and in the future. It calls for a sort of sublime foolishness, a reckless trust. In marriage there are no guarantees. You must take your chance. You must gamble on your health, your crops, your job. You must commit yourself to a leap in the dark. You must stake your all on the future.

Ireland's racial experience, I suggest, acts as a brake on this trust, this foolishness, this blind confidence. We tend to play for safety, to defer taking the plunge, to wait until things improve. So we marry late, or stay single, and put the blame on circumstance.

And, ironically enough, this timorousness, which has its roots in the past, tends to affect the present and the future. Men are often loath to take wives and beget children because they fear that they will not be able to provide for them properly, but one of the greatest factors in economic development is the need to provide for wife and children. A family is often a burden, but it is more often a spur. It gives a man something to work for. It compels him to look about him. The real pioneer is the young married man whose only wealth is human livestock: when the covered wagon rolled westward, the real driver was the infant at the breast.

It may then be doubly true to say that Ireland's marriage rate is closely connected with its material prosperity, for our scarcity of young married folk deprives us to a considerable extent of one of the greatest incentives to enterprise and economic progress. For myself I place this lack of confidence in the future very high in the list of human and social factors which have contributed to Ireland's poor showing in the marriage-statistics tables, and I think that in a Christian country like this our young people should have more trust in God and more faith in themselves. Our history may explain our timorousness, but it is high time that we rid ourselves of the dead hand of the past.

Another cause that has contributed to Ireland's poor showing in the marriage statistics is an exaggerated concern for that ancient and necessary institution known as the family; and once again it has its roots in our history. In the past, children had to emigrate or move to the cities as soon as they were fit to earn. Dire poverty drove them, and they went so that their younger brothers and sisters would have food in their stomachs and clothes on their backs.

But this tradition outlived the causes which made it necessary, and Irish children are still regarded as foreign investments. They leave home and bring their tethers with them. They are expected to be branches of the old firm. It is right that children should send money home, if they can afford it, and pay a little off an old debt, but it should not be a payment in perpetuity. There should be a limit to filial duty, but it is a sad fact that many of our young people who go to America, or England, or even to Dublin or Cork keep sending money to homes that have no real need of it and remain single all their lives as a result.

Respect for the family is a fine thing, but it can easily be stretched into injustice. Many Irish parents fail to realize that the rights of an existing family are limited by the rights of potential families and that children have a duty to themselves and to the future as well as to their parents and the past.

Another feature of Irish family life that makes for fewer and later marriages is the habit of keeping one of the girls at home to help in the running of the house. Her sisters become typists, or nurses, or teachers; they meet young men and marry in due course; but Cinderella stays at home. Not because she is less clever or less good-looking than her sisters, but because convention lays it down that somebody *must* stay at home.

She stays there until her parents die, and she inherits the house. Sometimes she marries the man who has grown old waiting for her, but more often she takes in lodgers and spends her leisure time knitting socks for her nephews and nieces.

Self-sacrifice of this kind is a high and noble thing—but on certain conditions. And the conditions are that it must be necessary and must be voluntary. But often it isn't necessary, and often it isn't voluntary—except in the sense that Cinderella doesn't fully realize her fate until her acquiescence is taken for granted and it is too late to make a move.

I am not suggesting now that aged parents should be left to fend for themselves. But I am suggesting that parents should think twice before they condemn a girl to spinsterhood. I think too that the job of staying at home and keeping house should not be imposed on any girl. If she accepts it of her own free will, well and good—again provided that the sacrifice is necessary. But the duty of looking after parents in their later years should not devolve on one girl of a family unless she accepts it willingly and with her eyes open. For the duty and the responsibility, in so far as there is a duty and responsibility, belong to the whole family and not to one member of it. This habit of tying a girl to the house is far too common in Ireland, and it has the sad effect of crossing one girl in every three or four from our list of potential wives and mothers. The country is full of spinsters who are little better than drudges and who are expected to dance attendance on their married brothers and sisters when they bring their children to visit the old homestead.

It has been suggested that the Irish regard for celibacy and respect for priests and nuns have led many of our people to consider courtship and physical love as shameful things and marriage as an inferior state. There may be something in this contention, but I think that it has been over-emphasized, for the God-given urge to mate and have children has not atrophied in us. I do agree, however, that many Irish parents keep far too strict an eye on their sons and daughters and that Irish courtships have often to be done by stealth.

This attitude, obviously, is not good either for morals or for marriages. It bottles up natural feelings, and it leads to a frame of mind in which the intention to marry is regarded as something to be confessed or admitted, rather than announced. But I think that this attitude on the part of some parents has no significant effect on the marriage rate. It may make courtship more difficult, but it does not keep young people from marrying.

To some extent, however, it may keep them from marrying young. One of our commonest parental admonitions is "You're time enough yet," and its meaning often is that a man should keep his thoughts from the women until his hair has started to go thin and that a girl should walk demurely until some well-doing man begins to show serious intentions. This attitude reduces marriage to mere expediency. Marrying for marrying's sake is a wildly unnatural thing. A young person should get married not because he (or she) has reached marrying age (whatever that may be) but because he wants more than any other thing on earth to marry some particular person.

I am not denying the dangers of early infatuation or of unsuitable early marriages. But I do think that when many Irish parents say, "You're time enough yet" they are thinking not of their children but of themselves and that their real intention often is to keep Mary at home for a few years yet to give a hand with the milking or to keep Paddy single until Johnny is priested.

Much has been said about the Irish mother's desire "to have a priest in the family." I think that too much has been said about it. For every Irish mother who wants a priest in the family puts a tail to the wish— she says, "If God wills it." But there have been cases where brothers and sisters have had to slave to provide a young cleric with clothes and holidays and pocket money and were expected to make no move toward marriage until after his ordination. This, when it happens, is a double injustice: it is not fair to the other members of the family, and it is certainly not good for the priest.

It has been suggested, too, that some Irish priests have thundered too

long and too violently against "company keeping" and that immoder-
ate denunciations from the pulpit have tended to turn this perfectly
respectable term for a perfectly legitimate activity into a euphemism for
something dark and hideous. And I fear that this mistaken zeal is by
no means uncommon. Sin is sin, and it must be condemned; and people
cannot sin in company unless they keep company; but we cannot keep
young people pure merely by trying to keep them apart.

The trouble about sermons of this kind is that they apply to the few
and unsettle the many. References to the "dark road" and the "lonely
place" may be justified and may sometimes be necessary, but if two
young people get the idea that they can never be alone together without
grave danger, they are getting a very wrong idea. If we are to have marriages, we *must* have company keeping, and the "lonely place" is not
stronger than the grace of God.

In many Irish parishes, unfortunately, the young people are left to
fend for themselves. There are no dances, no dramatic societies, no social
activities. In providing opportunities for young people to come together,
not just for an annual bun fight, but regularly, our priests could give a
lead. Many of them, thank God, do give such a lead, and the number of
parish-minded priests is increasing. But in many districts the old tradition of admonitions and awful warnings still persists, and young people
are expected to sit at home and watch their mothers knitting. And in
these districts, inevitably, the marriage rate is nothing to boast about.

One feature of our emigration figures is the high percentage of
women who emigrate; and many women emigrants go no farther than
England, where they find work as hospital wardmaids or domestic
servants. And yet, in Ireland, there is a shortage of wardmaids and domestic servants. Wages for this type of work are higher in England than
in Ireland, admittedly, but many of our young women leave the country not just to get better money but to have a better time and to get
away from a drab and joyless environment. This drain could be stemmed
to some extent if Irish rural life were brighter and if a determined effort
were made in every parish to provide amusements and amenities which
would give young people an opportunity of meeting and marrying.

Now that I have considered the reasons—economic, social, and historical—for Ireland's low marriage rate and high marrying age, it might
be well to say something about what is being done and what might be

done to remedy the situation and to give a prognosis. The condition of the patient has given rise to some alarm—is he going to live or die?

And first of all I must say that so far as things economic are concerned the matter is receiving attention. Many of our big ranches have been broken up into smaller holdings. Families from the western seaboard have been given farms in royal Meath, with free implements, free seeds, and special money grants to tide them over the transition period. More and more industries are being established, and many manufactured articles—wallpaper, cutlery, plastic goods, and aluminum ware, to mention but a few—which we used to buy from England are now being made at home. This industrial development is powered by water-generated electricity from the Shannon, the Erne, the Liffey, and the Lee and from four turf-fired stations. Electricity has reached most of our villages and many of our farms, and modern comforts are finding their way into rural homes. We can claim therefore that rural life is being brightened in more ways than one.

A state-financed maternity and hospitalization service is about to be introduced, under which free treatment and money grants will be available for working-class mothers; and children's allowances are paid to all parents irrespective of income.

One thing that we might do, and have not done, is to curb the unhealthy growth of Dublin and transfer some of our government departments and factories to the provincial towns. We cannot afford our unwieldy, top-heavy capital, and decentralization would be bound to help the country as a whole.

But the problem, in the last analysis, is one not of factories and people but of men and women. We must win free of the racial despair that came with the Famine. We must have more trust in God and in ourselves. We must look to the future and forget the past.

My own feeling is that all this is bound to come. For our pessimism was born of nine hundred years of political struggle and foreign domination, and our fear of hunger—which, though quite unconscious, makes some of us afraid to set off on the wild adventure of marriage without the guarantee of material prosperity—is due to the fact that for much of that time our people had to exist on the little that was left after the rent was paid.

We are an old nation but a young state, for it is a bare thirty years since we got rid of the foreigner and wrote our own name above the door; and thirty years is a short time where the habits and character of a people are concerned. But we have made headway during those thirty years, and the end is not yet. In one sense we are barely beginning.

One mistake which we must guard against is the complacent belief that improving economic conditions will of themselves, and inevitably, change our character and habits for the better and that more prosperity must necessarily make for more marriages; for a wrong attitude may remain after the factors which explain it or excuse it have disappeared. The Department of Agriculture and the Department of Industry and Commerce may bring us better crops and higher dividends; the Department of Social Welfare may pay our doctors' bills; but no civil-service planning or land-rehabilitation schemes will give us more or earlier marriages unless we change our way of thinking, and change it now.

Our priests could help by remembering when they are in the pulpit that a marriage is more than a deed of partnership, that love-making is the usual preliminary to it, and that company keeping has its place in the scheme of things. Young people must be warned, of course, and sin must be condemned, but we have had a spate of warnings and condemnations and not nearly enough in the way of positive steps to see that young people should have opportunities of coming together and that the God-given attraction between the sexes should result in a crop of early marriages.

Our parents could help by not expecting their children to make contributions in perpetuity to the family exchequer, unless in cases of dire necessity. And they should not sacrifice one daughter to the "house" or the "family" unless it is understood that she is free to marry like any of the others. Many of them, too, might have more confidence in God and in goodness and not behave as if a courting son or daughter were necessarily courting disaster. Parents should expect their children to marry, and to marry in reasonable time, and should condition their minds to this very natural and desirable possibility. Some Irish mothers accept the death of a husband with more resignation than they do the marriage of one of their children and realize too late that their own selfishness has left a daughter on the shelf for good.

And what of our young people themselves, our potential fathers and mothers? They too might have more courage, might fight harder against this "racial despair" that is the legacy of the Famine. Marriage is a serious business, and it should not be entered into lightly, but every marriage is based on "Here goes in God's name." So many factors are involved that there can be no guarantee of success or even of material prosperity. Indeed it is much like saving your soul—you do your best and take every precaution, but you can never be absolutely sure in advance. Every marriage is a gamble, and the stakes are very high, but the courage to take the gamble is part of the process of growing up to the size that God meant us to be, and undue prudence is a want of confidence, not only in ourselves, but in Him.

One final point. A wise old priest I used to know years ago was fond of saying facetiously, "Next to the grace of God there's nothing like the hard cash." I do think that we might have more marriages, and earlier marriages if we were a more thrifty people. For we aren't thrifty. We spend too much on amusements, and we spend too much on drink. We are no longer a drunken people, but too many of our young men regard an hour in a public house as the only civilized way of bringing each day to an end. The result is that the period of courtship is unduly prolonged and marriage has to wait on the price of the wedding—and this is a state of affairs for which we cannot put the blame on the Famine.

Most of the social and human factors responsible for our poor marriage statistics might be summed up in the word "selfishness": the selfishness of parents who do not want to let their children live their own lives; the selfishness of young people who put too much value on comforts and amusements; the selfishness of young men who spend too much on drink; and that deeper selfishness which makes a person sink into himself and shrink from the responsibility of bringing children into the world. If we set ourselves to correct these faults and replace selfishness by trust and generosity and courage, we would improve not only our marriage statistics but also our national character. We would be not only more numerous but more prosperous and there would be a blessing on all our undertakings.

I end, as I began, on a note of optimism. We have reached the lowest level, and I am confident that the upward climb will soon begin. We were until very recently a subject people, and now we are free. We are not affected to any appreciable degree by that vice of artificial birth-prevention that has stained almost every country but our own. We are slowly but surely building up an economic structure that must in time arrest the flow of emigration.

Other people, I know, have taken a gloomier view and have suggested the need for immediate remedies for a desperate situation. I am willing to endorse the remedies, but I do not think that the situation is as desperate as all that. And I will have no hand in sending out invitations to the funeral, for God is good, and we aren't dead yet.

OUR BLOCK

17 ———————————————————————————

Miriam Rooney

Miriam Loughran Rooney was born in 1897 in New York and spent her childhood in Massachusetts. She studied at Trinity College, Washington, D.C., and took her Ph.D. degree at the Catholic University of America. Since her marriage to Middle Westerner John F. Rooney she has made her home in Chicago, where she has kept busy, raising a family of five children and teaching child psychology at Mundelein College.

"Teaching," she writes, "filled in whatever chinks there were in a busy day and the two jobs complemented each other; child psychology in theory and in practice. The five children range in age from 10 years to 25 years. The twenty-three- and the twenty-five-year-old are married and have three children each. That makes six to offset the score of the Vanishing Irish.

"Seventeen-year-old Maura, the only girl, is at St. Mary's College, Notre Dame, and Sean, fifteen, is at Quigley, studying for the priesthood. Miceal, ten, is the only one left to keep me abreast of the new developments in child psychology. May their Gaelic names, of which they are proud, always remind them to do their share in keeping alive the culture of Ireland."

In addition to raising her good-sized family and teaching, Miriam Rooney takes an active part in cultural affairs and has written two books, "Concomitants of Amentia" and "Historical Development of Child Labor Legislation in the United States."

OUR BLOCK. IT'S A GOOD OLD IRISH NEIGHBORHOOD AND A GRAND JESUIT parish. But it's slowly giving way to the more prolific races. There are the McDonoughs. You know the McDonoughs that lived at 2411? I saw Sarah the other day. She's a lonely soul. She looks as though she were seeing ghosts all the time. I guess she lives with ghosts all the time. She was telling me about her family—all gone now. She, an old maid of seventy, is the last of the line.

"Oh, what a grand time we used to have when we were young. There were eight of us—eight kids. Mother was cooking and baking for us all the time. She was a wonderful mother. Now she's gone and it's lonely. Except for me, she saw all her children die before her. You knew Tom the best, didn't you? But you didn't know Mary. They were the cards. Mary was so full of life, there was no holding her down.

"The boys all liked Mary, but Mother didn't think any of them was good enough for her. Well, one night she ran away—out to Hollywood, no less. It broke Mother's heart. The next we heard she'd been married and divorced. Picked up with some no good hanger-on who already had a wife. What happened to her? She died. But Mother wouldn't let any of us go to her. When you transgress the law of God, you're punished. Mother was tough as steel. Right was right, and wrong was wrong, and there was no condoning it.

"But Tom was the one who broke my heart. I loved him so. He was so good-looking, and he loved life. And he loved little Karen Andersen across the street. She was a platinum blonde, the real thing. Mother used to say, 'Don't bring any of those dirty Swedes into my house. Why don't you find yourself a good Irish girl?' And Tom would say, 'I can make her Irish by marrying her, and I can make her a good Catholic, too.'

"Sure enough, they used to go to Mass every morning, hand in hand if no one was looking. One day Mother got on her high horse and forbade Tom seeing her again. And he didn't. When Mother cracked the whip, we obeyed. Karen? Oh, she married that guy across the street— some said he was a bookie. I don't know what he was except that he was no good. He used to beat her up. The carryings-on were awful. Poor Tom!

"Tom went off to the Jesuits. Mother always wanted a son in the Jesuits. Of course he didn't stay. He came back. I guess when you knew him he had taken to the bottle. First the drink, and then T.B. Between them they got him. Poor Mother, Tom was a terrible disappointment to her. I guess we all were. We all turned into a morose bunch of sour-pusses."

"Didn't any of you ever marry?"

"No—only Mary. I told you about her hooking up with a man already married—in California. After that, none of us dared bring a man into the house. No man was good enough for her girls. No girl was good enough for her boys. We all died off. There's hardly a month without a death anniversary in it. Mother was a great old warrior. Things weren't easy for her. My father was an easygoing, gentle soul who never made much money. But she had great plans for us all. Well, that's the way it goes."

Did you hear about poor Mrs. Callaghan? The children all used to call her Aunt Mary—yes, and her husband was Uncle Mike. They loved the children so. They never had any of their own. He started out a bricklayer when he first came from Ireland. He turned into a wealthy contractor. But somewhere along the line they lost everything they had. Aunt Mary has been getting very frail in body and mind. Things were getting rather bad—worse than we knew. Last week he took her to the Psychopathic and had her committed. Of course it broke his heart. And Heaven only knows what it is doing to her. I saw him. I asked him, "Haven't you any relatives, Uncle Mike? Haven't you any children anywhere?"

"No, no children. We never had any children."

"And you loved children so."

"I know. It's hard to talk about. Mary was so young when I married her. I thought she'd come round sooner or later to accept what marriage meant. But she never did. Put it down to this. I was an omadhaun, and she was an ignoramus."

What was he trying to tell me? Married fifty-three years and the marriage never consummated!

"Have you any brothers or sisters, Uncle Mike?"

"Oh, yes, but none of them ever married. Mother lived until she was one hundred and one, and she kept her family around her. But one of my sisters is coming to help me out now in my trouble. She was a teacher. She's retired now. She's a grand girl."

His old eyes shone with pride.

"And let me tell you, the man that gets her will get a treasure!"

Uncle Mike was very outspoken for an Irishman of his generation. Certain things just were never mentioned.

A little bride who lived next door to us was eagerly awaiting the first visit of her mother-in-law. Mrs. Dolan, Sr., arrived. She was a small, wiry woman of strong character. She was given a room papered with woolly lambs and A B C blocks.

Her new and terribly happy young daughter-in-law explained, "We just had to have a nursery. Jack and I can hardly wait until we have it filled."

The mother-in-law's shocked reply was "You dirty thing!" It is hard even to write the words. It is hard to comprehend the mind that spoke them.

I remember an old Irish neighbor saying to me one day, "I blush when I go to Mass and see that brazen young couple, the Moriaritys, going up to the communion rail every morning—and they with a new child every year!" The nonchalance of a pregnant mother waddling happily into church every morning called forth the bitter invective "The hussy!"

When the bride of a few months starts telling the world her exciting news, there is widespread disapproval among certain good old Irish. The boldness of it! But isn't the thrill of it like nothing else? Doesn't such world-rocking news yearn to be shouted from the housetops? Didn't Mary herself hurry to her cousin Elizabeth because she couldn't wait to share her wonderful news?

Loretta lives across the way. She's married to a "black Protestant." He's a wonderful lad. Loretta, for a Catholic, is not quite what she should be. Of course, she's always the life of the party. She has a collection of off-color jokes. They're not very funny. Neither is she. She's sad. She has no children, and she'd make a wonderful mother. She's a regular Pied Piper to the children on our block.

A lot of us have wondered about her and sensed a tragedy somewhere. I think I found it. One evening when Loretta was being particularly noisy and crude, I said to Jack, "I like you, Jack. You're so good." "Good," he repeated bitterly, "of course I'm good. I'm St. Joseph, or didn't you know?"

I suppose Loretta's Irish mother failed her as so many Irish mothers fail their children. I know of few who have had the courage and patience and wisdom to build in their children right attitudes toward sex. If sex means nothing but wrongdoing, impurity, transgression, perversion, it is hard to see in it the work of God instead of the devil. A confusion results which sometimes is not straightened out in a lifetime.

Two excellent movements have arisen in this country to counteract the tragedy of ignorance—Cana and the Christopher records. How would the Christopher records be welcomed in Ireland? How would Cana Conferences be received? I don't know. But it's a thought.

Sister Una is at the convent. Whenever I stop by, she gives me a good cup of tea. We talk about Ireland.

"Sure and it's a wonderful place. No, I can't say I do get lonesome for it. I was lucky to get away. We all want to come out to America. Some of us get as far as England. Some of the lucky ones get to America. My poor sister, the one that stayed with my mother—there's always one that has to stay with the mother—she died last year. My mother's still living. No, my sister never married. She would have if my mother had died first. She couldn't leave the old lady."

"But she did leave her."

"Yes, God took her."

"But why didn't she marry? Then your mother would still have an interest in this life."

"Why would she marry?"

"Well, why not?"

"I'll tell you why not. Marriage means a lot of children, and a lot of hunger, and a lot of work. There's no food to feed them. There's no vacuum cleaners and washing machines. There's not even any water except what we went down to the well to get and carried home in a bucket. Sure when they're young and in love marriage looks all right, but when they get older they count the cost."

All these things—the strange attitudes toward marriage, sex, purity, toward God and procreation; the good old mother who thought that certain things should never be talked about; the matriarch who kept her family infantile, who thought that no one was good enough for a son or a daughter of hers—all these things add up to one startling result. They all add up to this: the blossoms withering on the stalk; the family tree dying; the race slowly but inevitably vanishing. I hadn't thought of it in these terms. I had thought of it only as individual tragedy, on our street. But one street is so like another.

This summer, I was on the Irish Mail traveling third class from London to Dublin via Holyhead, the Irish Sea, and Dun Laoghaire. Such a mass of scarlet-cheeked, curly-headed children! They were all over the place—the Tobys and Michaels and Davids and Desmonds and Jims. For a moment I thought, "Vanishing Irish?" They were vanishing all right, behind coils of rope and under stairways. But thank Heaven they are very much alive and fine custodians of the spirit of Ireland. With them the race will live.

I sat happily on a coil of rope, sharing it with the mother of Toby. She was young and pretty but almost toothless. There was sorrow in her eyes. Her husband was tall, thin, gaunt, morose. Some worry oppressed them both.

"Do you live in Ireland?"

"We used to."

"You're going back?"

"Just for a visit. It's the first time we've been back since we left to get married. My mother's never seen the children. We hope they'll soften her heart. She's old. I want her to see my children."

That was all. I thought of the lively Toby and his brothers and sisters and parents several times. I hoped all went well with them on their visit back to the homeland. I thought of them especially one night when I took a mystery trip on a bus from Dublin—out along the Bray road to St. Kevin's country. The bus guide might have come out of Hollywood, he was so typical. He'd point to a little thatched cottage and say, "There's quite a story about that little cottage. A boy lived there and he went out to America, and when he came home on a visit, this is what he said."

At that he would burst into song, and all on the bus would chime in. It was a glee club on wheels. Such fun! The Irish seem to fall into song at the drop of a hat. Of all ways to make a stranger feel at home and at one with the world, this is it—all singing together. A priest sat beside me. His rich baritone filled the chorus. When we stopped at a little inn nestled in the hills, we drank a pot of tea together and talked.

"Father, is it true, all this talk of the vanishing Irish?"

"Indeed it is true, and more's the pity."

"But why? They love life so much. Why should they vanish?"

"There are several reasons. There's nothing to keep the young folks home. Sure there's an awful lot of scenery, but the young people want jobs. Those that stay at home don't get married very young, if at all. And all young things like to get married. The Irish mother likes to keep her children around her. She doesn't want to lose them. Then there's the matter of the dowry. No self-respecting Irish girl will get married without it."

"How much does she need?"

"Oh, she should bring about a thousand dollars into her new home. Otherwise she feels that she enters it as a servant and not as an equal. It's pretty hard to accumulate a thousand dollars, leastwise while you're young. So the marriage age is deferred until late in Ireland, that is, generally speaking."

"But don't the young people rebel? Doesn't the impetuous, hot blood of youth make them struggle against tyrannical mothers and tyrannical traditions?"

"Oh, I don't know as they think of it like that. It's the way things have always been. There are some who rebel and fight for their freedom to marry and live lives of their own, but they go over to England. They're not the ones who stay at home."

Once more I thought of Toby's mother sitting beside me on a coil of rope.

"Let me tell you a story." Father was speaking again. "I was a chaplain during the war. A young lad whom I knew in the war asked me to dinner the other night to meet his mother and father. He was a fine strapping lad of twenty-seven. His parents were sixtyish, I should say. Before dinner the lad said to me, 'Father, I'm in love. An Irish girl right here in Dublin. Speak to my mother for me, will you Father? She's dead set against it.'

"Well, I did speak to his mother—a fine outspoken woman she was. But she was sure dead set against the marriage. Says she, 'But the girl hasn't a cent of dowry. How would she feel going into a man's house and bringing nothing with her? If she's the right sort, she wouldn't want it either. Anyway, my son is only twenty-seven. He has another ten years before he should be thinking of getting married.' And all the future world of Irishmen, waiting to be born by the hand of God working through the love of men and women—all doomed to nonexistence by words like these."

Why should there be a future world of Irishmen? How tragic if there weren't! Nowhere can you find such simple love of God and such child-like open expression of that love. On a Dublin bus that wanders down from Phoenix Park along the banks of the Liffey, one passes three churches. Three times Our Lord in the Most Blessed Sacrament is adored joyously and openly. It is not a secretive nod of the head or a swift tip of the cap.

The conductor as well as every man in the bus holds his hat devoutly and slowly and reverently makes the sign of the cross. The women, too, all bow their heads and make the sign of the cross almost in unison. To us with our secret ejaculations and our rosaries hidden in our pockets, this open profession of faith is like a crashing chord, a waterfall, some-thing refreshing, beautiful, tremendous. The open profession of faith and the easy way they burst into song! Love of God and love of beauty go hand in hand in Ireland.

Then there's their love of a laugh. There's wit and fun in the most ordinary of conversations. On a very crowded train going from Dublin to Limerick, a thin little conductor was trying to squeeze through the mob. As we tried to make one space serve for the two of us, he said,

"Oh, what a terrible job for a bit of a man like me!"

"If you were any larger, you'd never make it," I replied pleasantly.

"Sure that's the truth, but I hope I'm wearing my right side out."

"Oh, you must be. I like the side I see."

"Well, there's never any sense in showing your seams."

By that time he had squeezed past and was spraying his smile over the next crowded compartment. Love of God, love of beauty, love of people, love of laughter, all go hand in hand in Ireland.

Isn't there humor in the signs I saw in food-shop windows in Dublin? "Let us send a box of food to your hungry friends in England." There's truth in it, too. On both sides of the Irish Sea I heard that the English come over for a good meal at the Gresham. But it hurts when the Irish lads and lasses fill the factories of England and the retired English colonels and their ladies fill the castles and lovely country homes of Ire-land.

The things that are Irish must stay Irish. The Irish have things to give the world that no other people ever can or ever will give. You will always have French gaiety, German constancy, and Italian love of beauty. But where will you find all these things together, and the love of God surmounting all?

If Ireland is to live, it must not become an old folks' home, a place for retired colonels and their ladies. It must be a young folks' paradise, where they can do more than sing of love, where they can fall in love and marry, find jobs, and work for their wives, their children, and their homes. Their love and reverence for God and His creation must be strong enough to carry over to His plan for procreation.

GETTING ON THE HIGH ROAD AGAIN

18

Bryan MacMahon

When "The Lion Tamer," a collection of twenty-two short stories, appeared in 1949, Bryan MacMahon became well known almost overnight to readers in the United States. It was an immediate success and placed the author in the front ranks of Ireland's gifted younger writers.

The inspiration for these charming stories came chiefly from the country around his native town of Listowel, County Kerry, where he was born on September 29, 1909. "Our house," he reports, "was actually on the market place and the horse fairs were held outside our door so that I could not avoid feeling the fresh impact of the countryside. I did my best to pick up the speech modes of the farmers and when I set them down on paper I found they were really beautiful."

By profession MacMahon is a teacher in the National Schools at Listowel. He is also a collector for the Irish Folklore Commission, taking down the folk tales just as they are told to him. In 1936 he married Kathleen Ryan, and they now have five children. With his wife he ran a bookshop in Listowel from 1939 to 1948.

In 1945 he received the Bell award for the best short story of the year with "The Good Dead in the Green Hills." His three-act tragedy "The Bugle in the Blood" was produced in 1949 by the Abbey Theatre. His first novel, "Children of the Rainbow," appeared in 1952 and was widely acclaimed on both sides of the Atlantic.

MacMahon is sensitive to the color in the Irish life around him—in tinkers, ballad singers, custom, sky, bog, fair, and market place—and *the color and speech patterns of the locality are reflected in his writings. At the forge and at the saddler's shop he catches the proper thrust and parry of words and the delightful art of oblique reference. Many of his stories and plays are broadcast over Radio Eireann and the BBC, and his feature "I Was Born in a Market Place" attracted wide attention. MacMahon and his family reside in Listowel, Ireland.*

I DETEST STATISTICS. I BELIEVE THAT FIGURES CAN BE PRESSED INTO PROVING OR disproving any given theory. Accordingly in examining this vexed question of the too few, too late marriages in Ireland, I deliberately avoid figures and choose to draw my conclusions from the life about me.

Everywhere in the Irish countryside I see middle-aged men who have never married. Chaffed about it, they offer you the bitter tag of "feeding another man's daughter." Meanwhile schools are being amalgamated or closed altogether, and soon we shall have an Ireland without the hallooing of children or the laughter of women at peace. Our humorous magazines and very many of our plays poke fun at this state of affairs. To me the resultant laughter has the queer sound of laughter in a wake room: in this case the corpse on the board is Ireland.

The matchmaking system, which has had coals of fire heaped upon its head, resembled a complicated game of patience with young nubile people as cards in the matchmaker's hands. The appearance of a key card should ensure a series of swift moves. ("Mary's waitin' to get her money; the fortune comin' in with her brother's wife will carry her into Connor's of Castleacre. That'll let the Connor girl into the Glebe farm in Ballymehan." And so on. . . .)

It is possible to follow a fortune the round of a parish and find it unbroken at the end of the mating season of Shrove. But, cumbersome and exhausting as this system was, with its incursions into "clear title," it *did* provide a solution of sorts. The most regrettable feature of its decay is that there is no other system left to take its place.

(The old shawled woman sitting beside me in the motorcar has fallen silent. Her gaze is riveted on a thatched farmhouse far down the valley. We are alone in the vehicle. Suddenly the old woman breaks silence. "Many the sleepless bitter night that farmhouse cost me," she says. "When I was twenty-one, I got an account of a match from the man of that farm. The good ground I loved, but I could never warm to the man. Night after night I used to walk to this turn of the road and stand here looking down at the lamp lighting far below. At last I rejected him. To this day I can't pass this place without reliving some of the trouble I went through long ago.")

Why, it may be asked, has the matchmaking system fallen into decay? Some observers have it that Romance, as we now understand it, was an artificial emotion brought into being by the troubadours and minnesingers of mid-Europe. (Our great love stories come down to us from pagan times.) Owing to the fact that we live on the periphery of Europe, this popular conception of love, because of the time lag involved, has but latterly reached our shores.

On its arrival in Ireland it waged semisuccessful war on our own traditional system, causing our young people to revolt against the old mating ways. Horror of matchmaking crystallized in anecdote: a man lighting a match in a dark boreen to discover which of three girls he had been matched with; a lame sister being substituted for an unblemished sister at the altar rails on the wedding morn.

Thus it was that the young Irish found themselves poised between two worlds. Magazines, popular songs, plays of an outmoded English vintage, the talk of returning emigrants—all these poured scorn upon the old ways of finding a life partner. Thus, semiashamed of matchmaking, and complete neophytes in this new art of love, the Irish sit glowering in their chimney corners. Their confusion they conceal beneath the saws of a bitter wisdom. A more facile solution is to sit in a public house, where, by the law of tradition, there is small danger of feminine company.

But this is but one in a series of causes contributing, large and small, to national decay. The petty tyranny of parents, the taciturn relations obtaining between father and son, the disproportionate influence of the mother on the children—these are factors which also demand examination.

While the ties binding mother and son are strong, the relations between father and son in the Irish countryside are exceedingly tenuous. Father and son appear to have little to say to one another. There are exceptions, I concede, but the rule still holds. The eldest—sometimes it is the youngest—son remains at home in the hope of eventually gaining possession of the farm. The father, on his part, is resolved to hold fast to authority until the last possible moment. Taciturnity is the logical outcome of this tug of war.

With age, the father grows more tyrannical; jealousy of being superseded gnaws at him constantly. He is at the mercy of hereditary forces derived from centuries of struggle for the land and dependency on a landlord's whim. When at last the son marries, it is a sad commentary upon the Irish interpretation of the fourth commandment that the privileges of the old pair have to be hammered out in the inner room of a solicitor's office before even a jittery peace can be established in a country homestead. Even then, as often as not, the old man's motives for yielding are dominated by the idea of his receiving the old-age pension.

Where the son is valiant enough to marry without the land being handed over, the breakfast table deteriorates into a series of wrangles as to farming procedure. The old fellow holds fast to his point of view, and the womenfolk keep pleading with the son to yield for the sake of peace. When the latter of the old pair passes away, the son is found to be devoid of initiative and as often as not turns out to be an exact replica of the old farmer who preceded him.

In his time, De Valera has made statements of varying degrees of wisdom. Two statements of his appear to me to be wisdom itself. The first was that in Ireland there should be brewed a light popular beer to supplant to some extent stronger and weaker beverages; the other was that at the gateway of each Irish farm there should be erected a cottage or dower house wherein the old farmer and his wife could live after having given up possession of the farm to their son. These sensible suggestions were greeted as a source of fun by a host of professional jesters.

Emigration continues to be an open wound through which the brilliant arterial blood of Ireland is constantly leaking. No well-wisher of our country can remain unmoved on reading paragraphs such as the following:

KERRYMAN, September 17th, 1952.

"GLENBEIGH AND GLENCAR NOTES.

"Many of our young people here who signed on with the British Sugar Beet Corporation have been called up and batches of them can be seen leaving the Railway stations every day for the past week. Many of these young boys, who are leaving home for the first time, may never return."

KERRYMAN, October 4th, 1952.

"GLENBEIGH AND GLENCAR NOTES.

"Addressing the congregation at Mass on Sunday last, The Very Reverend D. Griffin deplored the big flow of emigration from the parish. Something, he said, would have to be done immediately to find employment for those who through domestic circumstances had to remain at home. With this objective he proposed to hold a public meeting in the Hall at 8 o'clock on Friday night."

(It is interesting to learn, from subsequent Notes, that Father Griffin's efforts seem to have met with some success.)

Emigration! The word is on every lip. It's in the balladry of heartbreak. Our solution? When anything goes awry in Ireland, a government ponderously establishes a commission, and by the time this commission has issued its report, the fluid situation has considerably altered. The tragedy lies in the great chasm between "What are we going to say?" and "What are we going to do?" To my mind, the man who builds a ball alley, runs a rural drama group, or canvasses for the extension of electricity to his rural area is doing more than all the commissions in creation.

Two alert farmers' sons, from adjoining farms, had the habit of knocking at the door of my bookshop every Sunday afternoon so as to pick up a few westerns I had parceled since the previous day. In our town there are two cinemas: on Sundays during the winter these two young men first went to the afternoon matinee at one cinema, then had a modest tea in an "eating house" down the town, afterward proceeding to the evening house at the second cinema. I became very friendly with these young men.

One afternoon they surprised me by saying they were going away the following morning to take up work on a government scheme on a bog in the Midlands. I asked them if they hadn't a good time at home. One told me the story which held good for both. This young man drew two horseloads of turf a day to the nearest railway station, thus earning for his father £3 per day during the postwar years. This went on for six days of the week during the turf season. On Saturday nights the father grumbled as he gave the son 2s. 6d. or 3s. pocket money: this amount of money enabled him to go to the pictures on Sunday and have a few cups of tea. In deadly earnest each of the young men assured me that to each of their fathers the cost of production of a rail of turf was something like 5d. or 6d.

They complained that they were little better than slaves. They were off to the Midlands, they said, where they would be several pounds a week richer for doing less arduous work than they were doing at home. They intended buying bicycles on the installment plan and touring the Central Plain on week ends. A year later, at an All-Ireland Final in Dublin, I happened to meet them. They professed themselves delighted with the change. They also said that the success of their initial adventure had made them resolve to cross to England. The last I heard of them was that they were working in a British foundry.

Last Sunday at church, just as the priest was about to come to the altar, a girl, faultlessly dressed, minced up the passageway seeking a place, her young, well-dressed husband close behind her. With a start I recognized her. She was a maid who had left our town for England some years before, being then gawkish and shy. To all intents she was now a lady! As she passed the pews, the young girls of our town became brilliantly alert. The incident was a sermon without words.

True, there always has been emigration from Ireland; latterly, however, this emigration has taken on a new and less desirable aspect. An Irish speaker from West Kerry put the difference pithily when he said, "America! that was a *noble* emigration!" Over the years the Irish have beaten out their own pathways in America: the result is that today an Irish immigrant to the United States feels about him the pulse beat of home.

The pattern of Irish life in the shoddy towns of industrial England has yet to reveal itself; it seems rather a pity that the rural Irish did not emigrate to rural England. In this English emigration, as in any emigration, there are three stages. First, the unhappy-in-England stage. Second, on the return on holiday to Ireland, the vague-disappointment-with-Ireland stage. The final return to England as often as not marks the beginning of disillusion heralding the abandonment of hope for happiness in either country. In this last lies the tragedy.

What of the mother influence on the children? "Get out of the puddle!" This is the commonest cry of the Irish mother to her sons and daughters. Girls growing up see their mothers living in what they conceive to be slavery. There is the footing of turf, the boiling for farm

animals, the drawing of water. The Irish farmer seems mortally afraid
to take his wife to a place of amusement—a trait far more marked on
the western seaboard than in the Midlands—for the sole reason that he
dreads the censure of his neighbours. ("Mark my words, he won't last
long at that gait of go!")

The only occasion on which the farmer's wife may with impunity
visit the village hall is on the occasion of the showing of a "holy" picture.
The hard-working Irish farmer is prudence itself, but the error is that
the prudence is often carried to an undesirable extremity. He will keep
on saving money for the rainy day, but when that rainy day is upon
him, he will protest, "This is certainly not the day I had in mind!"

Receiving £98 for beasts at a fair, he will ask a friendly shopkeeper
for the loan of £2 so as to bank the round £100. And while the farmer
is prudently setting aside money for the purpose of driving a harsh bar-
gain for his daughters in the matrimonial market, those same daughters,
watching the maid strut up the church, are secretly counseling themselves to "get out of the puddle"!

"Ah!" confides the old woman of the house to a crony when discussing the arrival of a new daughter-in-law on her kitchen floor, "isn't it a
dreadful thing to think of a strange woman puttin' her hand into your
tay canister?" This comment indicates more than the jealousy of the
mother for the son's wife, which is a common factor in human behavior
everywhere. Irish history and the traditional poor reception for the
supplanter are also implicit in that comment. "Another person to be in
the place where you are accustomed to be; that is the keenest pain that
can be suffered in the world." So speaks one of Padraig Pearse's characters in one of his stories.

Nor is the Irish countryside devoid of social strata. The conception
of starting from scratch is reserved for the American adventure. A young
married couple starting in life with nothing but love and health is
reckoned a slur upon both the families concerned. Let a farmer's son
marry a dowerless laborer's daughter, no matter how gay or handsome
or hard-working that girl may be, and straightway sufficient money is
given them to pack the young pair off to Oregon or Arizona. Strange to
say, the boy and girl appear to take their sentence with calm philosophy. It is an inherited pattern of their life.

This snobbery of Irish country life is more marked in the Midlands, where a large unmated family clings to the land like a surfeit of lampreys. Secondary education, the traditional means of escape leading to the vocations and professions, they ignore as valueless. Horse racing is their sole diversion. About a well-endowed marriage of one of their members they preen inordinately.

" 'Tisn't for lyin' in bed in the mornin' we married you!" runs the complaint of the spokesman of three middle-aged brothers to the bride-of-a-week whom, they had decided, one should take unto himself for the common domestic weal. A joke this, but the kernel of truth remains.

"Don't marry for money, but marry where money is!" is the never-ending advice of the Irish mother to her son. The idea that a good wife without money is better than an indifferent wife with money would appear to be entirely foreign to the nature of the Irish rural parent.

The pity of it is that it is the farmer's stubborn son who broods over the ashes of his dying fire. Patrick Kavanagh has portrayed one of these in his poem "The Great Hunger." It is a harsh indictment since the subject called out for harshness. The prolific Dubliner, mating at mating time, ensures that the population of the capital is constantly on the increase, and thus is perpetuated the curse of a top-heavy nation, city-thinking and city-acting. What of the time when the country is no more? When no rude flower of folk art will come up out of the cow dung, blossom in an art form, and wilt and die in the city alleys? What then?

Implicit in the marriage contract is a merging of self, a partial surrender of certain rights, a pooling, a denial, and a bond. In other words —in one light, and that the wrong one—it is a limitation upon freedom. No country has for so long cleaved to the abstract idea of freedom as has Ireland. And here again the devilish overcompensatory factor enters, giving too much force to this abstract conception of freedom. Marry and we're tied, we say to ourselves in our secret hearts.

With this terrible problem confronting it (there can be no creed if there are no people), what has the Catholic Church in Ireland to say?

Jansen gave his name to a heresy. Yet he was not himself a heretic but rather lived and died in the bosom of his Church. Associated with the heresy of Jansenism were the principles of an exaggerated moral and disciplinary rigorism under the pretext of a return to the primitive Church. The Celtic spirit, despite or rather because of its essential volatility (the higher the ball bounces, the farther will it fall) would appear to me to provide an ideal field for the culture of Jansenism.

The penances of the early Celtic monks were severity itself. Mount the crag above Christ's Saddle on Skelligs Rock off the Kerry coast, and there, poised 750 feet above the sea, consider to what limit of penitential exercises our forefathers were prepared to go. Today, when the idea of physical penance would appear to be repugnant to the entire world, such laudable manifestations of physical denial as the exercises of Lough Derg and Croagh Patrick are beacons amid the darkness.

But the danger is that by a flaw in the Celtic nature we are apt to be led by overcompensation into penitential excesses; then it is that the traits of Jansenism are there to fill lacunae in our nature. Significant in this context is the presence of four refugee doctors of the Sorbonne on the staff of Maynooth College in its early and formative years. The teachings of the Rev. J. Delorth, Andrew Darré, Louis Delahogue, and Francis Anglade cannot but have in some measure colored, even as a grain of permanganate of potash colors a glass of clear water, the whole course of Irish seminary life and consequently the whole body of Irish lay thought.

In the Ireland of today the conception of sin is everywhere, even from the earliest years. Send a child of four years of age or so to an Irish school, and on his return on the very first day he will begin to cry out, "That's a sin!" This from the mouths of children running free in God's sunlight! Up to the current year each schoolgoing child of the diocese in which I teach has had to memorize questions and answers of a long-outmoded catechism which must have caused millions of Irish boys and girls to see the God of starfish and dawn light as the surly tapster of Omar Khayyám. From this catechism for twenty-two years I have taught Irish children "to pray for kings and for all who are in high station" even though the last king of Ireland has been dead for almost a thousand years. The sonorous and thunderous was explained in turn by the sonorous and thunderous: "Explicit belief is a belief accompanied by a definite distinct knowledge of the particular truth in which a person believes. . . ." Open at random a page in *Catechism Notes*, designed to *explain* the catechism, and one chances as early as page 4 on passages so abstruse that I once successfully defied a clever lawyer to reduce them to simple terms.

True, in many dioceses the old catechism has latterly been replaced, and the change, long overdue, is undoubtedly for the better. However, reading Question 256, page 62, of the *New Catechism*, "What are the chief dangers to chastity?" and its answer, "The chief dangers to chastity are: idleness, intemperance, bad companions, improper dances, immodest dress, company keeping and indecent conversation, books, plays and pictures," one is tempted to ask whether company keeping as such, without the use of a pejorative qualifying adjective, can be reckoned a danger to chastity. It can scarcely be argued that the word "immodest" qualifies "company keeping" as well as it does "dress"; else the adjective "indecent" would surely be redundant. The bracketing, by commas, of the terms "company-keeping" and "indecent conversation" could also possibly convey to a child's mind that all books, all plays, and all pictures are among the chief dangers to chastity. The term "company-keeping" itself is probably the source of the trouble: it is one of those compound words in the coining of which we Irish excel ("flag-walloping," "pratie-snapping," "cabin-hunting" are other examples of the same genus), and unfortunately it would appear to have different shades of meaning even as between parish and parish. Would it be proper to ask whether a term such as this—for it may well be the jewel upon which a million Irish courtships may swing—should be clarified so as to make a clear distinction between laudable and reprehensible courtship, and possibly the whole question recast so as to obviate the danger of error by misinterpretation?

For generations denied a catechism pervaded by the loveliness of God wherein euphony and accuracy united to form a picture of indelible beauty in an immature mind, we Irish have always been over-conscious of the thundercloud of sin above our heads. And since our priests are sprung from among us, their virtues and faults (which are ours, too) appear larger under the glass of holy orders. Time and again in my youth I have heard it thundered from country pulpits, "It is a mortal sin to be in a lonely place with a girl." Possessed of a heckling mind, I have often been tempted to rise in my pew and say aloud, "Excuse me, Father: it is *not* a mortal sin to be in a lonely place with a girl." Looking back twenty or thirty years, it would appear to me now as if the whole artillery of our Irish church had been brought to bear on that mysterious subversive force—the "company keepers." If from any pulpit there had been slight reference to company keeping of a laudable nature—as of course there must have been—my adolescent mind did not adequately register it. Never can I recall there being placed before me the possibility of connubial happiness, the essential incompleteness of single man, or the essential incompleteness of single woman.

Twenty or thirty years ago—that was the time when open-air dancing at the crossroads was in full swing. I do not say that these dances were entirely without blemish, but they were as near to being so as blemished human nature will ever allow. One does not raze a house to the ground if a window is broken; yet this system of dancing was smashed largely as a result of a campaign by the clergy. Wooden roadside platforms were set on fire by curates: surer still, the priests drove their motorcars backward and forward over the timber platforms; concertinas were sent flying into hill streams, and those who played music at dances were branded as outcasts.

How clearly I recall a band of laughing boys and girls on a fine Sunday afternoon dancing "sets" on the floor of a ball alley by the sea. Suddenly the cry of "The priest!" is heard. The dancers scatter in terror; the lame fiddler bobs brokenly after the others. Even at that time to my young mind the incident didn't make sense. I thought it would be more fitting if the priest sat on a chair at the edge of the platform and smiled at the dancers, the while he paired them off in his shrewd mind.

I recall with sorrow now, but with what then seemed to me to be the refinement of humor, the spectacle of a fat man jammed in the end window of a boathouse whence an afternoon dance had scattered in alarm: there fixed forever in my memory is that fat man poised for the blow from the sacerdotal umbrella. I once saw a parish priest at dusk wearing a postman's cap so as to steal up on company keepers. The most colorful pattern in the Western world—canoe racing, running, jumping, swimming—was smashed by a pastor's edict.

When later a more enlightened priest endeavored to revise this day of days in the parish and asked the older people to reorganize it, he was met with the hollow complaint, "Aye, Father, but can you take the curse off the sea?" A sad reply this since, despite everything, there is implicit in it the inalienable loyalty of our people to the priesthood. I can name a town where for a considerable number of years the pastor placed a complete ban upon dancing of every description; the result was that the young folk skulked out of their own parish after nightfall and sought dances farther and farther away from home and supervision.

What was the result? When the open-air dancing was abandoned, men of independent minds, many of them returned exiles, appreciating that the meeting of boys and girls will go on as long as the world lasts, raised up tin sheds glorified by the name of dance halls. This they did in many cases in defiance of the pastor's orders. In these "halls" young folk danced until the small hours.

Before long the state stepped in to demand that these places conform to certain regulations: one of the first casualties of regulation was the dance in the kitchens of the country houses, where a small charge was made to cover the expenses of the musicians. These kitchen dances were in the nature of family gatherings: everyone was known, and there was an innate traditional supervision. The surviving platforms then came under government fire. If at the present moment a man sets up an open-air dancing platform in the form of a few boards at a race meeting or patteran and charges a few pence to the young people to dance on those boards, he must first apply to the court for a license and near the platform must be displayed a legend reading "LICENSED UNDER ACT OF OIREACHTAS FOR PUBLIC DANCING."

It seems true to say that this emphasis on the sins of the flesh, thundered out at mission after mission, has rendered the Irish people among the most chaste in the world. But again as the result of the fatal Celtic trait of overcompensation, this chastity has projected itself beyond what is right and in many instances has ended by warping virtue into vice. Many a young Irish bride has suffered mental agonies in being unable to make the mental adjustments necessitated by the marriage state.

And curiously enough, it may be noted here, very many factors, earthen though they may be, leading toward marriage among Irish countryfolk, would appear to me to be of pagan origin. Superficial consideration of this fact presents the unthinking with the wrong idea that the Church has no reply whatsoever to the question of the beautiful but complex relations obtaining between man and woman.

Laudable company keeping—what form does it take? I have asked my friends who are priests. They reply, "First let the boy or girl bring the proposed partner into the home!" To my lay eyes this step toward a solution appears naïve: in Ireland such a step would be reckoned tantamount to a formal engagement. An Irish girl is slow to "get her name up" on what may prove to be a passing whim and thus impair her further prospects of marriage.

If the girl is desirable in every particular except that of dowry, it is almost certain that she will be insulted out of hand by one or the other of the parents on her first appearance in the boy's home. Also, the manifestations of love are so acutely personal that they are hard put to blossom in the presence of a third party, least of all in the presence of dowry-conditioned parents. That solution might hold good in other countries: it is very doubtful that it would work in Ireland.

Despite the fact that mothers occasionally pay lip service to the desirability of the married state, at every opportunity they din into their sons' and daughters' ears that there is no life to equal the priestly or conventual one. Confiding in one another, mothers say, "Have a son a priest an' be shortenin' your time in Purgatory!" or "Arrah, put your daughter in a convent, woman, an' have her away out of all the troubles o' this bitter world!" The end is glorious, but the motive would appear to be imperfect.

In the Irish countryside the clerical student is the young god. A play like *Maurice Harte* brings home to us the frightening result of pushing a young man beyond God's calling of him. If a girl goes to a resident boarding school, the nuns, being human and having the idea of the perpetuation of their community close to their hearts, will place the conventual life before her in its most attractive form.

And here it is fitting to note that, by an ironic twist of fate, one of the loveliest books possible on conventual life (and a selection of the Catholic Book Club of America to boot), *Land of Spices* by Kate O'Brien, was banned by the Irish censors. I have been a bookseller and am not unacquainted with the subtleties of pornography, nor am I one of those who demand that there should be no censorship of books whatsoever; yet the banning of this beautiful novel filled me with a sense of dismay that the subsequent "unbanning" did nothing to dispel.

This condition of affairs regarding marriages in Ireland is seen to be doubly tragic when it is realized that Irish girls make excellent wives. They are "content with little and happy with more." They are loyal, home-loving, and as a general rule not careerists. An Englishman recently confessed to me that he had come to Ireland to seek an Irish wife.

Lowering his voice, he said, "My work takes me away from home for weeks on end. While I'm away, my Irish wife will be faithful. Couldn't trust the others—see?" I saw. It was a wry but honest tribute. Nor is the average Irishman, once he has taken the initial step, anything but the most loyal of husbands. But, a factor often forgotten, one person's revolt against inertia is not sufficient; he or she must find and love a partner of the opposite sex also willing to revolt. In other words, the penny of chance must be tossed twice and must win twice before a single marriage is made.

Diagnosis over, let us attempt to write the prescription which we hope will lead to recovery.

One night in Sweden (the Swedes are vanishing, too, but from different causes) I accompanied two girls to a café in the hills. Explanations as to the object of our journey were forthcoming, but since I was not fully conversant with the language, I did not then quite grasp what was going on. On reaching the café we went straight to a table where already were seated two young men and a young woman. The young men stood up and clicked their heels, and introductions were made all round. We sat down to a meal which was followed by dancing.

After the dance there was a conversation in which all seemed vitally interested. Then, after further bowing and heel clicking, we parted. On the road home I gathered what it was all about. In Sweden there exists an organization which arranges holiday contacts between young men and women of vouched-for good character. In a modified form this might be acceptable in Ireland. It is not a very desperate remedy for what is admittedly a desperate evil.

There seems little doubt that the soil of Ireland is grossly underproductive. We should be able to feed 8 million people without difficulty. To my mind, the two most important agricultural factors, both needing fanatical agricultural organizers to shout aloud at every crossroads in the land, are drainage and soil analysis. Drainage must be undertaken on the basis of each river basin since it is not sufficient to remove water from one man's land and transfer it to his neighbor's. And each single drop of water must be capable of being traced from the point where it touches the ground until it reaches the sea.

I once went for an airplane ride over the countryside surrounding my native town. Below me among the brown boggy acres I spied a farm as green as emerald. It puzzled me how this could be. Later I made inquiries and found that in Famine days the starving people from all over the area had been gathered into an old workhouse on this farm. Their time was occupied in draining and manuring the land. One hundred years later the good fields bear the impress of their work.

I would be less than candid if I stated that successive governments have been blind to these questions: at the moment of writing, the catchment area in which I live is in the throes of a gigantic drainage scheme. Yet, somehow, one has the sad feeling that thirty valuable years of national endeavor have been lost and that this and similar dramatic gestures should have been made long before now and on the basis of the nation as a whole.

Last summer I spent my holidays in West Kerry—in a Gaelic-speaking area, allegedly a government "white-headed boy." The flanks of the south-facing hills were covered with purple loosestrife, brilliant above other water-loving plants. The whole place seemed sadly in need of drainage. And strange to say, at the present time when the land of Ireland cries out for workers and when almost every operation of farming is buttressed with public moneys, vast sums are also being paid out in unemployment relief. To me this does not make sense. A farmer needs workmen: workmen need work. These two parties should be brought together under some scheme whereby the farmer would have his land drained and the worker would receive a wage adequate to support himself, his wife, and his family in Christian dignity.

Any young agricultural inspector—almost all these young men have degrees in agriculture and are sprung from farming stock themselves—will give you examples of the traditional reluctance of the Irish farmer to adopt new methods. Soil analysis is reckoned a pipe dream; lime will be taken, if it is spread on the field.

Recently an inspector told me that he informed a certain farmer that the soil of his land was deficient in lime. Rather unwillingly one load of lime was accepted and scattered on a corner of a beet field: the yield in that corner was astonishingly high compared with the yield in the area outside it. Only then did the farmer believe. Not all the farmers are like this: there are some small few whose splendid homes and rich fields constitute outriders for the Ireland of our dreams.

Two admirable organizations, mainly rural in outlook, Macra na

Feirme and Muintir na Tire, hold promise of great things to come. Both advocate scientific advance in agriculture and in particular welcome rural electrification, which, as is obvious, decreases the drudgery of farm life. If you are of the opinion that, in Ireland, rural electrification needs small advocacy you are mistaken. I know one thickly populated rural area which, about fifteen years ago, was offered, and refused electricity: to the present day a few lively spirits in that area are still canvassing for sufficient consumers to tempt the Electricity Supply Board to renew the previous offer.

When I asked an old countrywoman how she liked the electricity which had just been installed in her thatched farmhouse, she said, "Ach! the cost of it spoils the taste of it!" After I had proved on paper that the cost of the electricity was in fact less than her previous expenditure on paraffin, the old lady stumped off muttering something about paying a hatful of money *together.* On this question of rural electrification the only mental grumble I have is that I do wish that it were possible to place transformers out of sight of the main roads in our lovely countryside and so prove that progress and beauty are not incompatible.

Still seeking a remedy and now touching upon the aspects that have to do directly with our religion, the time has come to state a brutal truth. It is this: the priest who has lost the faculty of effort and who no longer considers Ireland a mission country is an extremely misguided man. The priest—he is the last to realize it himself—moves in a peculiar dimension, for he is "of" and "not of." The tone of an ordinary conversation is often tempered by the "collar"; the moment a priest's back is turned, discussion can take on new tones.

In this field of low marriages in Ireland there is room for a lifetime of delightful work for each young apostolic-minded priest, more fruitful a millionfold than competence at poker or the lowering of a golf handicap. The priest who has the tendency to rest upon parochial sycophants or coteries is a drag upon Irish Catholic effort. But the priest who walks on his own shoe leather from door to door in his parish, being a common factor of every praiseworthy activity, reckoning each man and woman he meets a creation of individual beauty, discovering and appraising for himself, will find himself welcomed as a king in the Irish small town and countryside.

Wherever people, and especially young people, forgather, the priest should be there, endeavoring to feel as they feel, being a dun thread running through the bright fabric of their lives. Respect for the priest in Ireland is too real and too good to find itself threatened by the arrogant or the subterranean-minded, by the muddle-headed or the indolent. Priest and people must be one.

The pastor whose rural school appears on the medical officer of health's black list, without making a genuine effort to see that the children of his parish are educated in hygienic surroundings, is railing to the enemies of his Church scrap iron which may one day be returned to him or to his successors in Christ in the form of shot and shell. The school children may not see it now but, later in life, having traveled, will realize with bitterness that they were denied congenial surroundings during the most formative years of their lives.

Other factors, varying in degree of importance, are worthy of consideration. It is regrettable that the powerful Gaelic Athletic Association, numerically the largest amateur sporting organization in the world, should be almost exclusively male. The social side of this organization could be considerably extended so that boys and girls could mingle in congenial surroundings at Victory dinners, *ceilidhthe,* or Reunions. Also, one of the brightest phases in rural Ireland at the moment is the fact that almost every village in the land can boast of a dramatic society. The number of marriages I personally have known because of contacts made through drama is astonishing.

I do not advocate that drama societies should be reckoned as marriage bureaus, but at least this indicates that sharing of aesthetic interest may lead to friendship and finally to love and marriage. Factors having to do with the fostering of the native, such as the revival of the Gaelic language, the traditional dances, and the ballad, in addition to strengthening national fiber, lead also to a realization of the pity of pities it would be if the Irish people were to vanish from the face of the earth.

But above all the Faith must be harnessed to the task, since in Ireland Faith conditions our every single activity, both swim and journey, both meal and raking of the fire—all begun and ended in the name of God. But the present is not the time for smothering flaws in an otherwise admirable Christian society. In the Ireland of today the most damnable fallacy is the negative one of taking the Faith for granted. It is a most congenial fallacy since adherence to it requires no further effort save only an occasional routine condemnation.

It is almost equaled by another misapprehension, namely, that the Catholic Church is a house made of glass and that the faintest bugle blast of well-intentioned criticism will send it breaking into smithereens. The expression of a hard, even what on occasion may seem a harsh, faculty of Catholic criticism is a prime necessity. It will force us to appreciate that we are dealing with a disease which has glazed the very many prismatic colors of the Irish character. But it cannot be overstressed that the realization of our full danger is the prime step toward setting the feet of our people on the high road once again.

THE ROAD AHEAD

19

John A. O'Brien

THE TESTIMONY OF THE WITNESSES IS COMPLETED, AND THE CASE NOW RESTS with the readers. Every witness has done his best to ferret out the causes of population decline in Ireland and among her children abroad, and especially to solve the strange enigma of a race that believes passionately in family life and yet produces more old bachelors and old maids than any race in the civilized world. It will be helpful to summarize briefly the testimony of these highly qualified witnesses as to the causes of these disturbing conditions and the methods of remedying the situation. We shall add a few concluding observations of our own.

First as to the facts. There is unanimous agreement as to the tragically few marriages and the pathetically late ages at which they occur. In both these items Eire has the worst record in the civilized world. On the brighter side is the fact that the Irishwomen who do marry have a higher than average birth rate so that, if all emigration were stopped, Eire would register some increase in its population.

This, however, it has never achieved for any decade during the past hundred years, for emigration drains 10,000 to 20,000 of its youth each year. The first census in more than a century that did not report a decline was for the half decade ending 1951, when the microscopic gain of 0.02 was registered. But, as Archbishop Walsh points out, the question may be raised as to whether or not even that tiny gain may not be traceable to a larger than usual number of foreigners flocking into Ireland.

Even if Eire is unable to stem emigration and it continues in about the same degree as in recent years, a very substantial growth of the population could be achieved if the men and women married in the same proportions and at the same ages as in other countries. Hence it is an oversimplification of the problem and false to say, as some of the apologists for the present situation do, that emigration is the sole cause of Eire's declining population. Emigration is one of the causes, and an important one, of a century of unbroken population decline. But it must not be allowed out of a sense of false pride or for any other reason to obscure the other equally great and even more disturbing cause: the scarcity and the lateness of marriages.

This strange phenomenon should be dragged out into the open, and upon it should be focused the spotlight of public discussion, intensive study, and constructive action. Emigration, after all, merely transfers a group of young men and women from one country to another. They have being and life at least, and they can make their contribution to civilization and human welfare wherever their lot is cast.

The failure of twice as many people in Eire as in any other country to marry deprives even of life and existence thousands of boys and girls who would be born each year if marriages occurred in about the same proportion and at the same ages as in other countries. It is therefore a much greater evil than emigration.

It not only deprives thousands of life itself, but it also condemns hundreds of thousands to frustrated, abnormal, empty lives—fighting all their days the driving urges and the hungers which God and nature have put into their very being and made articulate in their nervous systems as well as in their hearts. Perhaps the most pathetic aspect of the whole tragic situation is that the women of Ireland, who crave wifehood and motherhood as much as, if not more than, the women of other races, are pulled willy-nilly into a spinsterhood not of their choosing. Is it any wonder that after enduring their plight for decades they are now fleeing from the island of bachelors so that Eire now has one of the lowest proportions of women to men of any country in the world?

Moreover this wholesale practice of celibacy has repercussions of a disturbing nature far beyond the Emerald Isle. It seems to have become so embedded in the Irish character as to become a racial trait affecting the habits of the Irish in other lands. How else can one account for the disproportionate number of old bachelors and old maids among the Irish in the United States, Canada, England, Australia, New Zealand, and every other land where they have settled? They did not acquire that trait in those lands, for it does not exist among other racial groups in any of them. They brought it with them like a strange hemophilia that threatens them with extinction.

What is its origin? To this problem, the root of the whole difficulty, we have devoted much thought and study. Unfortunately little, if anything, has been written upon the subject. Only in recent years have investigators into the causes of Irish decline come face to face with the disturbing realization that there is a pathological trait, a psychic trauma, in the Irish ethos which lies back of the abnormal proclivity toward wholesale celibacy.

We have considered a hypothesis. The years of the Famine—when more than a million people died, when members of a family saw father and mother, brothers and sisters starving day by day, eating grass in a futile effort to stave off death—seared the Irish soul with a horrible memory. It started them in terror on that wild, frenzied flight from the island which reached the proportion of tidal waves in the forties and fifties of the last century and which has continued in a lesser degree to the present time. Are there still stirring in that racial memory the subdued echoes of horror at seeing loved ones die and a resulting hesitance to enter into a relationship which might expose others to a similar fate or at least to grave insecurity? It is an interesting speculation which arose in our mind, and several of the contributors, we were interested in noting, have likewise speculated along these lines.

Personally, we think the hypothesis is, however, more fanciful than true. We have made repeated inquiries among Irishmen and -women in Eire and in America to ascertain whether or not they were even remotely conscious of any such influence. All rejected the hypothesis completely. True, the pull and tug upon them might conceivably lie in the subconscious and thus escape their detection. But we doubt the possibility of transmitting through inheritance such psychic shocks, traumas, and inhibitions. Otherwise we would come into the world riddled with phobias and scared stiff with all the accumulated fears and terrors experienced by our ancestors through uncounted centuries. Fortunately for us none of these experiences work their way into the germ plasm, and each of us starts with a clean slate.

We shall do better, we think, if we stick to the known facts. The Famine and its horror are facts. During the years following the Famine, with the continued scarcity of food, wholesale evictions from homes, and the hard conditions of life under an alien rule, the number of marriages declined sharply. That decline continued for decades. Even after living conditions improved, Irish farmers gained title to their land, and the country finally achieved independence in the form of the Irish Free State, great numbers of Irishmen and -women continued to pass up marriage.

It would seem that over the years the practice of celibacy by large numbers became a part of their social customs, their traditions, and their way of life. Few factors are more powerful in regularizing an irregularity and in normalizing an abnormality than custom. Polygamy, formerly practiced among the Mormons in this country, is a capital illustration of this.

Recall, too, how such ridiculous and irrational practices as dueling as a method of settling disputes and the ordeal by fire to determine guilt or innocence became woven into the social mores of nations. How astonishing it is to reflect that the use of the ordeal, common among primitive peoples, became woven into the customs of the people of Europe and persisted as part of the judicial procedure as late as the thirteenth century and sporadically much later. No matter how irrational and abnormal the practice, once it becomes woven into the customs of a people it achieves normalcy and respectability.

So it is with the practice of bachelorhood and spinsterhood among the Irish. Started during the years following the Famine, continued for many years, it gradually became an integral and accepted part of the way of life of the Irish, a custom deeply entrenched in their traditions and outlook, clothed now with respectability and stirring no questions or suspicion concerning its initial irregularity and inherent abnormality.

The great historian Herodotus, writing in the fifth century B.C., tells of some Greeks who came upon a family of primitive people eating the body of their father, who had just died. When they expressed horror at the sight, the natives asked, "What do you do with the bodies of your relatives?"

"We bury them in the ground," replied the Greeks.

"How horrible!" exclaimed the shocked natives.

"Thus custom," comments Herodotus, "is the lord of all."

Another factor tending to deepen and extend the wholesale practice of celibacy in Ireland is the enormous reverence for the priesthood and the religious life which obtains among the Irish. It is without parallel anywhere on earth and produces far more vocations than in any other nation. Nearly every family aspires to have either a priest or a nun among its members, and preferably both. With veneration of the religious life comes unwittingly but inevitably veneration for the celibate state, with which the religious life in the Catholic West is always associated.

Add to this the fact that priests, brothers, and sisters are most numerous in Ireland and touch the life of the people at almost every turn. They teach in the schools, operate the hospitals and charitable institutions, minister in the churches, and are conspicuously present in the life of the individual from the cradle to the grave. Naturally they stress the ideals of the religious life, reflect the viewpoint of the religious concerning the dangers of contact with those of the other sex, and etch upon the consciousness of their pupils their own outlook on life and their own distinctive scale of values, incentives, cautions, and taboos. Unconsciously the young grow up with an outlook on life not substantially different from that of their celibate spiritual teachers, guides, and counselors.

Thus is the ideal of celibacy inextricably interwoven into the pattern of their emotions, thoughts, dreams, and aspirations so that they tend in this regard to react like monks and nuns wearing lay garb and living in the world instead of in the cloister. Hence it was that a bishop remarked to Dr. James J. Walsh, puzzled at the discovery of such disproportionate numbers of old bachelors and old maids among the Irish in America, "There is an inherent love of celibacy that reigns in every true Irish heart."

Early in life the young in Ireland become accustomed to the presence of an abundance of unmarried men and women. They are as much a part of the Irish landscape as its green fields and running streams; in every family there is one, or several, and not infrequently many. Because of the insularity of their life, they grow up thinking of such conditions as normal, little realizing how anomalous they are as compared with all other civilized countries.

When the Irish migrate to other lands, they flock for the most part to Irish settlements, form parishes predominantly of their own, and thus perpetuate their old way of life in the New World. They have changed skies but not customs, viewpoints, or habits. Priests and religious from Ireland for the most part minister to them and their children, and thus much the same set of influences surrounds them here as abroad. The result is that the celibate pattern continues, diminished somewhat perhaps by the presence of other racial groups and their more marked proclivity toward marriage.

Pointing out that there is a noneconomic factor behind Eire's abnormally large number of old bachelors, Bishop McNamee says, "Many remain unmarried, who might easily support a family, because for one reason or other they had not the opportunity earlier in life and have now sunk into a lethargic and fatalistic acceptance of permanent bachelorhood." Mired in that state of frustration until middle life, a sort of sexual apathy and stupor, of which Mrs. Laverty writes, sets in, and they become like members of a third sex—neither men nor women, a sort of "ould Mary Annes." More sinned against than sinning, these old bachelors are the pathetic victims of social blindness and of archaic marriage conditions which should long ago have been buried in the depths of the Atlantic Ocean.

Thus it is apparent that social, educational, psychological, and religious influences, stemming from the milieu in which the Irish live, are largely responsible for their extraordinary proclivity toward celibacy. True, the economic factor also plays an important role. People can't marry if they haven't homes into which to move or jobs by which to support a family. This is true not only in Eire but also in every other country. But the economic factor must not be overstressed or singled out as the one factor which holds such an enormous proportion of the Irish people in the bondage of bachelorhood and spinsterhood.

Economic conditions in Eire are far better today than they are in other countries of Europe, to say nothing of the Orient, where far more people marry. They do not marry because they do not have the resolution or the determination to do so. It is the peculiar blend of economic and of noneconomic factors, a curious culture lag, unique in Eire, which alone explains the unique attitude toward celibacy and the resultant failure of such large numbers to marry.

If this simple and forthright analysis of the pronounced tendency of the Irish toward wholesale celibacy is right, and we think it is, then the prescription of remedial measures is simple enough. It is chiefly a matter of reeducation. Without changing a particle of the traditional teaching concerning the dignity and holiness of the religious life, there can and must be greater emphasis upon the dignity and sanctity of marriage and the family life. The young must be taught by their parents, teachers, and priests alike to look forward to marriage as their normal goal in life if they are not called to the religious life. After every talk about the religious life there should be one about family life. Indeed since the overwhelming majority are called by God to the domestic life, this might well be the subject of most frequent instruction for all but the few who have manifested signs of a religious vocation.

Seeking to arouse the old bachelors from their prolonged lethargy and to make them realize their divinely appointed duty of continuing the race, Alice Curtayne warns, "A race content to wither away, who do not marry simply because they are too indifferent to alter their state, is suffering from some sort of mental and physical decline, some enormous depletion of vitality. Their fathers before them were not so defeated; they had their homes and their families despite far more adverse circumstances. Pioneers in new countries usually marry although their positions and prospects may be far from roseate. How distant and unreal now seem the old slogans about *Ourselves Alone* and *Saving the Nation*. It is not the foreign enemy, nor Partition, that is likely to defeat us but the virus of death which we nurse among ourselves." Would that more of Eire's writers and leaders would echo that warning!

It would be well to tell the people of Ireland of the concern felt for them even by people of other races. Thus *Relations,* a French magazine published by the Jesuits in Montreal, Canada, in a recent article, "L'Irlande est inquiète," says, "Ireland whose national color is the youthful green of hope, has become the habitat of old men and old women. . . . Persecution strengthens the heart, the goodness of nature covers the fields anew, but to lose one's feeling for the family is to lose one's feeling for life itself." That is the tragedy of the people of Ireland today: they have lost the feeling and the craving for life itself.

"If I were a priest in Ireland," wrote an Irish priest in America to us recently, "I would preach frequent sermons on marriage. I left Ireland as a newly-ordained priest thirty-five years ago. On my last visit home I was heartsick at the thinning out of the ranks of the children in the

Carlow, Saturday, March 28, 1953.

WEDDING BELLS
SCARE THEM

STATISTICS show that marriage bells hold no appeal for farmers in South Kildare. In the past five years not a single farmer in the parish of Crookstown, Ballytore, has married.

Father P. Fitzpatrick, C.C., referred to the large number of bachelor-farmers in the parish in his St. Patrick's Day sermon at second Mass.

One hundred years ago, Fr. Fitzpatrick said, an average of thirty-four couples were married annually, and the population of the parish was 800.

To-day, with fewer marriages, scarcely two hundred people live in the parish.

The loss of the milling industry and the closing of Ballytore tannery, both of which gave good employment, account in part for the alarming 75 per cent. fall in population, for working men had to find jobs elsewhere.

This, however, does not explain the reticence of farmers to lead a bride to the altar. Farming, in recent years, has prospered beyond the most sanguine hopes, though improvements may still be possible.

The only hope now for a healthier marriage rate depends on the enlightened education of Young Farmers' Clubs.

schools and parishes of the district in which I was reared. Instead, I saw old bachelors and old maids on every side. They darken the landscape with the shadow of social decay and death. Every second or third homestead that I passed was occupied by old bachelors and spinster sisters.

"At Mass on my last Sunday there, I could restrain myself no longer. In my sermon I said: I leave Eire heartsick and sad at the decay of the family life, at the disappearance of children and at the failure of so many of you to assume the normal responsibility of the family life. Practically everyone of you, not called to the religious life, was called by God to the family life. The refusal of so many of you to heed that call means you are condemning Ireland to extinction. Whether you know it or not, you are committing racial suicide. You are doing what Oliver Cromwell and his minions were unable to do. You are disgracing the island that has sent missionaries to all the world by your widespread, stubborn refusal to heed God's command: 'Increase and multiply.' You are dooming Eire and its people to extinction."

How wonderful it would be if every priest in Ireland would preach a similar sermon and continue to do so every month until the tragic situation is corrected. How splendid it would be if every priest of Irish extraction on a visit from America, Australia, or New Zealand would reinforce the appeal of the local shepherds with similar sermons.

Bishop Fulton Sheen has set an example in this regard. When he visited Croghan, the little town from which his grandparents came, he was both shocked and saddened to learn that not a single marriage had taken place there for a whole year! Instead of speaking on the hackneyed theme of what the Irish have done for the world, he spoke on a subject vastly more urgent and important: the dignity, importance, and necessity of marriage. He explained the simple and elementary truth that if the Irish continue to turn deaf ears to God's supreme command, "Increase and multiply," they will soon vanish completely from the face of the earth.

If only a recording of that sermon, so simple and yet so eloquent, could be played and replayed to every congregation in Eire, would it not soon lose its pathetic reputation as the country with the fewest and the latest marriages in the civilized world? What has been said here applies in substantial measure to the Irish of the Diaspora. They all stand in need of similar sermons until their strange pathological reluctance to marry is washed, like an ugly spot, clean from the Irish character and temperament.

Seeking to arouse the Irish people to the doom to which they are sentencing their nation by their inordinate celibacy, Sean de Cleir writes in the Irish magazine, *Christus Rex*: "It is not easy to understand how a nation remarkable for the fertility of its married women has allowed the most fruitful country in Europe to become miserably depopulated. It is not easy to understand how a nation which has carried patriotism to exalted and even exaggerated extremes can regard the progressive physical decay of its people with complacency and without dismay. It is very difficult to understand how a people so gloriously rich in vocations to the religious life can be so slow in answering the call to the privileges and dignities of Christian parenthood. . . .

"Certainly no problem of the family is so perturbing, so stubbornly resistant of solution, as is the problem of celibacy and late-marrying amongst our farming community. Here there can be no question of so-called alien influence. This is a problem which, though it may be paralleled abroad, is peculiarly our own. And it is a spiritual problem. Here the modes and customs of marriage have developed in such a way that no man marries unless he owns land, even though he may spend the whole of his days working the land. If a man of the farming class inherits land early in life, he marries early. If he inherits late, he marries late. If he does not inherit at all, he does not marry at all. In effect the number of families is equated to the number of holdings and whole classes of men are effectually denied their right to marry and to establish families. When a purely material consideration is allowed to determine the lives, not of an individual here and there as will inevitably happen, but of a whole Catholic community, it is futile to talk of economic forces. No economic force could deny the men of Ireland their right to marry had they the will to exercise that right.

"There is here a disregard for the duties and the privileges of parenthood which ill becomes Catholic men. Parenthood is the normal vocation of the laity. What effect such widespread celibacy has on individual lives is a matter for those who have the care of souls. But any man who loves his country is free to deplore the deprivation of flesh and blood which it entails. One can only hope and pray that a more generous spirit will move these people, that a more manly determination will stir them, before this old nation perishes through lack of numbers."

Newspapers and magazines can continue and extend the educational campaign. Indeed there are signs in Eire that they are beginning such a campaign. When Seán O'Faolain's article, the substance of which is contained in his chapter in this book, appeared in *Life,* the newspapers were suddenly inundated with letters on this subject. Describing the reaction, a scholarly friend in Eire writes us as follows: "After the initial splash of cold water thrown in its face by the *Life* article, Ireland is at last swinging toward a proper sense of values. Everybody is endeavoring to speak on the low marriage rate question and the papers are full of letters. I haven't heard so much fuss about it in my lifetime and it's all to the good, although I think they'll begrudge you the credit for starting it. People are now discussing the matter calmly and out of this discussion something good will come. The following letter in *Times Pictorial,* a Dublin weekly, reflects the thought of those who look at the matter calmly and with open eyes and are not afraid to speak their minds:

'Sir: Did you see where a Dublin newspaper opened up a series of broadsides against Seán O'Faolain for his article, "Love among the Irish" in the American magazine, *Life,* the other week? I have just read that article, and quite frankly—and I am, I think, unprejudiced—I could see nothing wrong with it. I could not check with the figures he uses, because that's not my line, but his reasoning is sound as a bell. Love among the Irish is a shallow thing mixed up with "made" marriages, dowries, droves of cattle, pigs and sheep. This love of money and property may be no bad thing since we are rooted to the soil, but don't let us cod ourselves that it does not exist; that all is of the love made in Heaven.

'Can anyone deny that our finest young men and women are emigrating? Can anyone deny that the bachelors of Ireland are a toothless, gummy, shifty lot, as crude as you'll find them anywhere and with more feeling for an old pipe than for a woman who might help each one to a better life? Look at them, the old bachelors, I mean, loafing around a laneway and you'll see what I mean. They're afraid of life, or else they know nothing about it and they won't learn. Most of them know nothing about the virtues of a clean shirt, not to mention clean living in a state of holy matrimony, the way Seán O'Faolain would like to see them.

'The women of Ireland are a sorely tried lot. Virtue is preached at them from every corner—and I am not talking here about the Church—but what national happiness can one expect if the women of the country are being frustrated. This frustration is being elevated to the status of a national mission, and the state is slowly dying. The few young men who want to live their lives free of hide-bound restrictions are going away, and the girls are going away also because they cannot find that emotional outlet so dear to all women in this country. I pity the poor Irish women over 40 or 50 who are unable to make a new start in life; they must remain behind with the gummy old chaps, who are grand fellows in their own way, but would fly from marriage like the Devil from a paraffin torch placed to his posterior. (signed) "Imelda," Dundrum, Co. Dublin.' "

We care nothing about credit for the launching of the campaign throughout the English-speaking world to save Ireland from extinction and the Irish in other countries from continued dwindling. We ask the Irish to save both their brickbats and bouquets and devote their energies to the more urgent task of procreation and child rearing. All that we and the contributors to this volume are concerned about are results. We hope that the people of Eire will continue to discuss the subject in their homes, schools, churches, newspapers, and magazines, and ultimately in the Dail so that remedial measures can be launched speedily and on a national scale.

"I left Ireland," writes a well-known priest, "shortly after my ordination twenty-five years ago. About every five years I have returned to visit my family, of which I am the ninth and the youngest member. Half of my brothers and sisters are still unmarried and apparently will end their days as pathetic old bachelors and old maids. Coming from America where couples commonly marry between the ages of 21 and 25, and where all are encouraged to marry early if not called to the religious life, I am appalled not only at the abnormally large number of single people but also at their failure to look upon marriage as the normal state intended by God and nature for them.

"The enormous emphasis upon the so-called terrible danger of company keeping, the listing of it in the catechism as a danger to purity and as something to be confessed, and the thundering against it in pulpits are chiefly responsible for poisoning their minds against marriage and filling the country with bachelors and spinsters. I never heard a sermon on marriage as God's plan for the vast majority, on the incompleteness of life for the solitary man or woman or on the holiness of the married state. If Ireland is to be saved from bleeding to death because of its few marriages, the clergy must extol and encourage company keeping and, instead of scolding, praise and bless those who engage in it as a necessary preliminary to marriage. Early marriage should be fostered and encouraged. Indeed such couples should be held up as models for all."

"To help break the log-jam of excessive bachelors," he continues, "it would be well for the Government to import about 5,000 men—Italians, Lithuanians, Bohemians, Germans and Poles—who would marry young Irish girls and set an example for the marriage-shy bachelors of Eire. Their example, reflecting the custom of every other Christian country, would do more than a ton of abstract preachments. It would help bring Ireland into step with the rest of Christendom and save it from the extinction to which its bachelor and spinster mores are dooming it."

The teachings of the Church on the beauty, dignity, and holiness of marriage are clear and unmistakable. While an exceptional individual here and there may be called to the single state in the world, the overwhelming majority are called by God to matrimony, of which St. Paul says, "This is a great sacrament, but I speak in Christ and in the Church." By performing the duties of that holy state, human beings can not only scale the loftiest heights of holiness but also achieve the greatest joy and happiness in this life as well.

In the institution of marriage God has provided means for the legitimate satisfaction of the deep and abiding hungers He has placed in the heart of man. By neglecting to avail oneself of these divinely established means, man exposes himself to a thousand dangers and often finds himself seeking the satisfaction of the sexual hunger by methods contrary to the moral law. The frustration of these cravings during the whole of a man's life creates a thousand problems for his mental and moral health which are happily solved in the family life.

This point was brought out unexpectedly after a recent lecture of ours. We had just given a lecture to the students in the department of sociology at Notre Dame on the anomalies of the situation in Eire and at the end had paid a sincere tribute to the virtue and chastity of the Irish, despite their nonmarrying habits. Dr. Roger Bernier, an instructor in philosophy, made an observation on this point in the open discussion following the lecture.

"With no thought of reflecting upon the Irish," he said, "I would hold up as a better model the French-speaking people of the Quebec province from which I come. There virtually everyone marries and raises a large family. The bachelorhood in Ireland, of which you speak, is something which we would regard as abnormal and unhealthy for body, mind, and soul. I think our people have the best protection for their moral health, namely, marriage, the means provided by God Himself. Vast numbers of laymen and -women going through their whole life in a barren and witless celibacy, contributing no increase to Church or state, seems weird, pathological, and unnatural to us, and I hope that blight never spreads to the French-speaking people of Canada, who believe in life enough to pass it on generously to others."

The point which Dr. Bernier made is, in our opinion, a valid one, and it would be well to drive this home to the hundreds of thousands of bachelors and spinsters in Eire. Because of the insularity of their lives, as we have pointed out, few of the people there seem aware of the anomalous and abnormal situation they are in as compared with all other civilized nations. Here is an invaluable service which the priests and teaching brothers and sisters of Ireland could render. By focusing the attention of the people, young and old, upon the many benefits, blessings, and happiness of family life they could change the whole social, moral, and spiritual outlook of their people on this subject.

In no country in the world are the clergy so powerful and influential as in Eire. They are grand priests working among a great people who esteem and love them as do no other race. In their consecrated hands lies the precious opportunity of effecting a radical change in the non-marrying mores of their people. True, bishops in their Pastorals and priests in their sermons have pleaded for more and earlier marriages. But much can be done through conferences of priests with individuals who need help and guidance to achieve the goal of marriage.

How wonderful it would be if the priests of a parish called on each single man and woman and discussed the matter with them! Some might need help in finding congenial partners, others might have economic road blocks in their way, still others might need a bit of encouragement to take the step. Government measures which would help every able-bodied man to get a job with a family living wage might be enacted as a result of that mass effort of priest and people to solve Eire's Number 1 problem: too few and too late marriages.

Where private enterprise fails to provide jobs for all men willing to work, then it becomes the duty of the state, as the Holy Father has pointed out, to step in and to launch public work projects which will do so. Furthermore the remuneration of the workers must be sufficient to enable them to support a family in reasonable and decent comfort. Such is the unmistakable social teaching of our great pontiffs.

A Catholic country, such as Eire, has the opportunity to show the beneficial results of such teaching by translating it into a living reality. Above property rights come human rights, and among the most elemental of these are the rights to life, to marry, to work, and to secure for the same a family living wage. A Catholic country in which these elemental human rights are denied its citizens is a country which has somehow failed to implement the social teachings of all our recent pontiffs by appropriate legislative enactments.

This brings us to the economic factor. That it is an important factor in Eire's few and late marriages and in her emigration, as we have already pointed out, there is no doubt. While it doesn't explain the failure of the hundreds of thousands of well-fixed bachelors to marry, it does explain why thousands of jobless men either don't marry or why they postpone marriage till later years when they have achieved some security. At the present time the number of registered unemployed persons in Eire totals 88,853. But as not all who are unemployed and are anxious to obtain work are registered at the labor exchanges, it is likely, points out an editorial in *The Landmark,* the monthly journal of Muintir na Tire, that there are at least 100,000 unemployed and nearly all of them are in the towns and cities.

The contributors have already detailed many steps to be taken to improve the economic situation in Eire and they are too numerous to be repeated here. Father J. M. Hayes has presented at length the program of his great organization, Muintir na Tire, to stop the flight from the land by making the farms more productive and farm life less bleak and dreary. A kindred organization, Young Farmers' Club (Macra na Feirme) is doing a similarly splendid work, and both deserve encouragement and support. Eire is essentially an agricultural country, and the nation's leaders must bend every effort to bringing the latest scientific methods of agriculture, dairying, and poultry and cattle raising into operation on every farm.

Irish agricultural experts say that farming in Eire on the whole is very backward as compared with other countries and that scientific methods could double and in many cases even triple present production. Productivity per man-hour, per beast, per acre must be enormously increased.

"The solution," points out the *Irish Monthly,* "will lie along the road that will lead us to a 700-gallon cow milked by machine: an acre of grass giving three times the food-units the present acre does: a couple of million more pigs fattened on cooperative farms: 20,000,000 more fowl: and acres of more potatoes. And even to start along that road will need large doses of proper agricultural education given in 26 colleges, one in each county: intensive organization of farmers: and only then, but certainly then, lavish capitalization in the form of fertilizers, buildings and machines."

Education must not only supply the technical data and techniques for vastly increased production but also instill a new and deeper appreciation of farm life. The Most Rev. James Moynagh, Irish missionary Bishop of Calabar, Nigeria, stressed this point in a conference with us. "In a class of high-school students in Eire," related the bishop, "the teacher asked how many were planning on going into farming. Only one in the class of thirty raised his hand to indicate that was his intention. Whereupon most of the others snickered, showing their disdain for such work. I mention the incident to show how badly needed is a new attitude on the part of Irish youth toward farming as a career. We won't stem the flight from the land until we have convinced the young people of Ireland that farming can use the best brains and the most highly skilled scientists and technicians in the land. We're only scratching the surface now, but if we applied the latest scientific findings we could double and even triple the present productivity and the farm population as well."

In addition to tripling her agricultural output through the application of scientific methods and the more extensive use of cooperatives, Ireland needs to double and triple her industrialization. This requires capital, and private enterprise will need some "pump priming" in the form of government aid. We endorse the appeal of Father Hayes for aid for the extension of his Muintir na Tire plan to every farm parish and the appeal of Father Murray for help from American investors in much-needed industrial projects. In addition, we think Eire is deserving of help from the American government in the form of long-term loans with low interest rates.

We have poured millions into Titoland in the dubious enterprise of building up a barrier against communism. We have given billions to Great Britain to rebuild her war-shattered economy. We would like to see our government extend generous aid to Ireland, a mighty Gibraltar against the advance of communism, and help her in a huge agricultural and industrial program that would enable her to supply jobs with family living wages to all her people.

While Eire did receive generous aid under the Marshall Plan, she needs much more and is more deserving of it than any other nation in the world. While American taxpayers feel overburdened and disinclined to shoulder more of the load of bulwarking European countries against the advance of communism, it is well for us to remember that little Eire is one of the few nations which after World War I paid back every dollar which was loaned her. For more than a century Ireland has poured her lifeblood into America, and now she merits our unstinted help in stemming her population decline and in achieving higher levels of agricultural and industrial productivity.

With the resultant prosperity the emigration would stop or dwindle to a mere trickle, young men could marry at the normal ages of twenty-one to twenty-five as in other countries, and hundreds of thousands of homes could be built, especially in country districts, to provide for a growing population. Ireland sustained a population of 8 million more than a century ago. With intensive farming and vastly expanded industry, could she not support twice that number today? We would like to see a prosperous united Ireland with at least a tripled population so that she could take her place once again in the sun and extend her beneficent influence among all the nations of the world.

Eire is naturally much concerned over the separation of the six counties in Ulster from the rest of the country and desperately wants a united Ireland. We hope that such a union can be achieved through the wise statesmanship of leaders on both sides of the Border. Surely Irishmen can disagree in a friendly manner on many subjects and yet work together for a greater, a more prosperous and a united Ireland. The most disturbing aspect in the political picture to many of us, however, is the strange failure of so many of the Irish to show an appreciation of citizenship in the Irish Free State.

For centuries the Irish fought for freedom and independence. They showed a passionate attachment for the land when an alien government sought to evict them from their homes. When at long last the alien rule was ended and the Free State was established with a government of their own choosing, what happened? Did they exult with pride in their new citizenship and show that it was worth the centuries of struggle and bloodshed and the death of untold thousands of patriotic Irishmen?

On the contrary, they fled and they continue to flee in undiminished numbers from the land, to renounce their Irish citizenship and to espouse that of the United States, Canada, Australia, New Zealand, or any other country. Irish citizenship seems made of sand without a particle of cement. It is a strange contrast to the fierce pride of citizenship which burned within the American colonists when they had freed themselves from an alien rule. It is in sharp contrast to the passionate attachment to the land which burned within the Irish for centuries when they were struggling for freedom and self-government.

Economic pressures, of course, account for much of the emigration. But we can't but wonder if it isn't possible to rekindle that flame of patriotic devotion to Erin so that her children will become incandescent with the inextinguishable fire of a fierce and passionate pride in their Irish citizenship and cling to it with their very life. The irony of a nation with a profound religious belief in the dignity and beauty of marriage, from which so many of its members run in terror, like the devil from holy water, is matched only by the irony of their centuries-long fight for the freedom of their country from which, when it is achieved, they incontinently flee.

It was Davitt, we think, who said that the Irish would go down to Hell for the land. Once they acquired ownership of it under a government of their own choosing, however, they seem ready to go down almost to Hell to get away from it. The Irish race is one of paradox, enigma, and contradiction, and this last will rank with the most puzzling in their strange and mysterious history. Are they destined to be forever a ferment and a catalyst among the nations, roaming everlastingly over the earth like restless gypsies or some lost tribe of cosmic vagabonds aglow with Promethean fire, with never a permanent home? This restless wanderlust of the Gael is well depicted in *Cathleen Ni Houlihan,* wherein W. B. Yeats narrates the following conversation between the Old Woman, symbolizing Ireland, and some strangers she meets on the way.

PETER: It's a pity indeed for any person to have no place of their own.

OLD WOMAN: That's true for you indeed, and it's long I'm on the roads since I first went wandering.

BRIDGET: It is a wonder you are not worn out with so much wandering.

OLD WOMAN: Sometimes my feet are tired and my hands are quiet, but there is no quiet in my heart. When the people see me quiet, they think old age has come on me and that all the stir has gone out of me. But when the trouble is on me I must be talking to my friends.

BRIDGET: What was it put you wandering?

OLD WOMAN: Too many strangers in the house.

BRIDGET: Indeed you look as if you'd had your share of trouble.

OLD WOMAN: I have had trouble indeed.

BRIDGET: What was it put the trouble on you?

OLD WOMAN: My land that was taken from me.

PETER: Was it much land they took from you?

OLD WOMAN: My four beautiful green fields.

Now that three of her green fields and a part of the fourth are restored to her and the strangers are put out of her house, perhaps Mother Ireland can settle down, kindle the fire in the hearth, and put the lighted candle in the window to tell her wandering sons and daughters that she is at home to stay.

We should like to believe that the intensive development of agricultural education and its extension to all the schools, from the lowest to the highest, will kindle new interest in the land and help to chain the restless spirits of the Irish to their lovely green island. Every race needs a homeland to escape the feeling of cosmic waifhood. At long last the wandering people of Israel have established a national homeland which has become a spiritual Mecca to thousands of their refugee children. The Irish of the Diaspora need a spiritual homeland to which they can look with affection and pride and feel that their Mother is living still.

As we are writing the concluding lines of this book the following United Press dispatch from Dublin is appearing in the newspapers of America: "IRELAND HOLDS BACHELOR TITLE. Ireland has more bachelors and spinsters than any nation in the world, the Central Statistics Office says. A nation-wide survey showed that one of every four women never will marry partly because many Irish bachelors will never earn enough money to pop the question."

That is the gist of a news dispatch which has been appearing in newspapers throughout the English-speaking world year after year for decades. Prescinding from the dispatch's oversimplification of the causes of nonmarriage, there can be no questioning the fact that Ireland has a strangle hold on the title "Champion Bachelor and Spinster Country of the Civilized World." Such a dispatch is a challenge not only to the leaders of Church and State but also to every man and woman in Ireland to do everything possible to rid the country of the opprobrious title on which it has had a monopoly for more than a century.

To help them in that holy crusade, and it is as sacred as that which prompted the Crusaders of old to journey to Palestine to free the Holy Land from the hands of the Mohammedans, is the primary purpose for which this book has been written. The secondary purpose is to help the Irish of the Diaspora to rid themselves of the title of the least marrying race in the world.

From what has been said, it is clear that the nonmarrying mores of the Irish has the tragic effect of hemophilia, bleeding the race to death. Call that trait marriage shyness, an inherent inclination to wholesale celibacy, an ingrained reluctance to wed, a horror of sex, or whatever you will, it has already reduced the natives of Eire to a state of pernicious anemia, one step removed from death. It might with equal propriety be called a sort of racial cancer. It has a double malignancy: it kills off the living, and it foredooms thousands of potential boys and girls to the limbo of nonexistence. It is high time to eradicate this racial cancer from the Irish in every land; otherwise it will continue to drag the race to virtual extinction.

We end on a note of optimism and confidence. "We're Not Dead Yet" is the title of John D. Sheridan's chapter, and it symbolizes the spirit and the conviction of all participating in this cooperative study. For more than seven centuries the Irish fought a world power for their independence and freedom. It was a struggle against apparently hope-less odds, but it proved only the invincible power of a nation whose cause was just.

When the Irish see clearly that their real enemy today is not Parti-tion, nor any foreign foe, but the failure of so many of their people to marry, they will battle with the same unconquerable spirit which has carried their colors to victory on a thousand battlefields. Never was their cause more just. In former days they were fighting for the ownership of their land and for the freedom of their country. Now they are fighting for their very existence as a nation, fighting for life itself.

It is because we have a profound and deathless faith in the courage, ability, and intelligence of the Irish people and in the indomitable power of their national spirit when fully aroused that we have no seri-ous doubt of the ultimate victory. Though today Ireland has one foot, if not in the grave, at least very close to it, she will arise, join issue with the foe, and fight on to a glorious victory.

At a critical juncture in World War I when the German military machine was rolling like a mighty Juggernaut over France, apparently presaging her doom, Foch sent a wire to General Joffre which is credited with transforming the spirit of the French soldiery and turning the tide. "My right wing is dangerously threatened," he wired, "my center is giving way; it is impossible for me to move; the situation is excellent; I shall attack with all forces." And that is precisely what he did, and it marked the turning point of the war. With equal daring Ireland will mobilize her forces and attack on all fronts and change the tide from defeat to victory.

She will once again become a great, populous nation, fruitful in all good works. She will take her rightful place as a beacon light guiding the feet of the nations along the paths of peace, justice, and freedom, and her numerous children in all lands will rise up to call her blessed. "He that shall lose his life for my sake," said Our Lord, "shall find it." More than any other nation in the world Ireland has poured out her life's blood in bringing the glad tidings of man's redemption to all lands.

Like the Divine Master whom she has served so well, Ireland shall arise from her tomb of near extinction, glorious and strong with new and abundant life, to continue on a much larger scale her sublime mission. God and His Providence will be with her in the crucial days that lie ahead. Thus strengthened from on high, and with her children and her friends in all lands pulling and praying for her recovery, Ireland shall arise to resume her traditional role as the spiritual leader among the nations of the world.

INDEX